Appalachian Trail Guide to New Hampshire–Vermont

Appalachian Trail Guide to

New Hampshire–Vermont

Cynthia Taylor–Miller

Editor

ELEVENTH EDITION

APPALACHIAN TRAIL
CONSERVANCY

Harpers Ferry

Published by Appalachian Trail Conservancy
P.O. Box 807
Harpers Ferry, West Virginia 25425

Cover photo: Franconia Ridge, New Hampshire; Dan Stone
Half-title page photo: Stratton Pond, Vermont; Laurie Potteiger
Title-page photo: South of Clarendon Gorge, Vermont; Timothy Cummings
Please see page 352 for additional photography credits.

ISBN 978-1-889386-53-9

Eleventh edition
Printed in the United States of America on recycled paper.

Mixed Sources
Product group from well-managed
forests and other controlled sources
www.fsc.org   Cert no. SW-COC-002553
© 1996 Forest Stewardship Council
FSC

Contents

The Appalachian Trail

Welcome to America's best-known long-distance footpath, the Appalachian Trail. If you've never visited it before, you're in for a memorable time, and we hope this official guidebook will help you make the most of it. If you know the Trail, but not this part of it, we hope this book will help you discover new aspects of an experience that changes from state to state, mile to mile, and season to season.

Not long after the end of World War I, a Massachusetts regional planner named Benton MacKaye envisioned a footpath along the crests of the mountains from New England to the southern Appalachians. The work of scores of volunteers helped that dream become the Appalachian Trail, which extends more than 2,175 miles between Katahdin in central Maine

Climbing Killington's summit

and Springer Mountain in northern Georgia. Its terrain ranges from swamp-land to near-vertical rock scrambles that challenge the fittest wilderness trekker; its white "blazes" lead from small-town streets to remote mountain ridges days from the nearest road crossing.

The "A.T.," as it's called by hikers, is a linear trail that can be enjoyed in small pieces or large chunks. Hikers follow its blazes on round-trip day-hikes, on loop-hikes (where side trails connect with it and form a loop), on one-way "section-hikes" or overnight backpacking trips that cover short or long segments, or on end-to-end "thru-hikes" that cover the entire Trail. It is continuously marked, using a standard system of paint blazes and signs, and is cleared of undergrowth and maintained to permit single-file hiking. (Bicycles, horses, and motorized vehicles are not permitted along most of the route.) Many campsites and more than 250 primitive woodland shelters are located along the Trail, typically about a day's hike apart. The path itself is usually dirt, or rock, or grass, and only very short segments are paved or wheelchair-accessible.

This remarkable footpath is much more than just a walk through the woods. When it was first begun in the 1920s and completed in the 1930s, it was little-known and rarely traveled. Large parts of it were on private property. Since 1968, it has been a part of the same national park system that includes Yellowstone, Yosemite, and the Great Smoky Mountains. Its official name today is the Appalachian National Scenic Trail, and 99.6 percent of it runs over public lands. Hundreds of roads cross it, and scores of side trails intersect with it. In some parts, the Trail "corridor" is only a few hundred feet wide; in other parts, entire mountains are protected by it.

Unlike other well-known national parks, there's no "main entrance" to the A.T., with a gate and a ranger collecting tickets. You can begin or end your hike at hundreds of places between its northern and southern ends. As the longest, skinniest part of America's national park system, the A.T. stretches across fourteen different states and passes through more than sixty federal, state, and local parks and forests. Maybe the most important difference between the A.T. and other national-park units is that it was built by volunteers, and volunteers still are responsible for keeping it up. The A.T. relies on a system known as "cooperative man-agement" rather than on a large, paid federal staff. Yes, there are a handful of National Park Service staff members and a ranger assigned

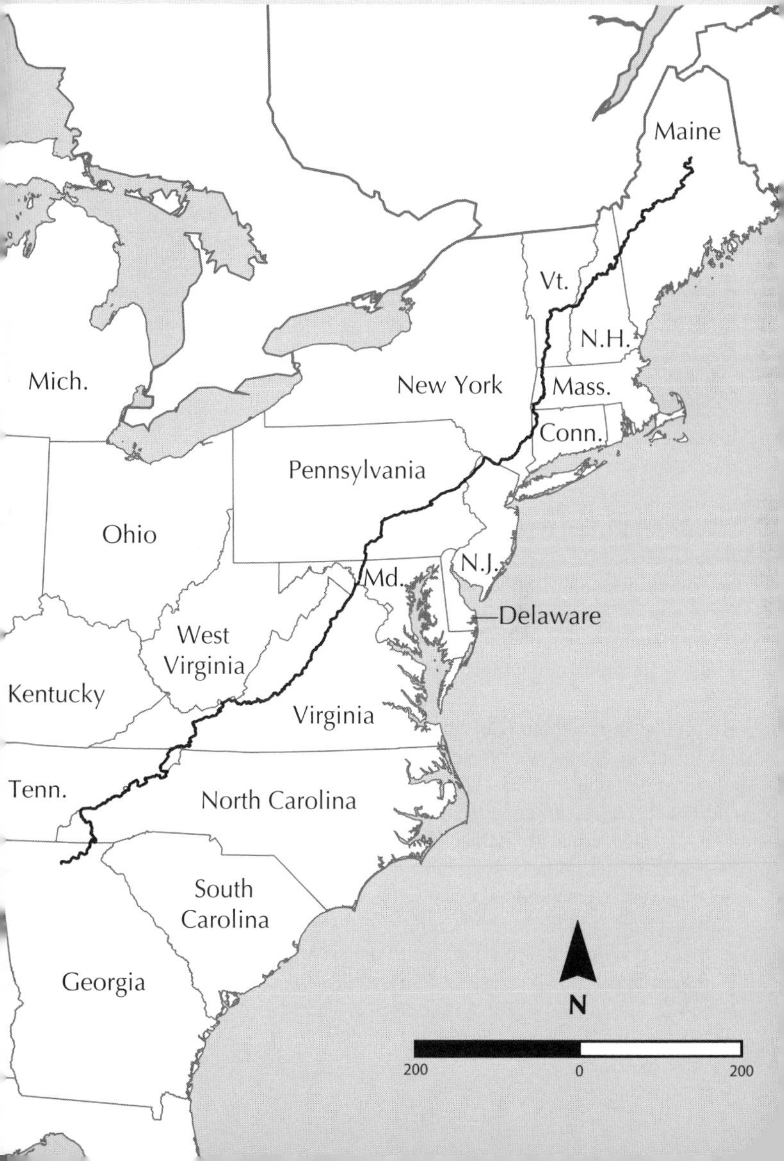

Maine

Vt.

N.H.

Mass.

Conn.

New York

Mich.

Pennsylvania

Ohio

N.J.

Md.

Delaware

West
Virginia

Kentucky

Virginia

Tenn.

North Carolina

South
Carolina

Georgia

N

200   0   200

Volunteer Trail maintainers

to the Appalachian Trail Park Office in Harpers Ferry, West Virginia, but thousands of the people who maintain, patrol, and monitor the footpath and its surrounding lands are outdoor lovers like you. Each year, as members of thirty maintaining clubs up and down the Appalachians, they annually volunteer almost two hundred thousand hours of their time looking after this public treasure. They would welcome your help.

About the Appalachian Trail Conservancy—We are the volunteer-based organization that teaches people about the Trail, coordinates the work of the maintaining clubs, and works with the government agencies, individuals, and companies that own the land that the Trail passes over. The membership of the Appalachian Trail Conservancy (ATC) includes hikers and Trail enthusiasts who elect a volunteer Board of Directors every two years. Members' dues and contributions help support a paid staff of about forty-five people at the ATC headquarters in Harpers Ferry; at regional offices in New England, Pennsylvania, Virginia, and North Carolina; and at a sales distribution center, also in West Virginia. Our Web site, <www.appalachiantrail.org>, is a good source of information about the Trail. Information about contacting the Conservancy is at the back of this book.

Maine Appalachian Trail Club—www.matc.org
Appalachian Mountain Club—www.outdoors.org
Dartmouth Outing Club—www.dartmouth.edu/~doc
Green Mountain Club—www.greenmountainclub.org
AMC Berkshire Chapter—www.amcberkshire.org
AMC Connecticut Chapter—www.ct-amc.org
New York–New Jersey Trail Conference—www.nynjtc.org
Wilmington Trail Club—www.wilmingtontrailclub.org
Batona Hiking Club—members.aol.com/Batona
AMC Delaware Valley Chapter—www.amcdv.org
Philadelphia Trail Club—m.zanger.tripod.com
Blue Mountain Eagle Climbing Club—www.bmecc.org
Allentown Hiking Club—www.allentownhikingclub.org
Susquehanna Appalachian Trail Club—www.satc-hike.org
York Hiking Club—www.yorkhikingclub.com
Cumberland Valley A.T. Club—geocities.com/cvatclub
Mountain Club of Maryland—www.mcomd.org
Potomac Appalachian Trail Club—www.potomacappalachian.org
Old Dominion Appalachian Trail Club—www.odatc.org
Tidewater Appalachian Trail Club—www.tidewateratc.org
Natural Bridge Appalachian Trail Club—www.nbatc.org
Roanoke Appalachian Trail Club—www.ratc.org
Outdoor Club at Virginia Tech—www.outdoor.org.vt.edu
Piedmont Appalachian Trail Hikers—www.path-at.org
Mount Rogers Appalachian Trail Club—www.mratc.org
Tennessee Eastman Hiking Club—www.tehcc.org
Carolina Mountain Club—www.carolinamtnclub.com
Smoky Mountains Hiking Club—www.smhclub.org
Nantahala Hiking Club—www.maconcommunity.org/nhc
Georgia Appalachian Trail Club—www.georgia-atclub.org

Tips for enjoying the Appalachian Trail

Follow the blazes—The Appalachian Trail is marked for daylight travel in both directions, using a system of painted "blazes" on trees, posts, and rocks. There are some local variations, but most hikers grasp the system quickly. Above treeline, and where snow or fog may obscure paint marks, posts and rock piles called "cairns" are used to identify the route.

A blaze is a rectangle of paint in a prominent place along a trail. White-paint blazes two inches wide and six inches high mark the A.T. itself. Side trails and shelter trails use blue blazes; blazes of other colors and shapes mark other intersecting trails. Two white blazes, one above the other, signal an obscure turn, route change, incoming side trail, or other situation that requires you to be especially alert to changes in direction. In some states, one of the two blazes will be offset in the direction of the turn.

If you have gone a quarter-mile without seeing a blaze, stop. Retrace your steps until you locate a blaze. Then, check to ensure that you haven't missed a turn. Often a glance backward will reveal blazes meant for hikers traveling in the opposite direction.

Volunteer Trail maintainers regularly relocate small sections of the

White blaze

Double blaze

path around hazards or undesirable features or off private property. When your map or guidebook indicates one route, and the blazes show another, follow the blazes.

A few cautions—The A.T. is a scenic trail through the forests of the Appalachian Mountains. It is full of natural splendors and is fun to hike, and parts of it run near roads and across fairly level ground. But, most of the Trail is very steep and runs deep in the woods, along the crests of rocky mountain ridges, miles from the nearest houses or paved roads. It will test your physical conditioning and skills. Plan your hike, and prepare sensibly.

Before you set out to hike the Trail, take a few minutes to review the information in this guidebook. It is as current as possible, but conditions and footpath locations sometimes change in between guidebook editions. On the Trail, please pay close attention to—and follow—the blazes and any directional signs that mark the route, even if the book describes a different route.

Although we have included some basic tips for preparing for an A.T. hike in the back of this guidebook (see page 298), this is not a "how-to" guide to backpacking. Many good books of that sort are available in your local bookstore and library. If you've never hiked before, we recommend that you take the time to read one or two and to research equipment, camping techniques, and trip planning. If your only hiking and camping experience is in local parks and forests, be aware that hiking and

Post   *Cairn*

camping in the mountains can be extremely strenuous and disorienting and has its own particular challenges. You will sometimes encounter wildlife and will have to make do with primitive (or nonexistent) sanitary facilities. Remember that water in the backcountry, even at water sources mentioned in this guidebook, needs to be treated for microorganisms before you drink it.

Responsibility for safety—Finally, know that you are responsible for your own safety and for the safety of those with you and for making sure that your food and water are safe for consumption. Hiking the A.T. is no more dangerous than many other popular outdoor activities, but, although the Trail is part of the national park system, it is not the proverbial "walk in the park," and help may be some distance away. The Appalachian Trail Conservancy and its member clubs cannot ensure the safety of any hiker on the Trail. As a hiker, you assume the risk for any accident, illness, or injury that might occur there.

Leave No Trace—As more and more people use the Trail and other backcountry areas, it becomes more important to learn to enjoy wild places without ruining them. The best way to do this is to understand and practice the principles of Leave No Trace, (shown at right), a seven-point ethic for enjoying the backcountry that applies to everything from a picnic outing to a long-distance expedition. Leave No Trace, Inc., is a nonprofit organization dedicated to teaching the principles of low-impact use. For more information, contact Leave No Trace at <www.lnt.org>, or call (800) 332-4100.

1. **Plan ahead and prepare**. Evaluate the risks associated with your outing, identify campsites and destinations in advance, use maps and guides, and be ready for bad weather. When people don't plan ahead, they're more likely to damage the backcountry.

2. **Travel and camp on durable surfaces.** Stay on trails and don't bushwhack short-cuts across switchbacks or other bends in the path. Keep off fragile trailside areas, such as bogs or alpine zones. Camp in designated spots, such as shelters and existing campsites, so that unspoiled areas aren't trampled and denuded.

3. **Dispose of waste properly.** Bury or pack out excrement, including pet droppings. Pack out all trash and food waste, including that left behind by others. Don't bury trash or food, and don't try to burn packaging materials in campfires.

4. **Leave what you find.** Don't take flowers or other sensitive natural resources. Don't disturb artifacts, such as native American arrowheads or the stone walls and cellar holes of historical woodland homesteads.

5. **Minimize campfire impacts.** Campfires are enjoyable, but they also create the worst visual and ecological impact of any backcountry camping practice. If possible, cook on a backpacking stove instead of a fire. Where fires are permitted, build them only in established fire rings, and don't add rocks to an existing ring. Keep fires small. Burn only dead and downed wood that can be broken by hand—leave axes and saws at home. Never leave your campfire unattended, and drown it when you leave.

6. **Respect wildlife.** Don't feed or disturb wildlife. Store food properly to avoid attracting bears, varmints, and rodents. If you bring a pet, keep it leashed.

7. **Be considerate of other visitors.** Limit overnight groups to ten or fewer, twenty-five on day trips. Minimize noise and intrusive behavior, including cell phone use around others. Share shelters and other facilities. Be considerate of Trail neighbors.

How to use this book

We suggest that you use this book in conjunction with the waterproof Trail maps that were sold with it. Information about services available in towns near the Trail is updated annually in the *Appalachian Trail Thru-Hikers' Companion*. Mileage and shelter information for the entire Trail is updated annually in the *Appalachian Trail Data Book*.

Although the Trail is usually well marked and experienced hikers may be able to follow it without either guidebook or map, using the book and the maps will not only help you keep from getting lost or disoriented, but will also help you get more out of your hike.

Before you start your hike:

■ *Decide where you want to go and which Trail features you hope to see.* Use the book to help you plan your trip. The chapter on loop hikes (page 292) lists a number of popular day-hikes and short trips that have proven popular with hikers along this part of the Trail. The introductions to each section give more detail, summarizing scenic and cultural highlights along the route that you may wish to visit.

■ *Calculate mileage for linear or loop hikes.* Each chapter lists mileage between landmarks on the route, along with details to help you follow the path. Use the mileage and descriptions to determine how far you must hike, how long it will take you, and where you can camp if you're taking an overnight or long-distance hike.

■ *Find the Trail.* Use the section maps included in the guidebook to locate parking areas near the A.T. and the "Trailheads" or road crossings where the footpath crosses the highway. In some cases, the guidebook includes directions to nearby towns and commercial areas where you can find food, supplies, and lodging.

After you begin hiking:

■ *Identify landmarks.* Deduce where you are along the Trail by comparing the descriptions in the guidebook and the features on the waterproof maps to the landscape you're hiking through. Much of the time, the Trail's blazes will lead you through seemingly featureless woodlands, where the only thing you can see in most directions is trees, but you will be able to check your progress periodically at viewpoints, meadows, mountain tops, stream crossings, road crossings, and Trailside structures.

■ *Learn about the route.* Native Americans, colonial-era settlers, Civil War soldiers, nineteenth-century farmers, pioneering railroaders, and early industrial entrepreneurs explored these hills long before the A.T. was built. Although much of what they left behind has long since been overgrown and abandoned, your guidebook will point out old settlements and forest roads and put the landscape in its historical context. It will touch on the geology, natural history, and modern-day ecosystems of the eastern mountains.

■ *Find campsites and side trails.* The guidebook includes directions to other trails, as well as creeks, mountain springs, and established tenting and shelter sites.

Areas covered

Each of the eleven official Appalachian Trail guidebooks describes several hundred miles of the Trail. In some cases, that includes a single state, such as Maine or Pennsylvania. In other cases, the guidebook may include several states, such as the one covering northern Virginia, West Virginia, and Maryland. Because so much of the Trail is in Virginia (more than 500 miles of it), a hiker needs to use four different guidebooks to cover that entire state.

The eleven guidebooks are:

Maine
New Hampshire–Vermont
Massachusetts–Connecticut

New York–New Jersey
Pennsylvania
Maryland and Northern Virginia
Shenandoah National Park
Central Virginia
Southwest Virginia
Tennessee–North Carolina
North Carolina–Georgia

How the guidebook is divided

Rather than trying to keep track of several hundred miles of the Trail from beginning to end, the Trail's maintainers break it down into smaller "sections." Each section covers the area between important road crossings or natural features and can vary from three to thirty miles in length. A typical section is from five to fifteen miles long. This guidebook is organized according to those sections, beginning with the northernmost in the coverage area and ending with the southernmost. Each section makes up a chapter. A summary of distances for the entire guidebook appears near the end of the book.

How sections are organized

Brief description of section—Each section begins with a brief description of the route. The description mentions highlights and prominent features and gives a sense of what it's like to hike the section as a whole.

Section map and profile—The map shows how to find the Trail from your vehicle (it is not a detailed map and should not be relied on for navigating the Trail) and includes notable roads along with a rough depiction of the Trail route, showing shelter locations. A schematic profile of the high and low points in the section gives you an idea of how much climbing or descending is ahead.

Shelters and campsites—Each chapter also includes an overview of shelters and campsites for the section, including the distances between shelters and information about water supplies. Along some parts of the

Trail, particularly north of the Mason-Dixon Line, the designated sites are the only areas in which camping is permitted. In other parts of the Trail, even where "dispersed camping" is allowed, we recommend that hikers "Leave No Trace" (see page 9) and reduce their impact on the Trail's resources by using established campsites. If camping is restricted in a section, it will be noted here.

Trail description—Trail descriptions appear on the right-hand pages of each chapter. Although the description reads from north to south, it is organized for both northbound and southbound hikers. Northbound hikers should start at the end of the chapter and read up, using the mileages in the right-hand column. Southbound hikers should read down, using the mileages in the left-hand column. The description includes obvious landmarks you will pass, although it may not include all stream crossings, summits, or side trails. Where the Trail route becomes confusing, the guide will provide both north- and southbound directions from the landmark. When a feature appears in **bold** type, it means that you should see the section highlights for more detail.

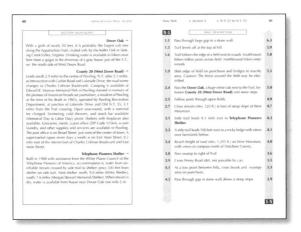

Section highlights—On the left-hand pages of each chapter, you will find cultural, historical, natural, and practical information about the **bold** items in the Trail description. That includes detailed information about Trailheads, shelters, and campsites, along with notes on the historical and cultural resources of the route, notes on landforms and natural history, and descriptions of side trails.

End of section—The northern and southern ends of each section are noted in **bold** in the Trail description and detailed in the section highlights at the beginning and ending of each chapter of the book, respectively. The information includes brief directions about how to find the Trailhead from the highway; information about where to park, if parking is available; distances to nearby towns and facilities; and notes on the services available near the Trail, such as grocery stores and restaurants.

Guidebook conventions

North or "compass-north"?—For the sake of convenience, the directions *north, south, east* and *west* in the guide refer to the general north–south orientation of the Trail, rather than the true north or magnetic north of maps and charts. In other words, when a hiker is northbound on the Trail, whatever is to his left will be referred to as "west" and whatever is to the right will be "east." For southbounders, the opposite is true.

Although this is instinctively the way A.T. hikers orient themselves, it can be slightly confusing for the first-time A.T. hiker, since the Trail does not always follow an actual north–south orientation. For example, you might be "northbound" along the Trail (headed toward Maine), but, because of a sharp turn or a switchback up the side of a mountain, your compass will tell you you're actually pointed south for a while. Nevertheless, in this guide, a trail or road intersecting on the left side of the A.T. for the northbound hiker will always be referred to as "intersecting on the west side of the A.T.," even where the compass says otherwise.

When the compass direction of an object is important, as when directing attention to a certain feature seen from a viewpoint, the guidebook will refer to "compass-north," "compass-west," and so forth.

Undocumented features—The separate waterproof hiking maps meant to accompany this guide generally reflect all the landmarks discussed here. Because the maps are extremely detailed, some features that appear on them, such as streams and old woods roads, may not be mentioned in the guidebook if they are not important landmarks. Other side trails that the hiker encounters may not be mentioned or mapped at all; in general, this is because the unmarked trails lead onto private property, and Trail managers wish to discourage their use.

Public transportation and shuttle services—Many sections of the Trail are served by persons providing shuttles to hikers, and some sections are reachable by public transportation. For the most up-to-date list of those services, please visit the Hike the Trail section of the ATC Web site, <www.appalachiantrail.org>.

Using the Trail in New Hampshire and Vermont

The more than 310 miles of the Appalachian Trail between the Maine and Massachusetts state lines include some of the oldest and most rugged sections of the entire fourteen-state route—running the gamut from alpine peaks and meadows to rolling farmland to "green tunnel" ridges, from Mt. Washington (the highest summit in New England) to the banks of the placid Connecticut River between the states.

Three clubs in those two states, all with staffs as well as volunteers, maintain the footpath and facilities and manage the surrounding lands in cooperation with ATC and federal and state agency partners: the Appalachian Mountain Club in the White Mountains, the Green Mountain Club in the Green Mountains, and the Dartmouth Outing Club in between.

 Appalachian Mountain Club—The A.T. between Grafton Notch (Maine 26) and Kinsman Notch (N.H. 112) is maintained primarily by members of the Appalachian Mountain Club (AMC), and some portions are maintained by the U.S. Forest Service (USFS). For further information on those sections of Trail, contact the AMC, Pinkham Notch Visitors Center, P.O. Box 298, Gorham, NH 03581; (603) 466-2721; <information@outdoors.org>. Its World Wide Web site is <www.outdoors.org>.

Founded in 1876 and the oldest nonprofit conservation and recreational organization in the United States, the AMC promotes the protection, enjoyment, and wise use of the mountains, rivers, and trails of the Northeast. Through its 75,000 members and regional chapters from Maine to Washington, D.C., the AMC supports the belief that the mountains and rivers have an intrinsic worth and also provide recreational opportunity, spiritual renewal, and ecological and economic health for the region. AMC encourages people to enjoy the natural world because it believes that successful conservation depends on this experience. In 1925, AMC leaders helped Benton MacKaye form the Appalachian Trail Conference (now Conservancy).

Randolph Mountain Club—The A.T. skirts the network of trails and shelters maintained by the volunteer members of the Randolph Mountain Club (RMC). The RMC maintains nearly 110 miles of hiking trails, principally on the northern slopes of Mounts Madison, Adams, and Jefferson in the Presidential Range of the White Mountain National Forest and on the Crescent Range in the town of Randolph, New Hampshire. The RMC maintains four shelters in the Northern Presidentials: Gray Knob, Crag Camp, the Log Cabin, and The Perch. The area within a quarter-mile of all RMC facilities and everything above treeline (where trees are 8 feet tall or less) are forest-protection areas (FPA). For further information on the RMC, contact Randolph Mountain Club, P.O. Box 279, Gorham, NH 03581; visit <www.randolphmountainclub.org>, or e-mail <info@randolphmountainclub.org>.

Path-making in the Randolph area dates back at least to the middle of the nineteenth century. Many Randolph trail-builders served as early officers of the AMC. Extensive logging in 1903 and the forest fires that followed shortly thereafter totally destroyed many of those earliest of trails. The original trail-builders had aged but still had a strong desire to see that the trails were restored. The RMC was founded in 1910 and incorporated in 1915. By the late 1930s, Forest Service policy no longer allowed private camps on national-forest land. The RMC took over Gray Knob and Crag Camp in 1939 and has maintained them for the public since, with caretakers in residence beginning shortly after World War II. The town of Randolph jointly maintained Gray Knob with the RMC until the early 1990s, when the club took it over completely.

The RMC board, which manages both the long-term and the day-to-day operations of the club, is completely volunteer. The nonprofit RMC is open to all, and it states that 95 percent of dues and contributions go directly back into trail work and maintaining staffed camp facilities.

Dartmouth Outing Club—The A.T. between Kinsman Notch (N.H. 112) and Vt. 12 is maintained by members of the Dartmouth Outing Club (DOC). For further information on this section, contact the Dartmouth Outing Club, P.O. Box 9, Hanover, NH 03755; (603)

646-2428; <thedoc@dartmouth.edu>; <www.dartmouth.edu/~doc>. This section is blazed with the standard white A.T. blazes, in addition to an occasional orange-and-black blaze marking DOC trails.

The Dartmouth Outing Club was formed in 1909 to "stimulate interest in out-of-door winter sports" and quickly grew to encompass the college's year-round outdoors recreation. It is the oldest and largest collegiate outing club in the country. Today, the club has more than 1,500 student members and about as many nonstudent members. The DOC organizes trips in the outdoors, provides outdoor leader and medical/safety education, and maintains more than seventy miles of the A.T. and its corridor boundaries. Membership in the DOC is open to all members of the Dartmouth community and to others who share common interests. In 1926, the DOC and its trail became a founding link in the new Appalachian Trail.

 Green Mountain Club—The A.T. between Vt. 12 and the Massachusetts–Vermont state line is maintained primarily by members of the Green Mountain Club (GMC); some portions are maintained by the U.S. Forest Service (USFS). For further information on this section, contact the Green Mountain Club, 4711 Waterbury–Stowe Road, Waterbury Center, VT 05677; (802) 244-7037; <gmc@greenmountainclub.org>; <www.greenmountainclub.org>. Additional information on the Trail from Mass. 2 in North Adams to the Connecticut River in Norwich is available in GMC's *Long Trail Guide*.

The history of the Green Mountain Club is the history of the Long Trail. The Long Trail is the oldest long-distance hiking trail in the United States and was, in its first decade, a role model for the Appalachian Trail. Conceived by James P. Taylor (1872–1949) as he waited one day for the mist to clear from Stratton Mountain, the Long Trail took its first step from dream to reality at a gathering of twenty-three people on March 11, 1910, in Burlington, when the Green Mountain Club was formed. In 1930, the final link of the Trail was cut to Canada. In 1971, the Vermont legislature passed a resolution recognizing the club as "the founder, sponsor, defender, and protector" of the Long Trail system and delegating to it responsibility for developing policies and programs for "the preservation, maintenance, and proper use of hiking trails for the ben-

Appalachian Trail Conservancy
Regional office—Lyme, N.H., (603) 795-4935
Main office—Harpers Ferry, W.Va., (304) 535-6331
<www.appalachiantrail.org>

National Park Service
Appalachian Trail Park Office—Harpers Ferry, W.Va., (304) 535-6278
<www.nps.gov/appa>

USDA Forest Service
<www.fs.fed.us>
White Mountain National Forest—Laconia, N.H., (603) 528-8721
 Androscoggin Ranger District, Gorham, N.H., (603) 466-2713
 Saco Ranger District, Conway, N.H., (603) 447-5448

Green Mountain National Forest—Rutland, Vt., (802) 747-6700
 Manchester Ranger Station, Manchester Center, Vt., (802) 362-2307

New Hampshire
Dial 911; if 911 is not available, dial the following local numbers:
New Hampshire State Police—(603) 846-5517; (603) 846-3333
AMC–Pinkham Notch—(603) 466-2721

Vermont
Dial 911; if 911 is not available, dial the following local numbers:
Bethel State Police—(802) 234-9933
Rockingham State Police—(802) 875-2112
Rutland State Police—(802) 773-9101
Shaftsbury State Police—(802) 442-5421

Massachusetts
Dial 911; if 911 is not available, call:
Massachusetts State Police—(413) 743-4700.

efit of the people of Vermont." Although different generations of Green Mountain Club members have faced different challenges—from pioneer trail-blazing to environmental concerns and land acquisition—the club's main responsibility remains the same today as it was in 1910: to maintain and protect the Long Trail for all Vermonters, now and into the future.

The Long Trail—The Massachusetts–Vermont state line is the southern terminus of the 272-mile Long Trail. The A.T. and Long Trail coincide for 105 miles to Maine Junction, just north of Sherburne Pass and U.S. 4. Like the A.T., it is a primitive footpath. It is steep, boggy, and rugged in the tradition of other early New England trails, like those the A.T. follows in the White Mountains of New Hampshire. It winds through wilderness terrain, densely forested with evergreens in higher elevations and northern hardwood trees in lower areas, passing a number of scenic mountain lakes. Although not as rough as the route in the White Mountains, the Long Trail terrain is strenuous and rewarding. *Please* avoid Vermont trails in "mud season," mid-April through Memorial Day. Hiking there in wet, sloppy conditions leads to serious Trail erosion.

Camping on the A.T. in Vermont—In Vermont, except in the Green Mountain National Forest and one state park, the A.T. runs inside a narrow corridor of land acquired to protect the Trail. In those sections, camping and fires are permitted only at designated sites. Some overnight sites charge a fee to help defray the cost of facilities maintenance.

Plant Life—Along the A.T. in Vermont, cutting living trees, shrubs, and plants is prohibited. Only downed trees may be used for fires.

Appalachian Trail Lands—Between the two large national forests, a protective corridor of land for the Trail and its resources has been steadily acquired over three decades by the National Park Service under the direction of the Appalachian Trail Park Office (ATPO), ATC's principal public partner. Generally in this area, ATPO has transferred administrative responsibility for those lands to one of the forests while delegating to ATC the day-to-day management responsibility.

Wilderness Areas—In New Hampshire, the Trail passes through the Great Gulf Wilderness, skirts the northern boundary of the Presidential Range–Dry River Wilderness, and closely parallels the northern and western borders of the Pemigewasset Wilderness. Those lands were set aside by Congress to preserve distinctive natural resources. No facilities exist in this area, but off-Trail camping is permitted.

In Vermont, the Trail passes through the Big Branch, Peru Peak, Lye Brook; and Glastenbury wildernesses. No entry permit is required, but the regulations concerning the remainder of GMNF also apply here.

Caretakers—In both New Hampshire and Vermont, AMC and GMC summer caretakers maintain and supervise several backcountry shelters, campsites, and tentsites in the White and Green mountains. At those areas, mentioned in the Trail description, a fee is charged to partially defray costs. Please cooperate with caretakers, and use trails and shelters in an ecologically sound manner.

Carry In/Carry Out—Carry out all trash and garbage. Rules governing AMC, DOC, and GMC facilities do not permit trash to be left behind. Please adhere to carry-in/carry-out practices in all backcountry areas.

State Parks—In New Hampshire, the A.T. passes through three state parks within the WMNF proclamation boundaries: Franconia Notch State Park, Crawford Notch State Park, and the summit of Mt. Washington. In state parks, camping is permitted only at designated campgrounds, huts, or shelters. Camping is not permitted atop Mt. Washington.

In Vermont, the A.T. passes through Gifford Woods State Park, established to ensure the preservation of certain virgin stands of hardwood forest. Camping is permitted at campsites and shelters.

Shelters—A number of Adirondack shelters (three walls, open front) that accommodate five to fourteen people are located along the Trail. Shelters are near water and have a fire pit and a privy. Many sites have tent platforms as well. Camping is permitted in the vicinity of most shelters. At some sites, a caretaker is in residence, and a fee is charged.

Overnight Sites

Trail Section	Miles from Grafton Notch	Miles from Maine Line		Site
Maine 13	4.6	10.0	+	Speck Pond Campsite and Shelter
Maine 13	9.7	4.9		Full Goose Pond Shelter and Campsite
Maine 13	14.1	0.5		Carlo Col Campsite and Shelter

Trail Section	Miles from Maine Line	Miles from Mass. Line		Site
N.H. 1	4.7	306.0		Gentian Pond Campsite and Shelter
N.H. 1	9.6	301.1		Trident Col Campsite
N.H. 2	18.4	292.3		Rattle River Shelter
N.H. 2	24.5	286.2	+	Imp Campsite and Shelter
N.H. 2	31.7	279.0	+	Carter Notch Hut
N.H. 2	37.6	273.1	+	Joe Dodge Lodge
N.H. 3	42.4	268.3		Osgood Tentsite
N.H. 3	45.4	265.3	+	Madison Spring Hut on Trail; Valley Way Tentsite
N.H. 3	46.3	264.4	+	RMC Crag Camp Cabin + RMC Gray Knob Cabin
N.H. 3	46.9	263.8	+	The Perch Shelter
N.H. 3	51.0	259.7	+	Hermit Lake Shelter
N.H. 3	52.5	258.2	+	Lakes of the Clouds Hut
N.H. 3	57.2	253.5	+	Mizpah Spring Hut; + Nauman Tentsite
N.H. 3	63.6	247.21	+	Dry River Campground
N.H. 4	66.5	244.2	+	Ethan Pond Campsite and Shelter
N.H. 4	71.3	239.4	+	Zealand Falls Hut
N.H. 4	75.5	235.2	+	Guyot Campsite and Shelter
N.H. 4	78.3	232.4	+	Galehead Hut

+ Fee sites

Trail Section	Miles from Maine Line	Miles from Mass. Line	Site
N.H. 4	81.0	229.7	+ Garfield Ridge Campsite and Shelter
N.H. 4	84.9	225.8	+ Greenleaf Hut
N.H. 4	88.7	222.0	+ Liberty Springs Tentsite
N.H. 4	91.3	219.4	+ Lafayette Place Campground
N.H. 5	94.2	216.5	+ Lonesome Lake Hut
N.H. 5	96.1	214.6	+ Kinsman Pond Campsite and Shelter
N.H. 5	100.1	210.6	Eliza Brook Shelter
N.H. 6	109.2	201.5	Beaver Brook Shelter
N.H. 6	116.0	194.7	Jeffers Brook Shelter
N.H. 7	124.6	186.1	Ore Hill Shelter
N.H. 8	131.7	179.0	Hexacuba Shelter
N.H. 8	137.0	173.7	Smarts Mountain Firewarden's Cabin
N.H. 8	137.1	173.6	Smarts Mountain Tentsite
N.H. 9	143.7	167.0	Trapper John Shelter
N.H. 9	149.4	161.3	Moose Mountain Shelter
N.H. 9	158.9	151.8	Velvet Rocks Shelter
Vt. 1	166.2	144.5	Happy Hill Shelter
Vt. 2	175.0	135.7	Thistle Hill Shelter
Vt. 3	186.6	124.1	Wintturi Shelter
Vt. 3	196.5	114.2	Stony Brook Shelter
Vt. 3	203.2	107.5	+ Gifford Woods State Park
Vt. 3	205.5	105.2	Tucker-Johnson Shelter
Vt. 4	208.4	102.3	Churchill Scott Shelter
Vt. 4	210.3	100.4	Pico Camp Shelter
Vt. 4	212.8	97.9	Cooper Lodge Shelter

*AMC huts: Reservations required, see page 27. **RMC sites:** No reservations accepted. Be prepared to pay. If space is not available, be prepared to camp.*

Trail Section	Miles from Maine Line	Miles from Mass. Line	Site
Vt. 4	217.1	93.6	Governor Clement Shelter
Vt. 4	222.9	87.8	Clarendon Shelter
Vt. 5	226.6	84.1	Minerva Hinchey Shelter
Vt. 5	231.7	79.0	Greenwall Shelter
Vt. 5	236.2	74.6	+ Little Rock Pond Shelter
Vt. 5	236.5	74.2	+ Little Rock Pond Tenting Area
Vt. 5	236.8	73.9	+ Lula Tye Shelter
Vt. 6	239.8	70.9	Big Branch Shelter
Vt. 6	240.0	70.7	Old Job Shelter
Vt. 6	241.5	69.2	Lost Pond Shelter
Vt. 6	245.7	65.0	+ Griffith Lake Tenting Area
Vt. 6	246.2	64.5	+ Peru Peak Shelter
Vt. 6	254.3	56.4	Bromley Shelter
Vt. 7	259.1	51.6	Spruce Peak Shelter
Vt. 7	262.2	48.6	William B. Douglas Shelter
Vt. 7	266.7	44.0	+ Stratton Pond, North Shore Tenting Area
Vt. 7	266.9	43.8	+ Stratton Pond Shelter
Vt. 8	277.4	33.3	Story Spring Shelter
Vt. 8	282.0	28.7	Kid Gore Shelter and Caughnawaga Tentsite
Vt. 8	286.3	24.4	Goddard Shelter
Vt. 8	294.8	15.9	Melville Nauheim Shelter
Vt. 9	300.7	10.0	Congdon Shelter
Vt. 9	307.9	2.8	Seth Warner Shelter and Primitive Camping Area
Mass. 1	2.3	1.8	Sherman Brook Campsite

+ Fee sites

Cabins—A cabin is a closed shelter with water, fire pit, and privy. Some have more elaborate facilities, such as bunks and wood stoves, and some have a caretaker with a fee charged. In Vermont, cabins are often called "camps." At some sites, a caretaker is in residence and a fee is charged.

Group Hiking—Organized groups can reduce their chances of arriving at already-crowded sites by contacting the local trail clubs. To notify the Appalachian Mountain Club, go to this Internet site: <www.outdoors. org/lodging/campsites/campsites-notification.cfm>; for the Green Mountain Club, <www.greenmountainclub.org/page.php?id=141>.

Groups hiking in the White Mountain National Forest or the Green Mountain National Forest are required to get an outfitter/guide permit from the USDA Forest Service; see "For More Information," page 349.

Hiking During Hunting Season—Most of the Appalachian Trail in New Hampshire and Vermont is on national-forest land where hunting is legal, subject to state laws. Deer season, typically in the months of October, November, December, and January, should be a time for special caution by hikers. In some areas, hunting is legal on the Trail itself. In sections where hunting is prohibited, hunters on nearby properties may wander near the Trail, not knowing that they are near the Trail.

Hikers should call ATC or check state Web sites or ATC's site, <www. appalachiantrail.org>, for detailed information about hunting seasons. ATC recommends that hikers wear plenty of highly visible "blaze orange" clothing when hunters are sharing the woods.

White Mountain National Forest

For two-thirds of its length in New Hampshire, the A.T. crosses the White Mountain National Forest (WMNF). The WMNF covers almost 800,000 acres in western Maine and New Hampshire, accommodating timber and wildlife management, watershed protection, and recreation. Inhabited for more than 10,000 years (archaeologists have found more than twenty prehistoric sites), the Whites became the core of a national forest established by presidential proclamation in 1918 after a long period of public agitation in reaction to the unregulated practices of logging companies that led to forest fires and damaged watersheds, affecting the mill towns downstream. Less than two decades earlier, 832 sawmills operated on what had been state public lands, and 17 logging railroads cross-crossed the state. Most of the land in the White Mountains in northern New Hampshire is a part of the WMNF.

In recent years, use of more than 1,200 miles of backcountry trails and facilities in the White Mountains has increased dramatically; more than 7 million people visit each year. Soil erosion, loss of vegetation, water pollution, and disposal of human waste have become major problems. In certain areas, scarred trees, eroded trails, and hardened campsites indicate that use is causing steady deterioration. Some areas may never recover. An example is on Franconia Ridge, where compaction and erosion from hikers' footsteps has left a broad, gutted footway. In other places, campers have cut trees, trampled vegetation, and polluted water. Those problems have necessitated regulations to lessen the impact camping and hiking have on plant life, soils, and water.

Forest Protection Areas (FPA)—To protect the forest's fragile ecosystems and allow damaged areas to rehabilitate, the USFS has designated parts of the A.T. in the WMNF as Forest Protection Areas (FPA). FPA information is provided for each section.

Camping and fires are prohibited inside FPAs. Outside FPAs, off-Trail camping and wood or charcoal fires are limited to areas below the alpine zone (where trees are 8 feet tall or less); at least 200 feet off the Trail, and one-quarter mile from any hut, shelter, tent platform, cabin, picnic area, campground, trailhead, lake, stream, or roads. Federal citations are issued for violations.

FPA information is posted at Trailheads. In the summer, USFS ridgerunners patrol the FPAs, offering assistance. For information and the backcountry camping rules for the current hiking season, contact the supervisor's office, White Mountain National Forest, or AMC's Pinkham Notch Visitors Center (see "For More Information," page 349).

Campsites—A "campsite" in the White Mountains generally refers to a site with a shelter like those elsewhere on the A.T., as well as water, toilet facilities, fire pit, and tent platforms. Tent platforms, if you have not camped on one before, are wooden platforms with cleats or rings with which to secure tents, instead of staking them down; they work best with free-standing tents and allow tenting on rugged or steep terrain. They also concentrate, or at least localize, soil compaction. Some campsites have a caretaker in residence, and a fee is charged.

Tentsites—"Tentsites" have only tent platforms or tent pads, with a fire pit, privy, and water. They are sometimes referred to as "primitive tentsites," which means sites are simply spots cleared for tents.

AMC Huts—These large, enclosed structures sleep anywhere from 36 to 90 people and are open as early as May, closing in late September or mid-October, depending on the hut. Two levels of service are provided. The "full-service" season lasts from the first Friday in June to late September or mid-October, depending on the hut. During the full-service season, a hut "croo," consisting primarily of college-aged outdoor enthusiasts, staffs each hut. An overnight stay includes bunk space, bathroom privileges (no showers), and breakfast and dinner prepared by the croo. The huts cater mainly to families and weekend hikers, and the croos usually schedule nightly entertainment programs or games. The "self-service" or "caretaker" season starts in early May and lasts until the first Friday in June at Greenleaf, Galehead, and Mizpah huts. Zealand Falls, Lonesome Lake, and Carter Notch offer caretaker service from late October through the winter months and then switch to full service from June through late October. Caretaker service means no meals, no bedding, and a single caretaker present in the morning and evening. With caretaker service, guests are required to bring their own sleeping bag and food but are welcome to use the kitchen facilities, including the oven, pots, serving dishes, and utensils. Contact AMC for current caretaker season rates; dates, type of service, and rates can almost always be found at <www.outdoors.org>. It is wise to make reservations as far ahead as possible, because all facilities are heavily used. Reservations open in November for the following year. For more information and to make reservations, call (603) 466-2727, Monday through Saturday, 9:00 a.m.–5:00 p.m. Eastern time.

Work-for-Stay Option for A.T. Thru-Hikers—AMC has a long tradition of providing room and board to A.T. thru-hikers in exchange for work at AMC facilities in the White Mountains. The guidelines are:

- The work-for-stay option is available at the huts, shelters, and Camp Dodge Volunteer Center. Work-for-stay is not available at Pinkham Notch Visitors Center/Joe Dodge Lodge.

- Work may not be available and is at the discretion of the AMC staff at the site.

- Work-for-stay is on a first-come, first-served basis. No reservations.

- If work is available, each site can accommodate two thru-hikers per night (four at Lakes of the Clouds Hut).

- Expect to work two hours at huts and Camp Dodge and one hour at shelters, usually after breakfast.

- Discuss what is expected of you with the hutmaster, shelter caretaker, or Dodge crew when you arrive, so terms are clear.

- As a courtesy to other thru-hikers, individuals limit their use of the work-for-stay option to no more than three huts and no more than three shelters. Stays are limited to one night.

Thru-hikers should call Camp Dodge, located four miles west of Pinkham Notch Visitors Center on N.H. 16, (603) 466-9469, to arrange a possible work-for-stay before stopping in. Thru-hikers can stay at regular guest quarters at the reduced member rates, whether or not they are members of the AMC. For more information, contact the AMC by telephone or on-line at <www.outdoors.org/thru-hikers>.

AMC Hiker Shuttle—An AMC hiker shuttle (fee) operates daily from June 1 to mid-September but only weekends from mid-September to mid-October. When planning your hike, it is recommended you take the shuttle at the start and hike back to your vehicle. Reservations are strongly recommended. Travel advice is available from the AMC Reservations Department, shuttle drivers, or the staff at any AMC destination. Along the A.T., the shuttle services Trailheads along N.H. 16 at Pinkham Notch Visitors Center and Nineteen-Mile Brook; along U.S. 3 at Liberty Spring/A.T. parking lot, Lafayette Place Campground West, Old Bridle Path, and Gale River; along U.S. 302 at Highland Center at Crawford Notch, Webster Cliff, Zealand Falls, and Ammonoosuc Ravine Trail; along U.S. 2 at

Valley Way/Appalachia; and in Gorham at the Irving Gas Station. See
<www.outdoors.org/lodging/lodging-shuttle.cfm>.

Parking Fees—In the WMNF, hikers need to display an annual pass
sticker on their windshields or be prepared to pay for a pass when parking at established trailhead parking sites that have a posted fee sign.
Almost all the proceeds from those passes are used for improvements
in the WMNF. Parking passes are available at WMNF ranger offices,
information centers, outdoor retail stores, and AMC's Pinkham Notch
and Crawford Notch visitors centers.

Green Mountain National Forest

For more than one-half its length in Vermont, from Vt. 140 south to the
Massachusetts border, the Trail passes through the Green Mountain
National Forest (GMNF). The national forest, established in 1932 after
uncontrolled logging and flooding despoiled the state, covers about
385,000 acres, stretching almost 100 miles from the Massachusetts line.
It is not only a recreational resource but provides for timber, wildlife,
grazing, and watershed protection. Camping is permitted in the GMNF.

In recent years, recreational use of the GMNF's backcountry also has
increased dramatically. In some places, shelters and trails are used by
greater numbers of hikers than the local environment can support. Trail
erosion, loss of vegetation, water pollution, and disposal of human waste
have developed into major concerns. Such problems necessitate regulations aimed at reducing the impact that camping and hiking have on
plant life, soils, and water.

Throughout GMNF, fires at designated sites must be built in the fire
pits provided. Outside the designated areas, fires are permitted on
national forest lands, but proper Leave No Trace techniques should be
employed. No campfire permits are required. Hikers are encouraged to
use portable stoves to reduce the impact at the campsites.

All visitors to the national forest are asked to keep the trailside and
overnight sites clean. Some Green Mountain Club shelter sites have areas
for gray-water disposal. All trash should be carried out. For further information on policies in GMNF, contact the supervisor's office, Green
Mountain National Forest (see "For More Information," page 349.)

A walk south along the A.T through New Hampshire and Vermont

The Maine–New Hampshire state line, which crosses the Trail through the middle of the Mahoosuc Range of eastern New Hampshire and western Maine, has no easy road access. For that reason, and because the range is usually hiked as one unit, this guide begins at Grafton Notch in Maine and covers the same section (Maine Thirteen) described at the end of the *Appalachian Trail Guide to Maine* and on the back of its Map 7. For similar reasons, this guide ends, not at the Vermont–Massachusetts state line but at the next road crossing to the south, in North Adams, Massachusetts.

Beginning in Maine, the southbound Trail ascends from Grafton Notch and traverses the remote and rugged Mahoosuc Range with many open summits. Along the way, the hiker must wind, crawl, and jump through the boulder-clogged and cave-ridden Mahoosuc Notch. Reaching the Maine–New Hampshire boundary, the Trail descends from the range and crosses the Androscoggin River Valley (Maine Section Thirteen and New Hampshire Section One). The Trail then climbs to the crest of the Carter–Moriah Range, which it follows to open Carter Dome before dropping at Carter Lakes into Carter Notch. From Carter Notch, the Trail rises sharply to Wildcat Mountain, then descends steeply over exposed ledges into Pinkham Notch, where the Pinkham Notch Visitors Center and the North Country headquarters of the Appalachian Mountain Club (AMC) are located (New Hampshire Section Two).

From Pinkham Notch, the Trail ascends and then drops through the Great Gulf Wilderness, climbing to the rocky summit of Mt. Madison, which marks the northern end of the much-storied, alpine Presidential Range, a rocky, tundra-covered ridge that is the highlight of the White Mountain National Forest. The Trail passes close to the summits of Mt. Adams, Mt. Jefferson, and Mt. Clay (Mt. Reagan) and then ascends to Mt. Washington (6,288 feet), the highest peak in the northeastern United States. From the summit of Mt. Washington, the Trail descends south, skirting Mt. Monroe, passing over Mt. Franklin, skirting Mt. Eisenhower,

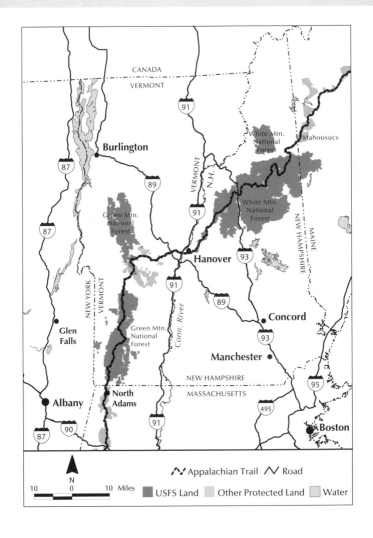

passing over Mt. Pierce (Mt. Clinton), and reentering the woods. It continues on this ridge, passing over Mt. Jackson and Mt. Webster before dropping into Crawford Notch State Park (New Hampshire Section Three).

From Crawford Notch, the Trail climbs to cross the lower flank of the Willey Range, passes through Zealand Notch, and then ascends to cross Zealand Ridge, Garfield Ridge, and the alpine Franconia Range, where it passes over Mt. Lafayette (5,249 feet), the highest peak in that area. The Trail drops from Franconia Ridge into Franconia Notch and Franconia Notch State Park (New Hampshire Section Four).

From Franconia Notch, the Trail once again ascends. It follows the crest of the wooded Kinsman Ridge to Kinsman Notch, where evidence of intensive glacial activity is preserved in the Lost River Reservation (New Hampshire Section Five). From Kinsman Notch, where the Dartmouth Outing Club takes over Trail-maintenance responsibility from the

Appalachian Mountain Club, the Trail makes a spectacular ascent to the summit of the massive, bald Mt. Moosilauke (4,802 feet), the southwestern edge of the White Mountains. From that summit, the Trail descends to Glencliff (New Hampshire Section Six).

Beginning at Glencliff, the Trail climbs Wyatt Hill, where it passes Wachipauka Pond and crosses the summit of Mt. Mist before descending to cross N.H. 25C. The Trail then passes over the summit of Ore Hill and descends to N.H. 25A (New Hampshire Section Seven).

From that highway, the A.T. climbs Mt. Cube, crosses Eastman Ledges, and then climbs to the firetower on Smarts Mountain (3,240 feet). The Trail descends steeply from the firetower, over Lambert Ridge to the Dartmouth Skiway, and then climbs Holts Ledge. Continuing on trails and woods roads through hardwood forest, pastures, and fields, the Trail passes over the north and south peaks of Moose Mountain and over Velvet Rocks to Hanover, home of Dartmouth College. After meandering through the town of Hanover, the Trail descends to the Connecticut River (400 feet), the border between New Hampshire and Vermont (New Hampshire Section Nine).

Climbing up from the Connecticut River, the Trail passes on roads west though the small town of Norwich, Vermont. It ascends Mosley Hill (1,180 feet), passes over the wooded crest of Griggs Mountain (1,570 feet), and descends along Podunk Brook to the White River at West Hartford (Vermont Section One). It crosses the White River on a highway bridge and passes over Bunker Hill (1,480 feet) on old roads before reaching the abandoned Kings Highway. West of Kings Highway, the

Franconia Ridge

Trail passes over Thistle Hill (1,800 feet), then crosses a number of roads, and reaches Vt. 12 (Vermont Section Two), where maintenance responsibility passes to the Green Mountain Club.

From Vt. 12, the route ascends to the Lookout (2,439 feet) and continues west across rugged terrain into Ottauquechee Valley, which is hemmed in by high ridges. From this valley, the Trail passes Thundering Brook Falls, Kent Pond, and Vt. 100 into Gifford Woods State Park, which has a stand of virgin hardwood forest. After passing through the park, the Trail rises steeply to "Maine Junction," its northern intersection with the Long Trail just north of U.S. 4; the routes of the two trails coincide between there and the Massachusetts border (Vermont Section Three).

From U.S. 4, the Trail climbs south across the Coolidge Range. Side trails lead to the summits of Pico Peak (3,957 feet) and Killington Peak (4,235 feet). The Trail reaches its highest point in Vermont just below Killington Peak, the second-highest summit in the state (Mt. Mansfield, at 4,393 feet, is the highest). From the Coolidge Range, the Trail continues south across rolling foothills and crosses a number of roads (Vermont Section Four).

Just south of Vt. 103, the Trail crosses a suspension bridge over Clarendon Gorge, ascends to the height of land on Bear Mountain (2,240 feet) and descends to enter the Green Mountain National Forest, which it had skirted just north of U.S. 4. South of Vt. 140, the Trail ascends by the Bully Brook cascades, enters the Robert T. Stafford White Rocks National Recreation Area, ascends the ridge of White Rocks Mountain (2,680 feet), skirts the western shore of Little Rock Pond, then descends along Little Black Branch to Danby–Landgrove Road (USFS 10) at a low point on the crest of the Green Mountains (Vermont Section Five).

Soon after USFS 10, the Trail travels nearly 12 miles through the Green Mountain National Forest's Big Branch and Peru Peak wildernesses. The Trail then rises to the summit of Baker Peak (2,850 feet), descends past Griffith Lake, passes over Peru Peak (3,429 feet) and Styles Peak (3,394 feet), and descends to Mad Tom Notch (2,446 feet). The Trail steadily climbs Bromley Mountain (3,260 feet) before descending and crossing Vt. 11/30 (Vermont Section Six).

From Vt. 11/30, the Trail climbs to Spruce Peak, reaches Prospect Rock (2,079 feet), enters the Green Mountain National Forest's Lye Brook Wilderness, and reaches Stratton Pond. As it leaves the pond on the

Coolidge Range in Vermont

western slope of Stratton Mountain, the Trail ascends to the Stratton firetower, near the point where Benton MacKaye is sometimes said to have first conceived the idea of an Appalachian Trail. The Trail leaves the summit of Stratton Mountain and descends to Stratton–Arlington (Kelley Stand) Road (Vermont Section Seven).

From the Stratton–Arlington (Kelley Stand) Road, the Trail ascends south along a ridge, rising to a firetower on Glastenbury Mountain (3,748 feet). It then enters the Green Mountain National Forest's Glastenbury Wilderness, continues along a wooded ridge, and drops steeply to Vt. 9. It then rises even more steeply on a rock staircase to Harmon Hill (2,325 feet) and follows a rolling ridge until it reaches the Vermont–Massachusetts state line on East Mountain (2,330 feet) (Vermont Sections Eight and Nine).

South of the state line, the Trail passes over the open rocky ridge of East Mountain, with no easy road access, then drops to the Hoosic River and Mass. 2 in North Adams. Massachusetts Section One begins at the state line. Because of the lack of road access at the boundary, this guide ends at Mass. 2 and covers Massachusetts Section One, as described in the *Appalachian Trail Guide to Massachusetts–Connecticut*.

New Hampshire

The Appalachian Trail in New Hampshire is a true gem of its route through New England. It follows the rugged ridgecrests of the White Mountains with spectacular scenery and extraordinary vistas. It includes long sections above treeline, where the temperature may change very suddenly and snow is possible in any season. The route ascends high, rocky, and barren ridges divided by steep, deep notches or valleys and often by sharp cols between high peaks. It also follows footpaths and woods roads through dense hardwood and coniferous forests and crosses rushing mountain streams.

Beyond the high peaks, between Glencliff and the Connecticut River to the west, traversing the White Mountain foothills along the Connecticut River Valley, the physical and cultural features characteristic of upland northern New England become strikingly evident. Many of the low ridges and rolling hills have reverted to woodland. The large fields and

clearings, cellar holes, stone fences, lilac and apple trees, cemeteries, and abandoned roads are evidence of a time, more than a century ago, when this was a prosperous area of farms and small hamlets.

Among the highlights of this state:

The Mahoosuc Range—The Mahoosuc Range is a northeast-to-southwest mountain chain extending from Grafton Notch, Maine, to the Androscoggin River Valley of New Hampshire. Many alpine bogs highlight the area, and open ledges provide splendid views.

Two guidebook sections of the Trail traverse this range, crossing eight major mountain peaks. The range is accessible by road only at its ends, and it is usually hiked in its entirety (Maine Section Thirteen and New Hampshire Section One). The total climb in either direction is approximately 8,000 feet.

The range is wild and rugged. Be prepared for frequent climbs and descents and a rough, wet footway. Do not underestimate the time necessary to traverse the range (three to five days).

View from Mt. Madison

The Trail crosses wet, boggy areas along the range, both high on the ridge and in sags between peaks. Although those bogs appear stable, even limited trampling will break down the vegetation and soil structure, leading to unpleasant, muddy areas. To keep hikers from widening the footway, extensive log walkways or bog bridges, also known as puncheon, have been installed. Use the walkways to prevent further harm and allow regeneration of the parts of the bog already damaged.

The northern part of this range is taller and narrower, with a well-defined ridgecrest, while the southern part of the range is a broad, ledgy, and lumpy ridge. Do not be deceived by the low elevations on the map profiles; this section of Trail is among the most rugged of its kind, a very strenuous Trail, especially for those with heavy packs. Be prepared for frequent climbs and descents, aided by wooden ladders on sheer rock, a rough and wet footway, and many rock scrambles. Although travel may be both boggy and wet along the ridge and between the peaks, the range has no major stream crossings, and water might be scarce. Some sections of the ridge above treeline, especially the one traversing Goose Eye Mountain, have significant exposure to bad weather.

Mt. Washington Summit—Most of Mt. Washington (6,288 feet), the highest peak in the United States north of the Carolinas and east of the Mississippi, is part of the New Hampshire state-park system (New Hampshire Section 3). The Mt. Washington Cog Railway, the world's first mountain-climbing railway and an engineering marvel in 1869, ascends from Marshfield Station three miles up the western ridge of the mountain to the summit (see also <www.thecog.com>). The Mt. Washington Auto Road (toll road), beginning on N.H. 16, winds eight miles up the eastern side of the mountain to the summit (see also <www.mtwashingtonauto-road.com>). Both corridors are private property.

The Sherman Adams Building on the summit is owned by the state and has a snack bar, souvenir shop, toilets, telephone, and post office. It also houses the Mt. Washington Observatory and Museum. Southwest of the summit is the Yankee Building, built in 1941 to house transmitter facilities for the first FM radio station in northern New England; it houses two-way radio equipment for various organizations. The old Tip-Top House, built in 1853, is west of the summit building and is usually open as a museum daily during the park's season.

Mt. Washington has long been a center of attention. The first path to the summit was cut in 1819 by a father-and son team, Abel and Ethan Allen Crawford, who later established the first tourist hostelries in the notch now bearing their name. In 1839, Thomas, a younger son of Abel, converted Crawford Path into a bridle path, the first of its kind to the summit. The first bridle path from the east was constructed between 1851 and 1861 and started at the Glen House, where the auto road begins. Major trails from the summit pass the remains of old corrals.

The summit stands well above treeline and, with the 20-mile ridge of the Presidential Range, forms an eight-square-mile arctic island in New England—the largest east of the Rockies and south of Canada—with permafrost, arctic flora resembling that of northern Labrador, and some of the most extreme weather in the world. The severe weather is caused by high winds and frequent, sharp temperature changes, influenced by air masses flowing from the south, west, and the St. Lawrence River Valley in the north.

The first weather observatory was established on the summit in 1870 and staffed by the U.S. Signal Corps until 1892. The present observatory was initiated in 1932 by Joe Dodge, former Appalachian Mountain Club (AMC) hut-system manager, and Bob Monahan, a Dartmouth College weather buff. On April 12, 1934, the observatory measured a wind velocity of 231 miles per hour, still the strongest wind speed ever recorded on land. The observatory is staffed all year, carrying out scientific experiments and recordings, including a morning report on the summit weather conditions (see also <www.mountwashington.org>). A snow vehicle is used for the weekly change of personnel in the winter. The observatory is not open to the public, but a museum on the lower floor of the Sherman Adams Building contains artifacts and exhibits of unusual flora and fauna. A museum fee supports the observatory.

Because of the violent weather, the Crawfords provided crude stone huts for shelter. The first summit house was built in 1852; the Tip-Top House, in 1853. Those small structures became inadequate, and the first large summit house was opened in 1874. A fire swept the summit in 1908, destroying the summit house and damaging the Tip-Top House.

Construction of the Carriage Road began in 1851, and it opened in 1861. Today, thousands of cars ascend the eight miles to the summit at grades of up to 12 percent.

The cog railway's trestle over Jacob's Ladder, at a 37.4-percent grade, is the steepest in the world. Sylvester Marsh built the 3.5-mile railroad and powered it by a coal-fired steam engine. The railway was honored at its one-hundredth birthday by designation as a national historical mechanical and civil-engineering landmark.

In 1937–38, a radio tower was installed on the summit. FM-radio broadcasts from the summit began as early as 1941, and, in 1954, a television transmitter was added. The Yankee powerhouse and the former WMTW-TV building were destroyed by fire in February 2003.

Until recently, the summit was privately owned. From early grants and purchases, it passed to Colonel Henry Teague of the cog railway, who left it to Dartmouth College. Most of it is now owned by the state of New Hampshire.

Crawford Notch State Park—In 1777, Timothy Nash spied a defile, in what was then considered an impassable wall of mountains, while he was hunting moose on Cherry Mountain. Soon after Nash's discovery, a road was built through Crawford Notch (New Hampshire Section Three). It was rough, crossing the Saco River thirty-two times. In some places, horses had to be lifted or lowered by ropes. As poor as it was, the route was far preferable to traveling around the White Mountains. The first cargo sent from the coast through the notch was a barrel of rum that arrived a great deal lighter than when it began its voyage.

In 1852, Samuel Willey and his family moved into the notch and opened a hostel. The next year, the calamitous "Willey Slide" shook the notch, taking the lives of the entire family. Tons of debris suddenly and violently slid and fell from the valley walls, partly determining the shape of the notch today. Despite the devastation of the slide, activity in the notch did not slow down—it was an important commercial route and a prime attraction for summer tourists.

Today, the notch is preserved in Crawford Notch State Park. The Willey House Site and Willey Slide are still visible one mile north of the Trail crossing. A snack bar and souvenir shop nearby are open mid-May to mid-October. AMC operates its Highland Center at the site of the original Crawford Hotel, and nearby is its historic Crawford Notch Depot Visitors Center, with displays and exhibits on the rich human and natural history of Crawford Notch and the White Mountains.

Treeline—Treeline in the Whites occurs at approximately 4,200 feet. Above this elevation, only stunted krummholz (spruce) and a wealth of alpine species prevail against the severe weather. This vegetation is extremely vulnerable to damage by foot traffic. In many places, obliteration of alpine tundra has given way to erosion, visibly scarring the mountainside. To prevent trampling vegetation and to allow successful regeneration of damaged areas, rock steps and low stone walls have been installed in many places. *Closely follow established treadway,* in order to keep impact to a minimum; those plants can withstand weather you would find unbearable but cannot survive your soles.

Franconia Ridge—The walk along the rocky spine of Franconia Ridge (New Hampshire Section Four)—anchored by Mt. Lafayette, formerly known as Great Haystack with its overview of the Pemigewasset Wilderness (see below), and Little Haystack—is one of the most dramatic, rewarding, and popular few miles of the entire New Hampshire portion of the Appalachian Trail. Mostly above treeline and spectacular for both its views and its rare and fragile arctic tundra, the ridge is a true prehistoric remnant. Not only is the tundra an island of the northern Canadian ecosystem left by the retreat of glaciers 12,000 years ago, just before humans started venturing toward New England, but it also is the flank of a volcano from perhaps a hundred million years ago that collapsed into itself.

While the eastern slopes slide into the vast woods of the "Pemi," the western drop precipitously into Franconia Notch State Park. For a brief period in June, the alpine flowers throw up little scatterings of color across the predominant green of the ridge. On some days, that display is accompanied by 100-mile visibility and the songs of Bicknell's thrush and more than 180 other bird species. It should also be noted that the ridge is fully exposed to lightning strikes and other violent weather—be prepared for that and to drop below treeline at the first sign of trouble.

The Pemigewasset Wilderness—In New Hampshire Section Four, the A.T. passes through the valley and along the ridges making up the western and northern edges of the Pemigewasset Wilderness, a 45,000-acre tract of now-undeveloped mountain land where forests were extensively logged from the nineteeneth century until just after World War II. In 1969, the U.S. Forest Service established much of this tract as the Lincoln Woods Scenic Area. It became a congressionally designated wilderness area in 1984.

On a clear day now, hikers can see south from Zealand, Garfield, and Franconia ridges into a densely forested landscape that was once a clear-cut area. The most striking evidence of past logging activity is the striated appearance of the forest, a result of logging roads having once been cut across the mountainside.

In Zealand Notch, hikers walk along the bed of the former Zealand Valley Railroad, used to transport timber out of the notch before 1900. Most of the timber logged in the White Mountains, including Zealand Notch and the "Pemi," was removed by one of seventeen railroads, and many other trails in the wilderness area follow former railroad rights-of-way. The Zealand Branch was known as the steepest and most crooked in New England. The Lincoln and East Branch Railroad (now the Kancamagus Highway), leading from Lincoln northeast into the wilderness area, was the longest, with more than 60 miles of track. Relics of logging and the railroads are still found in the forest.

During the logging years, forest fires swept the "Pemi" and left marks still visible today. In 1903, the Zealand Notch area burned. In 1907, a fire ravaged much of the "Pemi," burning both Zealand and Garfield ridges. Mt. Guyot and Mt. Garfield, now open summits, were both wooded until fire burned their forest cover. The forest is still in the succession stage of regrowth.

Franconia Notch State Park—This park, also in New Hampshire Section Four, was established to protect the area's spectacular natural features and geologic curiosities. The Basin, located one mile compass-north of the Trail crossing at its junction with the Basin–Cascade Trail, is a glacial pothole 20 feet in diameter, carved in granite at the base of a waterfall perhaps 25,000 years ago. The "Old Man of the Mountains," a 40-foot stone profile of a man's face formed by five former ledges of Cannon Cliffs and sometimes used as an iconic symbol for the state, collapsed and tumbled to the valley floor in May 2003. An aerial tramway soars to the summit of Cannon Mountain north of Profile Lake on U.S. 3. The Flume is a natural chasm 800 feet long with granite walls 60 to 70 feet high and only 12 to 20 feet apart. Boardwalk views are available within the gorge itself (fee charged).

Mt. Moosilauke—This glacially polished highlight of New Hampshire Section Six was a hunting ground for the Pemigewasset tribe of native Americans, to whom *Moosilauke* meant "high bald place." In the eighteenth century, European settlers farmed the Moosilauke area. The Indians retreated before the wave of settlement, the region was opened to land grants, and it was not long before much of the virgin forest was cleared for cultivation and timber.

About 1850, agriculture declined here, and the mountain became a logging and resort center. Two bridle paths were built to the 4,802-foot-high summit with its panoramic views, and, in 1860, a summit hotel, the Prospect House, opened. As the tourist business boomed, the Moosilauke Mountain Road Company completed the five-mile Carriage Road to the summit. When that hotel closed its doors in 1880, another one, the Tip Top House (1881–1919), opened.

Between 1899 and 1914, lumber companies stripped all but the most inaccessible timber from the western side of the mountain. Around 1920, that intensive logging ended, and the relatively young U.S. Forest Service purchased most of the land, although Dartmouth College owns 4,600 acres of the Baker River watershed, about a third of the mountain above the 2,000-foot mark. The summit includes about 100 acres of alpine tundra, but "the Gentle Giant" is known almost as much for its miles of cascading streams and side trails as it is for the views from the top of the Whites and Vermont and even into New York.

The Dartmouth Outing Club (DOC) adopted the Tip Top House in 1920 when it and a circular tract on the summit was given to the college. The Dartmouth Summit Camp burned down in 1942, but its foundation is still visible. The Carriage Road, rebuilt in 1994, is now used only by hikers, and the Ravine Lodge at the base of the mountain on the east is owned and operated by Dartmouth.

Grafton Notch (Maine 26) to Maine–New Hampshire State Line

14.6 MILES

For the Trail northward in Maine, consult the *Appalachian Trail Guide to Maine,* from which this description is derived.

The Trail in this section crosses rugged, mountainous terrain (see page 37). At the northern end of the Mahoosuc Range, from Grafton Notch to Old Speck, the A.T. coincides with the Old Speck Trail to its junction with the Mahoosuc Trail, just below the 4,180-foot summit of Old Speck. From there, the Trail passes Speck Pond, steeply descends the Mahoosuc Arm, and enters the giant, boulder-filled Mahoosuc Notch, which many consider the most challenging single mile of the entire 14-state Trail. Then, the Trail reaches the South Peak of Fulling Mountain, descends, climbs yet once again to reach treeline on the North Peak of Goose Eye Mountain, and climbs even more steeply to the East Peak of Goose Eye. The path descends steeply before ascending Mt. Carlo, then works its way through the boulders of the col to the Maine–New Hampshire state line. The elevation at Grafton Notch is 1,500 feet; at the state line, 2,972 feet. The highest point of the section, at 4,030 feet, is at the Mahoosuc Trail junction, just below the summit of Old Speck Mountain.

Road Access—Only the northern end of this section, on Maine 26, is directly accessible by vehicle. Parking is available (small fee).

Success Pond Road, which begins in Berlin, New Hampshire (see New Hampshire Section One), and ends near Grafton Notch, provides access to trailhead parking for several side trails that approach the Trail from the west. It is a private gravel road owned by a local paper company but open to public use.

The Trail also may be approached from the east by way of the Wright Trail (mile 12.0/2.6), which is reached by taking Sunday River Road to Bull Branch Road near Ketchum, Maine.

continued on page 46

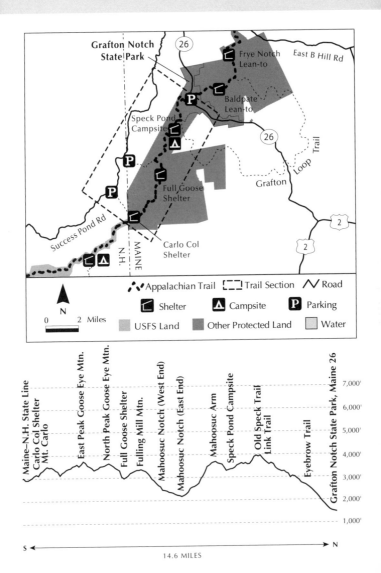

Grafton Notch State Park

(26)

Frye Notch Lean-to

East B Hill Rd

P

Baldpate Lean-to

(26)

Speck Pond Campsite

Loop Trail

Grafton

Full Goose Shelter

P

P

Success Pond Rd

Carlo Col Shelter

N.H.

MAINE

2

2

N

0   2 Miles

•••• Appalachian Trail   [___] Trail Section   ∧ Road

🏠 Shelter   ▲ Campsite   P Parking

USFS Land   Other Protected Land   Water

Maine–N.H. State Line
Carlo Col Shelter
Mt. Carlo
East Peak Goose Eye Mtn.
North Peak Goose Eye Mtn.
Full Goose Shelter
Fulling Mill Mtn.
Mahoosuc Notch (West End)
Mahoosuc Notch (East End)
Mahoosuc Arm
Speck Pond Campsite
Old Speck Trail
Link Trail
Eyebrow Trail
Grafton Notch State Park, Maine 26

7,000'
6,000'
5,000'
4,000'
3,000'
2,000'
1,000'

S ◄   ► N

14.6 MILES

Maps—Refer to Map One with this guide, Map 7 from the *Appalachian Trail Guide to Maine,* or AMC Map 6 (North Country–Mahoosuc Range). For area detail but not up-to-date Trail routes, refer to the USGS 15-minute topographic quadrangles for Old Speck Mountain and Bethel, Maine, and Success Pond and Gorham, New Hampshire, or the USGS 7½-minute topographic quadrangle for Shelburne, New Hampshire.

Shelters and Campsites—This section has three shelters with tent platforms for camping: Speck Pond Shelter (mile 4.6/10.0), Full Goose Shelter (mile 9.7/4.9), and Carlo Col Shelter (mile 14.1/0.5). *No camping is allowed in Grafton Notch State Park.*

Throughout this section, camping should be limited to the shelter sites and away from water sources. Off-Trail camping is limited. Do not camp in the fragile alpine bogs. State fire laws require that wood and charcoal fires be built only at designated shelter sites. At other places along the Trail, only stoves are permitted.

North of the Maine–New Hampshire state line, the Trail passes through Grafton Notch State Park and federal lands managed by the Mahoosuc Management Unit of the state Bureau of Public Lands. Most of the side trails are on private land.

Mahoosuc Notch

SECTION HIGHLIGHTS

Northern end of section →

The Trail crosses Maine 26 at a well-signed parking area (fee) at the height of land in Grafton Notch, 12 miles northwest of U.S. 2. Bethel, Maine (ZIP Code 04217), is 18 miles east on Maine 26 and U.S. 2, with public telephones, motels, restaurants, groceries, an outfitter, and a hostel. The village of Upton, with a small store near Umbagog Lake, is 7 miles west.

Old Speck Trail →

This 3.5-mile trail up Old Speck Mountain coincides with the A.T.

Eyebrow Trail →

Leads 1.2 miles west over steep and rough terrain and is an alternative to the lower part of the Old Speck Trail, passing along the edge of Eyebrow Cliffs. It is better suited for ascent than descent.

Eyebrow Cliffs →

Eyebrow Cliffs drops 800 feet to the floor of Grafton Notch.

Mahoosuc Trail→

Coincides with the A.T. along the entire 26.7-mile length of the Mahoosuc Range from the summit of Old Speck to Gorham, New Hampshire. *Mahoosuc* is thought to be Abenaki for "home of the hungry animals," which may refer to Mohegan–Pequot refugees who fled from Connecticut to Maine after the Pequot War of 1637. Another theory is that the word is Natick for "a pinnacle."

Old Speck Mountain →

It is a gentle climb 0.3 mile east to the flat, wooded summit. An observation tower and recently cleared summit plateau afford fine views. Old Speck is the fifth-highest mountain in Maine. Trail-north from this point, the A.T. is coaligned for 8 miles to Baldpate Mountain with the 30-mile Grafton Loop Trail.

N-S

TRAIL DESCRIPTION

0.0 The **northern end of section** (elev. 1,500 feet) is at Grafton Notch on Maine 26. ■ SOUTHBOUND hikers ascend **Old Speck Mountain** on the **Old Speck Trail** from the kiosk area on the north side of the parking lot. ■ NORTHBOUND hikers cross Maine 26 and enter woods, ascending toward Baldpate Mountain (see *Appalachian Trail Guide to Maine*). **14.6**

0.1 Reach northern junction with the **Eyebrow Trail** (elev. 1,550 feet). It rejoins the A.T at mile 1.2/13.4. **14.5**

0.3 Cross brook. Follow a series of switchbacks to/from the falls on Cascade Brook (elev. 1,580 feet). **14.3**

1.1 Cross brook for the first/last time in box canyon (elev. 2,500 feet). Last water southbound until Speck Pond, mile 4.6/10.0. **13.5**

1.2 Pass southern junction with the **Eyebrow Trail** (elev. 2,550 feet), which leads 0.1 mile west to **Eyebrow Cliffs** and rejoins the A.T. at mile 0.1/14.5. **13.4**

1.5 Cross crest of North Ridge (elev. 3,000 feet). **13.1**

3.0 Pass easterly outlook from top of hump (elev. 3,500 feet). **11.6**

3.4 Reach an excellent northerly outlook (elev. 4,000 feet). **11.2**

3.5 Junction of **Mahoosuc Trail** and **Old Speck Mountain** side trail (elev. 4,030 feet). ■ SOUTHBOUND hikers follow Mahoosuc Trail. ■ NORTHBOUND hikers follow **Old Speck Trail** away from summit. **11.1**

S-N

Speck Pond Shelter and Campsite →

Built in 1978 and maintained by the AMC. Caretaker; fee. Accommodates 8 in shelter and 30 on three single and three double tent platforms. Cookstoves only. Composting privy; bear box. Water source is a stream on the blue-blazed trail behind caretaker's yurt. Next shelter or campsite: south, 5.1 miles (Full Goose); north, 6.9 miles (Baldpate).

Speck Pond Trail →

Leads west 3.6 miles to Success Pond Road, 11.4 miles from Hutchins Street in Berlin, New Hampshire (see New Hampshire Section One).

Mahoosuc Notch →

A deep cleft between Mahoosuc Arm and Fulling Mill Mountain. Giant boulders fallen from the notch's sheer walls have clogged the floor. Ice is found in the caves here as late as July. As hikers follow the blazes, they must climb around and under house-sized boulders and through caves and, in some places, must remove their packs to do so. Traversing the notch is difficult and dangerous. Take care to avoid slipping on damp moss.

Mahoosuc Notch Trail →

Leads west 2.5 miles to Success Pond Road, 10.9 miles from Hutchins Street in Berlin, New Hampshire (see New Hampshire Section One).

Full Goose Shelter →

Rebuilt in 1970; maintained by the AMC. Accommodates 8 in the shelter and 17 on three single and one double tent platforms. Composting privy. Water source is a stream 250 yards on the side trail behind shelter. Do not camp near spring. Next shelter or campsite: south, 4.7 miles (Carlo Col); north, 5.1 miles (Speck Pond).

N-S	TRAIL DESCRIPTION	

3.7	Cross scrubby boulder slope (elev. 3,700 feet).	**10.9**
4.0	An intermittent spring is 100 feet to east (elev. 3,600 feet).	**10.6**
4.6	Reach **Speck Pond Shelter and Campsite** (elev. 3,430 feet) and junction with **Speck Pond Trail**.	**10.0**
4.9	Cross outlet of Speck Pond (elev. 3,400 feet), one of the highest ponds in Maine.	**9.7**
5.5	Reach open summit of Mahoosuc Arm and junction with the May Cutoff Trail (elev. 3,770 feet), which leads west 0.3 mile to Speck Pond Trail.	**9.1**
6.6	Cross brook and skirt southern slope of sheer-walled Mahoosuc Mountain (elev. 2,600 feet).	**8.0**
7.1	Reach northern end of **Mahoosuc Notch**, near Bull Branch of Sunday River (elev. 2,150 feet).	**7.5**
8.2	Reach junction with the **Mahoosuc Notch Trail** at the southern end of Mahoosuc Notch (elev. 2,460 feet).	**6.4**
9.2	Reach the bare crest of the South Peak of Fulling Mill Mountain (elev. 3,395 feet).	**5.4**
9.7	Pass **Full Goose Shelter** (elev. 3,030 feet).	**4.9**

SECTION HIGHLIGHTS

Wright Trail→

Descends 1.6 miles to meet its southern branch and another 2.5 miles to Bull Branch Road. *Directions for this as an access route:* 2.8 miles north of Bethel, Maine, on U.S. 2, turn north onto Sunday River Road. At a fork in 2.2 miles, bear right at signs for Jordan Bowl and covered bridge; at 3.3 miles, bear right again (sign for covered bridge); at 3.8 miles, continue past Artist Covered Bridge on left; at 6.5 miles, road turns to gravel; at 7.8 miles, turn left across the two steel bridges, and take immediate first right onto unsigned Bull Branch Road; at 9.3 miles, cross Goose Eye Brook on bridge; at 9.5 miles, trailhead sign is on left. Parking is farther up the road.

Goose Eye Trail→

Ascends west 0.1 mile to the open summit of the West Peak of Goose Eye Mountain (elev. 3,870 feet) with spectacular views, then descends 3.2 miles to Success Pond Road, 8.1 miles from Hutchins Street in Berlin, New Hampshire (see New Hampshire Section One).

Carlo Col Trail→

Leads west 2.6 miles to Success Pond Road.

Carlo Col Shelter→

Rebuilt in 1976; maintained by the AMC. Accommodates 16 at shelter and 25 at three single and two double tent platforms. Composting privy; bear box. Water from stream. Next shelter or campsite: south, 5.5 miles (Gentian Pond); north, 4.7 miles (Full Goose).

Southern end of section →

The nearest resupply point is the full-service town of Gorham, New Hampshire (ZIP Code 03581), 20.1 miles from the state line, with telephones, supermarket, coin laundry, restaurants, motels, hostels, outfitters, AMC hiker-shuttle stop, and bus service to Boston through Concord Coach Lines, (800) 639-3317, <www.concordcoachlines.com>. Gorham is reached by continuing 16.5 miles south on the A.T. to U.S. 2 and walking from there 3.6 miles west (see New Hampshire Section One).

N-S	TRAIL DESCRIPTION	
10.3	Reach treeline on the North Peak of Goose Eye Mountain (elev. 3,300 feet).	**4.3**
10.7	Reach open North Peak of Goose Eye Mountain (elev. 3,675 feet).	**3.9**
11.8	Pass northern junction with the **Wright Trail** (elev. 3,450 feet).	**2.8**
11.9	Cross the East Peak of Goose Eye Mountain (elev. 3,790 feet).	**2.7**
12.0	Pass southern junction with the **Wright Trail** (elev. 3,620 feet).	**2.6**
12.3	Pass junction of the **Goose Eye Trail** (elev. 3,800 feet).	**2.3**
13.7	Reach the open, southwest summit of Mt. Carlo (elev. 3,565 feet), with excellent views.	**0.9**
14.1	Reach a boulder-filled box ravine and the junction with the **Carlo Col Trail**, which leads 0.3 mile west to **Carlo Col Shelter** (elev. 3,170 feet).	**0.5**
14.6	The **southern end of section** is the Maine–New Hampshire state line (elev. 2,972 feet). ■ SOUTHBOUND hikers descend over a low hump beyond the border signs (see New Hampshire Section One). ■ NORTHBOUND hikers continue climbing beyond the border signs.	**0.0**

Maine–New Hampshire State Line to Androscoggin Valley (U.S. 2)

16.5 MILES

From the state line, the Trail in this section continues through the southern Mahoosuc Range, coinciding with the Mahoosuc Trail, then ascends Mt. Success. It descends to Gentian Pond, passes Moss Pond and Dream Lake, climbs Wocket Ledge to Page Pond, climbs Cascade Mountain, and joins the Centennial Trail. On it, the footpath reaches the eastern summit of Mt. Hayes on open ledges, then descends to the Androscoggin River Valley. The elevation at the state line is 2,972 feet; at U.S. 2, 760 feet. The highest point is on Mt. Success, at 3,565 feet.

Road Approaches—The Trail is not directly accessible by road at the northern end. Road access and parking is available at the southern end of this section at Hogan Road (mile 15.7), at the junction of Hogan and North roads (mile 16.0), and at the parking lot on U.S. 2 (0.2 mile north of mile 16.5 below).

continued on page 56

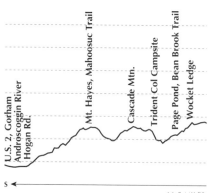

S ◄—

16.5 MILES

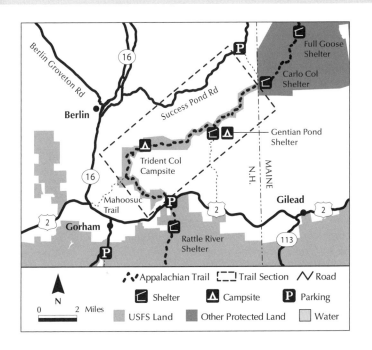

Appalachian Trail   Trail Section   Road

Shelter   Campsite   Parking

N

0   2 Miles

USFS Land   Other Protected Land   Water

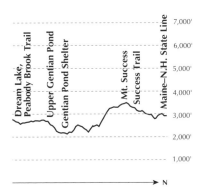

Several side trails approaching the Trail from the west have trailheads on the Success Pond Road (directions below). The two side trails closest to the state line are Carlo Col Trail, 0.5 mile to the north, and the Success Trail, 1.3 miles to the south of the border.

Success Pond Road, which begins in Berlin, New Hampshire, and ends near Grafton Notch, Maine (see Mahoosuc Range), provides access to trailhead parking for several side trails that approach the Trail from the west. It is a gravel logging road, often muddy and rough and not maintained in winter—owned by a local paper company but open to public use. It runs 19.4 miles from Hutchins Street on the east side of the Androscoggin River in Berlin to Maine 26, 2.8 miles north of the Old Speck Trailhead in Grafton Notch. The northern 1.8 miles are signed as the York Pond Road. Use extreme caution when traveling on this road and yield to the fast-moving logging trucks. *Directions to Success Pond Road*: 4.5 miles north of U.S. 2 in Gorham, on N.H. 16 in Berlin, follow Unity Street across the Androscoggin River on the Cleveland Bridge. At the east end of the bridge, Unity Street swings left and, at 0.7 mile, passes through traffic lights. At 0.8 mile, cross railroad tracks, and, at 0.9 mile, bear left; the road becomes Hutchins Street. At 1.6 miles, the road turns sharply left, and, at 1.9 miles, there is usually a sign on the left that reads "OHRV Parking 1 Mile." The gravel Success Pond Road is on the right (east) between large boulders. The first part of the road may be difficult to distinguish from dead-end branch roads, but, once out of the open area, it is well-defined, dusty, and dangerous. At 0.5 mile, bear left under a power line, and, at 1.0 mile, pass parking for the Success ATV Trail on the right. Trailheads are marked with the AMC's small, standard trail signs, often at diverging logging roads with no well-defined parking area, so look carefully. The lower parts of the trails originating on this road are often disrupted by new logging roads, so take great care in following your route. Be prepared for changing conditions.

Maps—Refer to Map One with this guide and AMC Map 6 (North Country–Mahoosuc Range). For area detail but not current trail routes, see these USGS 7½-minute topographic quadrangles: Shelburne and Berlin, New Hampshire.

Shelters and Campsites—This section has one shelter with a campsite and one tentsite: Gentian Pond Shelter and Campsite at mile 4.7/11.8 and Trident Col Tentsite at mile 9.6/6.9.

SECTION HIGHLIGHTS

Northern end of section →

"Welcome to Maine. The way life should be," says a sign here. The boundary is designated by yellow blazes in the trees running east–west from the Trail. The nearest resupply point is the full-service town of Gorham, New Hampshire (ZIP Code 03581), 20.1 miles from the state line, with telephones, supermarket, coin laundry, restaurants, motels, hostels, outfitters, AMC hiker-shuttle stop, and bus service to Boston through Concord Coach Lines, (800) 639-3317, <www.concordcoachlines.com>. Greyhound, <www.greyhound.com>, also has service in New Hampshire. Gorham is reached by continuing 16.5 miles south on the A.T. to U.S. 2 and walking from there 3.6 miles west.

Success Trail →

Leads west 3.0 miles to Success Pond Road at a point 5.4 miles from Hutchins Street in Berlin, New Hampshire.

Mt. Success →

Excellent 360-degree views, including Mt. Washington.

Gentian Pond Campsite and Shelter →

Shelter rebuilt in 1974 and maintained by the AMC. Accommodates 12 at shelter and 18 at three single and one double tent platform. Composting privy; bear box. Water is available from inlet brook to Gentian Pond, 300 yards south on Trail. Next shelter or campsite: south, 5.0 miles (Trident Col); north, 5.5 miles (Carlo Col).

Austin Brook Trail →

Descends east 3.5 miles to North Road in Shelburne, New Hampshire.

Upper Gentian Pond →

Named for moisture-loving wildflowers, gentians, common in North America. The gentian root extract is a major flavor component in New England's regionally popular soft drink, Moxie.

N-S

TRAIL DESCRIPTION

0.0 The **northern end of section** is the Maine–New Hampshire   **16.5**
state line (elev. 2,972 feet). ■ SOUTHBOUND hikers descend
over a low hump to a wooden ladder before climbing
steeply to an unnamed peak at 3,335 feet. ■ NORTHBOUND
hikers continue to climb north of the border signs (see
Mahoosuc Range above or Section Thirteen in the *Ap-*
palachian Trail Guide to Maine).

1.3 Junction with **Success Trail** (elev. 3,170 feet).   **15.2**

1.9 Over high scrub and alpine meadow, reach the open   **14.6**
summit of **Mt. Success** (elev. 3,565 feet).

3.3 Cross small brook (elev. 2,500 feet).   **13.2**

4.7 Reach **Gentian Pond Campsite and Shelter** and junction   **11.8**
with the **Austin Brook Trail** (elev. 2,166 feet).

5.1 Pass southwestern shore of **Upper Gentian Pond** (elev.   **11.4**
2,530 feet).

Gentian Pond Shelter

SECTION HIGHLIGHTS

Peabody Brook Trail →
Leads 100 yards east to intersect with Dryad Falls Trail and then descends 3.1 miles to North Road.

Dryad Falls Trail →
This 1.5-mile, yellow-blazed trail runs from the Peabody Brook Trail to the Austin Brook Trail, passing Dryad Falls, one of the highest cascades in the mountains—particularly interesting for a few days after a rainstorm, because its several cascades fall at least 300 feet over steep ledges. The falls were named by Eugene Cook, a pioneer White Mountains trail-builder and an incurable punster, referring to the fact that, unless it has rained recently, the falls are fairly dry.

Trident Pass →
Traverse ridge past three peaks that form the Trident, then past three gullies that may have water.

Page Pond →
Named after 19th-century hunter Yager Page. Beaver activity may cause wet conditions.

Trident Col Tentsite →
Primitive site rebuilt in 1978 and managed by the WMNF. Four tentsites accommodate 20. Composting privy; bear box. Water is available from a spring 50 yards west of the campsite. Next shelter or campsite: south, 8.9 miles (Rattle River); north, 5.0 miles (Gentian Pond).

Centennial Trail →
Constructed by the AMC in 1976, its centennial year; coincides with the A.T. for 3.1 miles.

Mt. Hayes →
The Mahoosuc Trail leads west 0.2 mile to the summit of Mt. Hayes, then descends 3.1 miles to N.H. 16, 1.3 miles north of Gorham.

N-S	TRAIL DESCRIPTION	

5.4	Pass northwestern shore of Moss Pond.	**11.1**
6.9	Cross inlet brook of Dream Lake, reach junction (elev. 2,610 feet) with **Peabody Brook Trail** to **Dryad Falls Trail**.	**9.6**
7.3	Cross Upper Branch of Peabody Brook (elev. 2,750 feet).	**9.2**
8.0	Fifty yards west (elev. 2,780 feet) is viewpoint on Wocket Ledge, a shoulder of Bald Cap.	**8.5**
8.6	Enter area known as **Trident Pass** (elev. 2,240 feet), passing to south of **Page Pond** over outlet on beaver dam.	**7.9**
9.6	Reach Trident Col (elev. 2,020 feet) and spur trail leading 0.1 mile west to **Trident Col Tentsite**.	**6.9**
10.7	Reach wooded summit of Cascade Mountain (elev. 2,631 feet).	**5.8**
11.5	Excellent views to south on steep, large, broken rock slabs and ledge.	**5.0**
11.9	Possible water in pass (elev. 1,960 feet) between Cascade Mountain and Mt. Hayes.	**4.6**
12.6	Junction of the **Centennial Trail** (elev. 2,550 feet) and Mahoosuc Trail below **Mt. Hayes**. ■ SOUTHBOUND hikers turn left and follow Centennial Trail. ■ NORTHBOUND hikers turn right and follow Mahoosuc Trail north from the summit of Mt. Hayes.	**3.9**
12.9	Reach eastern summit of **Mt. Hayes** (elev. 2,555 feet).	**3.6**
15.0	Cross brook (reliable water; elev. 1,350 feet).	**1.5**

SECTION HIGHLIGHTS

Hogan Road→

A small parking area is located on this gravel road, bordering the Lead Mine State Forest, 0.2 mile west of paved North Road.

North Road →

Parking is available on grassy area. Do not block road.

Androscoggin River→

The history of the Androscoggin has been one of degradation and recovery. It was once badly polluted by a variety of textile mills, paper-making factories, and other industries located along its banks. That situation helped inspire Congress to pass the Clean Water Act. The river has benefited greatly from environmental work and the departures of certain types of industry from the region but still has problems with industrial waste and mercury contamination.

Southern end of section →

The Trailhead is at the intersection in Shelburne of North Road and U.S. 2. A large parking lot can be found on U.S. 2, 0.2 mile south of the Trail, just beyond the highway bridge over the Rattle River. Theft and vandalism have been reported; do not leave valuables in cars. On U.S. 2, it is 1.8 miles west to White Birches Camping Park (telephone, campground, bunkhouse hostel). It is 3.6 miles west to Gorham (ZIP Code 03581), with telephone; supermarket; coin laundry; restaurants; motels; hostels; outfitters; AMC hiker-shuttle stop; and bus service through Concord Trailways Bus, 800-639-3317, <www.concordtrailways.com>, to Boston.

N-S

TRAIL DESCRIPTION

15.7   Reach **Hogan Road** (elev. 800 feet). ■ Southbound hikers   **0.8**
follow Hogan Road left for 0.3 mile to North Road. ■
Northbound hikers enter woods on right and begin climb
on **Centennial Trail**.

16.0   Reach **North Road** (elev. 760 feet). ■ Southbound hikers   **0.5**
turn right onto North Road for 0.5 mile. ■ Northbound
hikers turn left onto Hogan Road.

16.2   Cross **Androscoggin River** on Leadmine Bridge at Shel-   **0.3**
burne power plant and dam (elev. 750 feet).

16.4   Cross railroad tracks (elev. 755 feet).   **0.1**

16.5   The **southern end of section** is at U.S. 2 (elev. 760 feet).   **0.0**
■ Southbound hikers turn left, cross Rattle River on high-
way bridge, turn right into A.T. parking lot, and enter
woods on Rattle River Trail (see New Hampshire Section
Two). ■ Northbound hikers turn right on North Road.

Regulations—Throughout this section, the Trail is
mostly in a corridor jointly managed by the USFS
and AMC. Camping is limited to designated sites,
and off-trail camping opportunities are limited.
Do not camp in fragile alpine bogs. State fire laws
require that wood and charcoal fires be built
only at designated sites, and, at certain sites, only
camping stoves are permitted. Use dead and
downed wood only.

   South of the state line, the A.T. is on U.S. Forest
Service land jointly managed by the White Mountain National Forest and AMC, with the exception
of the lower mile of the Centennial Trail, which is
in New Hampshire's Leadmine State Forest. Most
side trails are on private land.

S-N

Androscoggin Valley (U.S. 2) to Pinkham Notch (N.H. 16)

21.1 MILES

The Carter–Moriah Range offers rugged hiking on an uninterrupted footpath. Eight significant peaks more than 4,000 feet high are crossed along the 10-mile ridge, with a precipitous drop into Carter Notch to the two small Carter Lakes that lie in a secluded hollow in the deepest part of the notch. Hiking along this section is extremely strenuous, and water may be scarce. From the Androscoggin River Valley, the Trail coincides with the Rattle River Trail up the ridge and, along the ridge, the Kenduskeag Trail, the Carter-Moriah Trail, a short jaunt on the Nineteen-Mile Brook Trail, and the Wildcat Ridge Trail. It then descends across the Wild Kittens (small peaks) and the Lost Pond Trail to Pinkham Notch. The major peaks are, from north to south, Mt. Moriah, 4,049 feet; North Carter, 4,530 feet; Middle Carter, 4,610 feet; South Carter, 4,430 feet; Mt. Hight, 4,675 feet; Carter Dome, 4,832 feet; and Wildcat, 4,422 feet.

continued on page 66

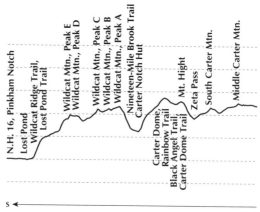

S ←

21.1 MILES

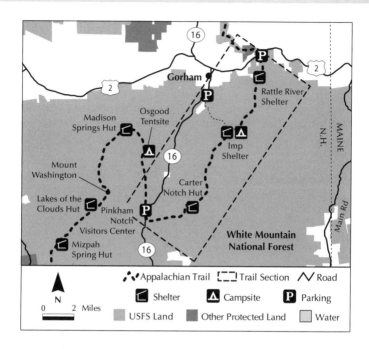

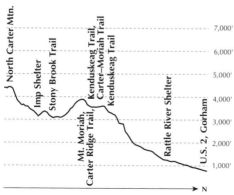

The best views are from bare Mt. Hight. The elevation at the U.S. 2 is 760 feet; at Pinkham Notch, 2,050 feet. The highest point is Carter Dome.

Road Approaches—Both ends of this section are on major highways.

Maps—For route navigation, refer to Map Two with this guide, or AMC Map 5 (Carter Range–Evans Notch). For area detail but not current route information, consult these USGS 15-minute topographic quadrangles: North Conway, Crawford Notch, and Mt. Washington, New Hampshire, and USGS 7½-minute topographic quadrangles for Carter Dome and Wild River, New Hampshire.

Shelters and Campsites—This section has two shelters—Rattle River Shelter (mile 1.9/19.2) and Imp Campsite and Shelter (mile 8.0/13.1)—and one AMC hut, Carter Notch (mile 15.2/5.9).

Ledge south of Wildcat Mountain

Northern end of section →

The Trailhead is at the intersection in Shelburne of North Road and U.S. 2. There is a large trailhead parking lot on U.S. 2, 0.2 mile south on the Trail, just beyond the highway bridge over the Rattle River. Theft and vandalism have been reported. Do not leave valuables in cars. It is 1.8 miles west to White Birches Camping Park (telephones, campground, bunkhouse hostel) and 3.6 miles west to Gorham (ZIP Code 03581), with telephones, supermarket, coin laundry, restaurants, motels, hostels, outfitters, AMC hiker-shuttle stop, and bus service to Boston through Concord Coach Lines, (800). 639-3317, <www.concordcoachlines.com>. Greyhound, <www. greyhound.com>, also has service in New Hampshire.

Rattle River Trail→

This trail coincides with the A.T. for 4.3 miles, from U.S. 2 to the Kenduskeag Trail in the Moriah–Shelburne col (mile 4.5/16.6).

Rattle River Shelter →

Built in the 1980s and maintained by the USFS. Accommodates 8. Privy. Water source is the river. Next shelter or campsite: south, 6.3 miles (Imp); north, 8.9 miles (Trident Col).

Rattle River →

The A.T. follows this four-mile river from its source between Middle Moriah and Shelburne Moriah mountains to the Androscoggin River in Shelburne.

Kenduskeag Trail →

Kenduskeag is an Abenaki word meaning "a pleasant walk." From Mt. Moriah to the Rattle River Trail junction, this trail is part of the A.T. The Kenduskeag Trail also leads east 2.7 miles over the summit of Shelburne Moriah Mountain to the Shelburne Trail, which leads north 5 miles to U.S. 2 and south 3.0 miles to Wild River.

N-S

TRAIL DESCRIPTION

0.0 The **northern end of section** is at U.S. 2 (elev.760 feet).　**21.1**
■ SOUTHBOUND hikers turn left and cross the Rattle River
on a highway bridge. ■ NORTHBOUND hikers turn right on
North Road (see New Hampshire Section One).

0.2 ■ Southbound hikers turn right off U.S. 2 into Trailhead　**20.9**
parking lot and enter woods on the **Rattle River Trail**. ■
Northbound hikers cross through the parking area and
turn left onto U.S. 2, crossing the Rattle River on a highway bridge.

1.9 Pass **Rattle River Shelter** (elev. 1,260 feet).　**19.2**

2.3 Cross the East Rattle River; may be difficult in high water　**18.8**
(elev. 1,500 feet).

3.4 Cross **Rattle River** (elev. 1,700 ft).　**17.7**

4.5 Junction with the **Kenduskeag Trail** (elev. 3,300 feet). ■　**16.6**
Southbound hikers turn right onto Kenduskeag Trail. ■
Northbound hikers turn left onto **Rattle River Trail**.

Black bear near Rattle River

S-N

SECTION HIGHLIGHTS

Carter–Moriah Trail →

The Carter–Moriah Trail leads west, soon reaching the rocky summit of Mt. Moriah (elev. 4,049 feet), then descends 4.5 miles to U.S. 2 in Gorham. From the Kenduskeag Trail junction near the summit of Mt. Moriah to Carter Notch, the Carter–Moriah Trail is part of the A.T. Water is very scarce on many parts of this trail, because it runs mostly on or near the crest of the ridge.

Imp Campsite and Shelter →

Built in the 1980s and maintained by AMC; caretaker, fee. Accommodates 10 at the shelter and 20 on four single and one double tent platforms. Privy; bear box. Water source is a brook near the shelter. Next shelter or campsite: south, 18.1 miles (Osgood); north, 6.3 miles (Rattle River).

North Carter Trail →

Descends west 1.2 miles to Imp Trail and 3.1 miles beyond to N.H. 16.

Zeta Pass →

Water is generally found in this pass. A good reliable spring is 0.8 mile west on the Carter Dome Trail (see below).

Carter Dome Trail →

Descends west 1.9 miles to the Nineteen-Mile Brook Trail, following the route of an old road that served the long-dismantled fire tower on Carter Dome. From there, it leads 1.9 miles to N.H. 16. The Carter Dome Trail coincides with the A.T./Carter–Moriah Trail for 0.2 mile and then diverges west, bypassing Mt. Hight.

Mt. Hight →

Between 1890 and 1903, a logging railroad operated along the Wild River, as far upstream as Red Brook, and along the Bull Brook and Moriah Brook tributaries. Soon after a very dry May 1903, a raging forest fire destroyed several thousand acres of timber and made possible the open summit and views one sees today.

N-S

TRAIL DESCRIPTION

4.7 Skirt to the east of the summit of Middle Moriah Mountain **16.4**
(elev. 3,640 feet).

5.9 Junction with the **Carter-Moriah Trail** (elev. 4,000 feet). **15.2**
■ SOUTHBOUND hikers turn left on Carter-Moriah Trail,
descending along the wooded ridge. ■ NORTHBOUND hikers turn right on the **Kenduskeag Trail**.

7.3 Reach junction with Stony Brook Trail, which descends **13.8**
west 3.6 miles to N.H.16, and Moriah Brook Trail (elev.
3,127 feet), which descends east 5.5 miles to the Wild
River Trail.

8.0 Spur trail leads 0.2 mile west to **Imp Campsite and Shelter** **13.1**
(elev. 3,120 feet). A stream crossing is south on the A.T.

9.7 Pass over wooded summit of North Carter Mountain (elev. **11.4**
4,530 feet).

9.9 Reach junction with **North Carter Trail** (elev. 4,500 **11.2**
feet).

10.2 Cross open ledges of Mt. Lethe (elev. 4,584 feet). **10.9**

10.5 Cross wooded summit of Middle Carter Mountain (elev. **10.6**
4,610 feet).

11.8 Cross wooded summit of South Carter Mountain (elev. **9.3**
4,430 feet).

12.6 Reach **Zeta Pass** (elev. 3,890 feet) and junction with the **8.5**
Carter Dome Trail junction. No camping.

13.2 Cross open summit of **Mt. Hight** (elev. 4,675 feet). **7.9**

13.6 Junction of the **Carter Dome Trail** and the Black Angel **7.5**
Trail (elev. 4,600 feet), which descends east 4.8 miles to
the Wild River Trail.

S-N

Carter Dome →

Highest peak in the Carter Range. The highest fire tower in New England, long gone, sat on this flat, scrub-fringed summit. The spot still allows good views to the west and north.

Nineteen-Mile Brook Trail →

The A.T. coincides with this path for 0.2 mile west to the Wildcat Ridge Trail junction, where the Nineteen-Mile Brook Trail leads 3.6 miles west to N.H. 16 (AMC hiker-shuttle stop).

Carter Notch →

A deep cleft between Carter Dome and Wildcat Mountain. The two small Carter Lakes lie in the secluded hollow, totally enclosed by rock walls. The huge boulders, known as the Ramparts, that surround the pond once were part of the rock walls.

Carter Notch Hut →

The AMC constructed this stone hut in 1914, and it is the oldest hut still in use. Full-service in summer only; self-service in fall, winter, and spring; reservations recommended; fee. Accommodates 40. Resident staff has trail information and weather reports. Hut includes small retail store with safety items, snacks, and water. It uses solar and wind power and Clivus composting toilets. The Wildcat River Trail descends 4.3 miles from Carter Notch Hut to the Carter Notch Road toward Jackson.

Wildcat Ridge Trail →

This is part of the A.T. from the Lost Pond Trail junction (mile 20.2/0.9) to the Nineteen-Mile Brook Trail junction in Carter Notch (mile 15.2/5.9). From that Nineteen-Mile Brook Trail junction, it is 3.4 miles west to N.H. 16 (AMC hiker-shuttle stop). From the Lost Pond Trail junction, it is 0.1 mile east to N.H. 16 at Glen Ellis Falls.

N-S

TRAIL DESCRIPTION

14.0   Reach open summit of **Carter Dome** (elev. 4,832 feet)   **7.1**
and junction with the Rainbow Trail, which descends east
2.5 miles to Perkins Notch and the Wild River Trail.

14.5   A fine spring is 60 yards to west (elev. 4,300 feet).   **6.6**

14.8   Pass viewpoint down into Carter Notch (elev. 4,000   **6.3**
feet).

15.2   Reach junction (elev. 3,388 feet) with **Nineteen-Mile**   **5.9**
Brook Trail, which leads 0.2 mile east to **Carter Notch**
Hut in **Carter Notch** and skirts the shore of Carter Lake.
■ SOUTHBOUND hikers turn right on Nineteen-Mile Brook
Trail, skirting shore of Carter Lake. ■ NORTHBOUND hikers
turn left on **Carter-Moriah Trail** and ascend to summit of
Carter Dome.

15.4   Reach height of land (elev. 3,388 feet) and junction with   **5.7**
Wildcat Ridge Trail. ■ SOUTHBOUND hikers ascend
steeply on switchbacks on Wildcat Ridge Trail toward
Wildcat Peak A. ■ NORTHBOUND hikers descend on **Nine-**
teen-Mile Brook Trail to Carter Lakes in **Carter Notch**.

S-N

Wildcat Mountain →

A heavily wooded mountain that rises at the southern end of the range, it has been nicknamed "Wildcat and her kittens" because of its five prominent summits, A through E, all rising more than 4,000 feet above sea level.

Wildcat Mountain Peak D →

The summit supports a look-out platform that provides extensive views of Tuckerman (left) and Huntington (right) ravines on Mt. Washington and of the northern Presidential Range.

Wildcat Mountain Ski Area Gondola →

When in operation, the gondola offers rides to and from the A.T. (fee). A rugged alternative is to descend 2.6 miles on a ski trail to the base lodge on N.H. 16. The Wildcat Ski Area base lodge is 2 miles west of the AMC Pinkham Notch Visitors Center.

Lost Pond Trail →

This short link trail, which coincides in its entirety with the A.T., runs from Pinkham Notch Visitors Center to the lower end of the Wildcat Ridge Trail.

Lost Pond →

More than 12,000 years old, Lost Pond offers stunning views to the west of Huntington Ravine, the source of some of the boulders now in and around Lost Pond.

Glen Ellis Falls →

Near N.H. 16, the main cascade is 70 feet high. Below it are several pools and smaller falls.

Square Ledge Trail →

Leads 0.5 mile to an excellent outlook from a ledge that rises from the floor of Pinkham Notch on the side of Wildcat Mountain.

N-S	TRAIL DESCRIPTION	

16.1	Cross **Wildcat Mountain** Peak A (elev. 4,422 feet), with views down into **Carter Notch**.	**5.0**
16.6	Cross Wildcat Mountain Peak B (elev. 4,330 feet).	**4.5**
17.0	Cross Wildcat Mountain Peak C (elev. 4,298 feet).	**4.1**
17.8	Reach Wildcat Col (elev. 3,770 feet).	**3.3**
18.1	Cross **Wildcat Mountain Peak D** (elev. 4,062 feet).	**3.0**
18.2	Pass **Wildcat Mountain Ski Area Gondola** (elev. 4,020 feet).	**2.9**
18.4	Cross 3 yards west of Wildcat Mountain Peak E summit (elev. 4,046 feet).	**2.7**
18.8	Cross steep ledge (elev. 3,500 feet) with views of ravines on Mt. Washington.	**2.3**
19.1	Side path to west leads to signed spring (elev. 3,250 feet).	**2.0**
19.4	Reach level, open ledge with fine views to the south, marked by a rock with "Sarge's Crag" engraved on it (elev. 3,000 feet).	**1.7**
20.2	Reach junction with the **Lost Pond Trail** (elev. 1,990 feet). **Glen Ellis Falls** is 0.1 mile east on the **Wildcat Ridge Trail**. ■ Southbound hikers turn right onto **Lost Pond Trail**, skirting the eastern shore of **Lost Pond**. ■ Northbound hikers turn left on **Wildcat Ridge Trail** and begin the steep climb up Wildcat Mountain Peak E.	**0.9**
21.0	Pass junction with **Square Ledge Trail** (elev. 2,020 feet). ■ Southbound hikers turn left over small marsh on a wooden bridge. ■ Northbound hikers turn right along the eastern bank of the Ellis River and the eastern shore of **Lost Pond**.	**0.1**

S-N

Pinkham Notch →

Named for Daniel Pinkham, a young, nineteenth-century farmer-turned-road-builder from the town of Adams (now Jackson), New Hampshire. The state gave Pinkham three years to build a road linking Jackson and Gorham through boulders, streams, dense timber, and steep, rugged terrain. He had nearly reached his goal when, in August 1826, heavy rains washed away two years of work. He eventually opened a toll road, but deep snows discouraged travel. This project was not a financial success for him.

Pinkham Notch Visitors Center →

AMC's North Country base, it is open all year, with an information desk, retail store, pack-up room, telephones, and showers. The dining room features a breakfast buffet, lunch grill, family-style dinner; reservations required. The Joe Dodge Lodge fee facility also is open year-round. Reservations are strongly recommended; private or shared bunk rooms. Accommodates 108, with meal service in the visitors center.

Southern end of section →

The Trail crosses N.H. 16 at Pinkham Notch at a large hiker parking lot. Theft and vandalism have been reported; do not leave valuables in vehicles. This Trailhead is a stop for the AMC hiker shuttle and Concord Coach Lines (see northern end of section). Greyhound, <www.greyhound.com>, also has service in New Hampshire. On N.H. 16, it is 9.0 miles east to Jackson (ZIP Code 03846), with telephones, restaurants, and bus service. It is 16 miles east to North Conway (ZIP Code 03860), with lodging, restaurants, groceries, coin laundry, outfitters, a cobbler, and bus stops. It is 12 miles west to Gorham and the northern end of the section.

N-S

TRAIL DESCRIPTION

21.1 Reach N.H. 16 at **Pinkham Notch** and southern end of   **0.0**
section (elev. 2,050 feet). ■ SOUTHBOUND hikers cross
N.H. 16 to **Pinkham Notch Visitors Center** (see New
Hampshire Section Three). ■ NORTHBOUND hikers cross
N.H. 16 and follow the **Lost Pond Trail**, crossing a
wooden bridge over the bog.

> ***Regulations**—Except for its northern 0.8 mile,
> where camping is not permitted, this section is
> within the White Mountain National Forest
> (WMNF). The WMNF has established a number of
> forest protection areas (FPAs)—formerly known as
> "restricted use areas"—where camping and wood
> or charcoal fires are prohibited throughout the year.
> No camping is permitted above treeline (where
> trees are less than 8 feet tall), except in winter, and
> then only where there is at least two feet of snow
> cover on the ground—but not on any frozen body
> of water. No camping is allowed within 0.25 mile
> of any trailhead, picnic area, or any facility for
> overnight accommodation, such as a hut, cabin,
> shelter, tentsite, or campground, except as desig-
> nated by the facility itself. In this section, that in-
> cludes Imp Campsite and Shelter, Carter Notch
> Hut, the intersection with the Carter Dome Trail at
> Zeta Pass, and N.H. 16 at Pinkham Notch. Permits
> are required for open fires outside designated fa-
> cilities on WMNF lands. They can be obtained from
> AMC at the Pinkham Notch Visitors Center (see
> "For More Information," page 349).*

S-N

Pinkham Notch (N.H. 16) to Crawford Notch (U.S. 302)

26.0 MILES

The Presidential Range in the White Mountain National Forest (WMNF) is the highest mountain group traversed by the Appalachian Trail north of Clingmans Dome on the North Carolina–Tennessee border. For most of the 12-mile distance between Mt. Madison and Mt. Pierce (Mt. Clinton), the Trail is above treeline. From Pinkham Notch, the Trail gradually ascends on the Old Jackson Road to the Mt. Washington Auto Road. It crosses the Auto Road, enters the Great Gulf Wilderness, ascends gradually on the Madison Gulf Trail, follows the Osgood Cutoff, and then ascends steeply on the Osgood Trail to a ridge above treeline and then the summit of Mt. Madison. Descending to Madison Spring Hut, it continues to follow the ridgecrest on the Gulfside Trail and ascends on the Trinity Heights Connector to Mt. Washington.

continued on page 78

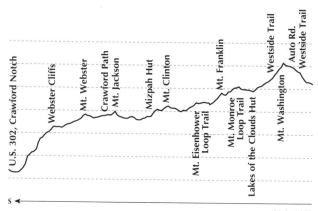

S ←

26.0 MILES

79

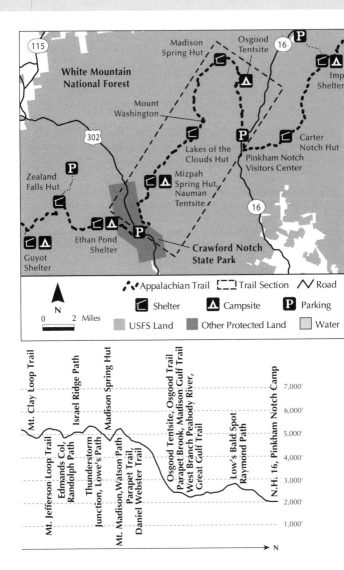

The Trail gradually descends on the Crawford Path, past Lakes of the Clouds, to Mt. Pierce. It reenters the woods and follows the Webster Cliff Trail across a sometimes-open ridge to Crawford Notch.

The major peaks traversed in the section, from north to south, are Mt. Madison, 5,367 feet; Mt. Washington, 6,288 feet; Mt. Franklin, 5,001 feet; Mt. Pierce (Mt. Clinton), 4,310 feet; Mt. Jackson, 4,052 feet; and Mt. Webster, 3,910 feet.

The alpine ridge of the Presidential Range is exposed to storms that rise rapidly and are often violent, with hurricane-force winds and freezing conditions, even in summer. The above-treeline sections where the A.T. follows the Gulfside Trail and Crawford Path are marked with frequent cairns, topped by yellow-painted stones (white blazes are less common); nonetheless, it is still possible to lose the Trail in fog or bad weather. Carry ample clothing, and, if weather becomes threatening, promptly descend to shelter by the shortest route. If severe weather is predicted (daily forecasts are available at Pinkham Notch Visitors Center, Madison Spring Hut, Lakes of the Clouds Hut, and Mizpah Hut), take the steep shortcut between Lakes of the Clouds and Pinkham Notch by way of Tuckerman Ravine, past Hermit Lake Shelters. That eliminates crossing the northern Presidential Range. However, even that route can be forbidding in bad weather (many deaths due to exposure and falls have occurred there) and should be approached equally cautiously.

The elevation change in this section is enormous, but it is mostly at the ends of the ridge. Many less significant climbs are along the ridgecrest. The A.T. passes over the highest Presidential summits but bypasses many others that can be reached by short loop trails, scarcely increasing the total distance traveled. The elevation at N.H. 16 is 2,050 feet; at U.S. 302 in Crawford Notch, 1,275 feet. The highest elevation is on the summit of Mt. Washington, second-highest peak in the East (after North Carolina's Mt. Mitchell).

Road Approaches—Both ends are accessible by vehicle. Seasonal road access is also available on the Mt. Washington Auto Road. Concord Coach Lines, <www.concordcoachlines.com>, and Greyhound, <www.greyhound.com>, both provide bus service in New Hampshire.

Maps—For route navigation, refer to Map Two with this guide; AMC Map 1 (Presidential Range); or the White Mountain National Forest map (1:250,000). For area detail but not current trail routes, refer to the following USGS 15-minute topographic quadrangles: Mt. Washington and Crawford Notch, New Hampshire.

Shelters and Campsites—This section has four shelters some distance off the Trail. At mile 8.7/17.3, side trails go varying distances to Log Cabin, Crag Camp, and Gray Knob. The Perch Shelter is 0.9 mile away on a loop trail (miles 8.8/17.2 and 9.3/16.7). This section also has three campsites: Osgood Tentsite (mile 4.8/21.2), Valley Way Tentsite (mile 7.8/18.2), and Nauman Tentsite (mile 19.6/6.4). One public campground, Crawford Notch State Park's Dry River Campground, is 1.8 miles from the Trail at the southern end of the section.

This section also has three seasonal AMC mountain huts: Madison Spring Hut (mile 7.8/18.2), Lakes of the Clouds Hut (mile 14.8/11.2), and Mizpah Spring Hut (mile 19.6/6.4).

Mt. Monroe

SECTION HIGHLIGHTS

Northern end of section →

The Trail crosses N.H. 16 at Pinkham Notch at a large hiker parking lot. Theft and vandalism have been reported; do not leave valuables in vehicles. This Trailhead is a stop for the AMC hiker shuttle and Concord Coach Lines [(800) 639-3317 or <www.concordcoachlines. com>] with service to and from Boston. Greyhound, <www.grey-hound.com>, also has service in New Hampshire. On N.H. 16, it is 9.0 miles east to Jackson (ZIP Code 03846), with telephones, restaurants, and bus service. It is 16 miles east to North Conway (ZIP Code 03860), with lodging, restaurants, groceries, coin laundry, outfitters, a cobbler, and bus stops. It is 12 miles west to Gorham (see New Hampshire Section Two).

Pinkham Notch →

The notch is a result of extensive erosion by the Laurentide ice sheet during the Wisconsinian Ice Age. Pinkham Notch was eroded into a glacial, U-shaped valley walled in by the Presidential, Wildcat, and Carter–Moriah ranges. For early European settlers, the notch was "discovered" in 1784 by Jeremy Belknap, but its isolation prevented development for years. The construction of N.H. 16 led to increased accessibility and a rise in tourism. Its location makes it a hub today for hiking and skiing throughout the Whites.

Pinkham Notch Visitors Center →

AMC's North Country operations base, it is open all year, with an information desk, the Trading Post retail store, pack-up room, telephones, and showers. The dining room features a breakfast buffet, lunch grill, family-style dinner; reservations required. The AMC hiker shuttle stops here.

Joe Dodge Lodge at Pinkham Notch →

This AMC fee facility also is open year-round. Reservations are strongly recommended; private or shared bunk rooms. Accommodates 108, with meal service in the visitors center.

N-S

| TRAIL DESCRIPTION |

0.0 Reach N.H. 16 at **Pinkham Notch** (elev. 2,050 feet) at   26.0
northern end of section. ■ SOUTHBOUND hikers cross N.H.
16, walk between the **Pinkham Notch Visitors Center**
and **Joe Dodge Lodge**, turn onto the **Tuckerman Ravine
Trail** for 88 yards, then join **Old Jackson Road** (trail)
straight ahead. ■ NORTHBOUND hikers cross N.H. 16 and
follow the Lost Pond Trail, crossing a wooden bridge over
the bog (see New Hampshire Section Two).

Lichen in Pinkham Notch

S-N

SECTION HIGHLIGHTS

Tuckerman Ravine Trail →
Leads 2.4 miles east to Hermit Lake Shelters and an additional 4.1 miles to the summit of Mt. Washington, bypassing the ridges above treeline.

Old Jackson Road →
It is part of the A.T. and is blazed in white. Because it also is used as a cross-country ski trail in winter, it is usually also marked with blue diamonds year-round.

Crew-Cut Trail and George's Gorge Trail →
Those two trails and Liebeskind's Loop, forming a small network of paths in the region north of Pinkham Notch Visitors Center, were originally located and cut by Bradford Swan. They provide pleasant walking with a modest expenditure of effort and pass through fine woods with small ravines and ledges.

Mt. Washington Auto Road →
The Mt. Washington Auto Road is an eight-mile toll road that extends from N.H. 16 at the Glen House in Pinkham Notch to the summit of Mt. Washington. The road was completed and opened to the public in 1861 (see page 38).

Madison Gulf Trail →
From the Mt. Washington Auto Road to its departure from the Great Gulf Trail (mile 4.1/21.9), the Madison Gulf Trail is the A.T.

Great Gulf Wilderness →
Congress designated the Great Gulf Wilderness in 1964. The Great Gulf is a glacial cirque, its walls formed by Mt. Washington, Mt. Clay, Mt. Jefferson, Mt. Adams, and Mt. Madison. It is drained by the West Branch of the Peabody River. *Because it is a designated wilderness area, the familiar A.T. white-paint blazes are not used. Take care to follow the correct trails.*

N-S

TRAIL DESCRIPTION

Great Gulf Wilderness

0.5 Pass junction of **Crew Cut Trail** (elev. 2,075 feet). **25.5**

1.0 Reach junction of **George's Gorge Trail** (elev. 2,525 **25.0**
feet).

1.8 Pass junction with Raymond Path, which leads 2.7 miles **24.2**
east to Tuckerman Ravine Trail, and then, 100 yards to
the south, Nelson Crag Trail (elev. 2,625 feet), which
leads 3.6 miles east to the summit of Mt. Washington.

1.9 Cross **Mt. Washington Auto Road** west of 2-mile post **24.1**
(elev. 2,675 feet). ■ SOUTHBOUND hikers follow the **Madison Gulf Trail** to enter the **Great Gulf Wilderness**.
■ NORTHBOUND hikers follow **Old Jackson Road** (trail),
pass through a gravel pit, and enter woods, leaving the
Great Gulf Wilderness.

S-N

Great Gulf Trail→

Leads 4.8 miles east at this point, following the West Branch of Peabody River into the Great Gulf Wilderness to rejoin the A.T. on the Gulfside Trail (mile 13.1/12.9). At mile 4.2, it leads 2.9 miles straight ahead, or east, to a trailhead on N.H. 16.

Osgood Cutoff→

This link trail, a part of the A.T., provides a convenient short-cut from the Great Gulf and Madison Gulf trails to the Osgood Trail. It is entirely within the Great Gulf Wilderness.

Osgood Trail →

At the A.T. junction (mile 4.8), the Osgood Trail leads 0.8 mile straight ahead or west (depending on direction of travel) to the Great Gulf Trail, which continues 1.8 miles to N.H. 16. The upper parts are very exposed to the weather, with rough footing. Made by Benjamin F. Osgood in 1878, this is the oldest trail now in use to the summit of Mt. Madison.

Osgood Tentsite→

Maintained by the WMNF. Three tent platforms accommodate 12. Privy. Water source is a spring on the Trail at a prominent boulder. Next shelter or campsite: south, 3.6 miles (Valley Way); north, 18.1 miles (Imp).

N-S   TRAIL DESCRIPTION

2.1	Spur trail leads 200 yards west to Low's Bald Spot (elev. 2,875 feet).	**23.9**

4.0 Northern junction with the **Great Gulf Trail** (elev. 2,290 **22.0**
feet). ▪ Sᴏᴜᴛʜʙᴏᴜɴᴅ hikers turn right to follow the Madison Gulf Trail/Great Gulf Trail, crossing the West Branch of the Peabody River on a suspension bridge. ▪ Nᴏʀᴛʜ-ʙᴏᴜɴᴅ hikers turn left and follow the Madison Gulf Trail.

4.1 Reach junction with the Madison Gulf Trail (elev. 2,300 **21.9**
feet), which becomes coaligned with the northbound A.T. but also leads east 2.6 miles east to the Parapet Trail near Madison Spring Hut. ▪ Sᴏᴜᴛʜʙᴏᴜɴᴅ hikers follow the Great Gulf Trail, descending the ridge and crossing Parapet Brook. ▪ Nᴏʀᴛʜʙᴏᴜɴᴅ hikers follow the Madison Gulf Trail/Great Gulf Trail, crossing the West Branch of the Peabody River on a suspension bridge.

4.2 Reach junction with the **Osgood Cutoff** at The Bluff (elev. **21.8**
2,300 feet). ▪ Sᴏᴜᴛʜʙᴏᴜɴᴅ hikers turn left and follow the Osgood Cutoff. ▪ Nᴏʀᴛʜʙᴏᴜɴᴅ hikers turn right, downhill, on the **Great Gulf Trail** and cross Parapet Brook.

4.8 Reach junction with the **Osgood Trail** at **Osgood Tentsite** **21.2**
(elev. 1,850 feet). ▪ Sᴏᴜᴛʜʙᴏᴜɴᴅ hikers turn left and ascend Osgood Trail, entering the alpine zone and leaving the wilderness area *en route* to the summit of Mt. Madison. ▪ Nᴏʀᴛʜʙᴏᴜɴᴅ hikers turn right and follow **Osgood Cut-off** along contour, leaving the alpine zone and entering the Great Gulf Wilderness.

Parapet Trail→

Leads 1.0 mile east to the Star Lake Trail, which leads 0.2 mile to Madison Spring Hut. Mostly sheltered from the northwest winds, it is probably a useful bad-weather route only if strong northwest or west winds are a major part of the problem.

Daniel Webster Scout Trail→

This trail, cut in 1933 by Boy Scouts from the Daniel Webster Council, descends 3.5 miles west to Dolly Copp Campground near the homestead of Hayes Copp, Pinkham Notch's first settler in 1827. With his wife, Dolly, he built a house in the then-uninhabited area, near where the campground stands today.

Howker Ridge Trail→

Leads 4.2 miles west to Dolly Copp–Pinkham B Road. The ridge's name is from a family that once had a farm at its base.

Mt. Madison →

Mt. Madison is named in honor of James Madison, the fourth president of the United States and lead drafter of the Bill of Rights, as well as much of the 1789 Constitution before it.

Watson Path→

Descends 1.5 mile west to the Valley Way. In bad weather, it is potentially one of the most dangerous routes on the Northern Peaks. It is very steep and rough, and, on the slopes above treeline, exposed to the full fury of northwest winds in a storm.

N-S

| TRAIL DESCRIPTION |

6.1 Reach treeline on the crest of Osgood Ridge (elev. 4,300   **19.9**
feet). *The A.T. is mostly above treeline for the next 12.7
miles south and should only be attempted in favorable
weather.*

6.8 Reach Osgood Junction (elev. 4,822 feet). The **Parapet**   **19.2**
Trail joins on the east and the **Daniel Webster Scout Trail**
joins on the west.

7.1 Reach junction with the **Howker Ridge Trail** (elev.   **18.9**
5,100 ft).

7.3 Reach the summit of **Mt. Madison** and junction with the   **18.7**
Watson Path (elev. 5,366 feet).

Mt. Madison

S-N

SECTION HIGHLIGHTS

Madison Spring Hut →

At treeline, nestled between Mounts Madison and Adams, this hut was constructed on the site of the AMC's first high-mountain refuge, built in 1888. Star Lake is nearby. A staffed, full-service fee facility only in season (summer); reservations recommended. Accommodates 52. Resident staff members have trail information and weather reports. The hut, which uses solar and wind power, has a small retail store with safety items, snacks, and water.

Valley Way →

J.R. Edmands constructed this trail from 1895 to 1897. In bad weather, it is the safest route to or from the hut, being well-sheltered most of the way. It leads 4.2 miles to U.S. 2 at the Appalachia parking area (AMC hiker-shuttle stop).

Gulfside Trail →

This trail, the main route along the Northern Presidentials ridgecrest, leads from Madison Springs Hut to the summit of Mt. Washington and coincides with the A.T for almost all of its length.

Valley Way Tentsite →

Maintained by the WMNF. Two tent platforms accommodate 8. Privy; spring. Next shelter or campsite: south, 2.6 miles (Crag Camp/ Gray Knob); north, 3.6 miles (Osgood).

Star Lake Trail →

Leads 0.2 mile east to the Parapet Trail and joins the Osgood Trail (mile 6.8/19.2) in 1.0 mile, bypassing the summit of Mt. Madison. Mostly sheltered from the northwest winds, it is probably a useful bad-weather route only if strong northwest or west winds are a major part of the problem.

N-S

TRAIL DESCRIPTION

Madison Spring Hut

7.8 Reach junction with the Pine Link Trail, which leads 1.2   **18.2**
miles west to Howker Ridge Trail. In 35 yards south, reach
Madison Spring Hut (elev. 4,825 feet). In another 35 yards
south, reach junction with the **Valley Way** on the **Gulfside
Trail**. The Valley Way leads 0.6 mile west to **Valley Way
Tentsite**. The **Star Lake Trail** also intersects here. ■ SOUTH-
BOUND hikers follow Gulfside Trail, leaving the wilderness
area. ■ NORTHBOUND hikers follow the Osgood Trail and
enter the wilderness area.

```
                    SECTION HIGHLIGHTS
```

Air Line →

This trail, completed in 1885, is the shortest route to Mt. Adams from a highway. From the northern A.T. junction, it leads 3.7 miles west to U.S. 2 at the Appalachia parking lot (AMC hiker-shuttle stop).

Mt. Adams →

Mt. Adams (elev. 5,799 feet) is named in honor of the nation's second president, John Adams. It is the second-highest peak in New England. Unlike Mt. Washington, Adams shows few impacts of human activity and, for that reason, may be preferred by backcountry hikers seeking a wilder experience.

Gray Knob Cabin →

Gray Knob Cabin, located just below treeline (elev. 4,370 feet), was originally built as a private cabin by in 1905. In 1989, that building was replaced. A closed cabin maintained by RMC with a caretaker; fee. Accommodates 15. Winterized with a woodstove; composting privy. Ample water. No open fires. Group limit is 10. Next shelter or campsite: south, 2.7 miles (The Perch); north, 2.7 miles (Valley Way).

Log Cabin →

The Log Cabin (elev. 3,263 feet), built in 1985, is the third building here, the first being a closed cabin built around 1890. A partially enclosed shelter maintained by RMC, with a caretaker; fee. Accommodates 10. Privy. Ample water. No open fires. Next shelter or campsite: south, 3.6 miles (The Perch); north, 3.6 miles (Valley Way).

Crag Camp Cabin

Originally built in 1909 as a private camp, it has been maintained by the RMC since 1939. In 1993, the original structure was replaced (elev. 4,247 feet). A closed cabin with a caretaker; fee. Accommodates 20. Composting privy. Ample water. No open fires. Group size limit is 10. Next shelter or campsite: south, 2.6 miles (The Perch); north, 2.6 miles (Valley Way).

N-S   TRAIL DESCRIPTION

8.1 Pass northern junction with the **Air Line** trail (elev. 5,125   **17.9**
feet).

8.2 Pass southern junction with the **Air Line** trail, which leads   **17.8**
east 0.5 mile to the summit of **Mt. Adams**.

8.7 Reach **Thunderstorm Junction** (elev. 5,490 feet), where   **17.3**
a massive cairn about ten feet high once stood. Lowe's
Path leads east 0.3 mile to the summit of Mt. Adams, 1.2
miles west to **Gray Knob Cabin**, and 2.1 miles west to
Log Cabin. The Spur Trail leads 1.1 miles west to **Crag
Camp Cabin**.

The pass between Mt. Adams and Mt. Jefferson

S-N

SECTION HIGHLIGHTS

Israel Ridge Path →

Named for an early hunter, trapper, and surveyor of the area, Israel Glines. From this junction, it leads 0.1 mile east to Lowe's Path and 0.2 mile to the summit of Mt. Adams. From the southern junction at mile 9.3/16.7, it descends 0.9 mile west to the The Perch Shelter and 4.6 miles to Bowman, New Hampshire, on U.S. 2.

The Perch Shelter →

Originally a birch-bark building built by J. Rayner Edmands in 1890 at 4,313 feet. That structure was completely destroyed by the hurricane of September 1938 (along with long swatches of the original A.T.). It was rebuilt in 1948 and has been renovated several times. Maintained by RMC with a caretaker; fee. Accommodates 8 at the shelter and 16 on four tent platforms. Privy. Ample water from Cascade Brook. No open fires. Next shelter or campsite: south, 11.2 miles (Nauman); north, 2.6 miles (Crag Camp/Gray Knob).

Edmands Col →

Named after J. Rayner Edmands, a charter member of the AMC and one of the first to build graded paths in the Presidentials, a number of which are noted above. A bronze plaque honoring his hard work has been placed here. He built a private cottage where The Perch Shelter is now located. This col, acting like a natural wind tunnel, is known for high winds and bad weather in all seasons.

Mt. Jefferson →

Mt. Jefferson (elev. 5,716 feet) is named in honor of Thomas Jefferson, the nation's third president.

Six Husbands Trail →

Leads east 1.5 miles, descending steeply into Jefferson Ravine and the Great Gulf Wilderness to the Buttress Trail and west 0.3 mile to the Mt. Jefferson Loop, 0.1 mile below the summit of Mt. Jefferson. The name honors the six successive husbands of Weetamoo, queen of the Pocasset Wampanoag tribe (1635?–1676). The Wampanoag sat with the Pilgrims at the first Thanksgiving dinner. In 1676, during

N-S	TRAIL DESCRIPTION	

8.8	Reach northern junction with the **Israel Ridge Path** (elev. 5,475 feet).	**17.2**
9.2	Pass unreliable Peabody Spring on west (elev. 5,220 feet). Just south of here, water at the base of a conspicuous boulder on the east of the Trail may be a better option.	**16.8**
9.3	Reach southern junction with the **Israel Ridge Path** (elev. 5,250 feet), which descends 0.9 mile west to the **The Perch Shelter**.	**16.7**
10.0	Reach **Edmands Col** (elev. 4,938 feet). Randolph Path leads 0.2 mile west to Spaulding Spring (reliable) and descends 1.1 miles to **The Perch Shelter**. Edmands Col Cutoff leads 50 yards east to Gulfside Spring (unreliable in dry seasons) and 0.5 mile to Six Husbands Trail.	**16.0**
10.2	Reach northern junction of Mt. Jefferson Loop (elev. 5,125 feet), which leads 0.3 mile west to summit of **Mt. Jefferson** and rejoins the A.T at mile 10.9/15.1.	**15.8**
10.5	Pass junction of **Six Husbands Trail** (elev. 5,325 feet).	**15.5**
10.9	Reach southern junction of Mt. Jefferson Loop (elev. 5,375 feet), which leads 0.3 mile west to summit of **Mt. Jefferson** and rejoins the A.T at mile 10.2/15.8.	**15.1**

SECTION HIGHLIGHTS

a King Philip's War battle between the English colonists and native Americans, Weetamoo drowned in the Taunton River while trying to escape. Her corpse was mutilated by the English and her head put on a pole.

Cornice Trail→

Leads 0.5 mile west to the Caps Ridge Trail, descending 2.1 miles to Jefferson Notch Road.

Monticello Lawn→

A comparatively smooth grassy plateau to the southeast of Mt. Jefferson, named after Jefferson's Virginia estate.

Mt. Clay (Mt. Reagan) →

Mt. Clay (elev. 5,533 feet) was named in honor of Henry Clay, Sr., a nineteenth-century legislator and statesman from Kentucky and the ninth U.S. secretary of state. In 2003, the state of New Hampshire passed legislation that said Mt. Clay "shall hereafter be called and known as Mt. Reagan," after the 40th president, Ronald W. Reagan. However, the policy of the U.S. Board on Geographic Names precludes considering commemorative names for geographic features for five years following the person's death; in this case, not before June 2009.

Mt. Washington Cog Railway→

The world's first mountain cog railway was built by Sylvester Marsh, who came up with the idea while climbing the mountain in bad weather in 1857. The railway, a rack-and-pinion system completed in 1869, allows the trains to operate on a steep gradient. President Ulysses S. Grant and his family were among the passengers in August of the first year. Using steam locomotives and beginning at 2,700 feet, the railway ascends three miles to the summit. Each three-mile ride burns one ton of coal and consumes 1,000 gallons of water. The railway is not subject to the state's air-pollution-control law.

N-S

TRAIL DESCRIPTION

| 11.0 | Pass **Cornice Trail** junction, and cross **Monticello Lawn** (elev. 5,325 feet). | 15.0 |

| 11.5 | Reach junction with Sphinx Trail (elev. 4,975 feet), which leads east 1.1 mile to the Great Gulf Trail. | 14.5 |

| 11.6 | Reach Sphinx Col (elev. 5,025 feet) and northern junction of Mt. Clay Loop, which leads 0.5 mile east to the summit of **Mt. Clay (Mt. Reagan)** and rejoins the A.T at mile 12.5/13.5. | 14.4 |

| 11.7 | Pass loop trail on west to reliable Greenough Spring (elev. 5,100 feet). | 14.3 |

| 12.2 | Reach junction with Jewell Trail (elev. 5,400 feet), which leads 3.7 miles west to Base Road. | 13.8 |

| 12.5 | Pass southern junction of Mt. Clay Loop (elev. 5,400 feet), which leads 0.7 mile east to summit of **Mt. Clay (Mt. Reagan)** and rejoins A.T. at Sphinx Col, mile 11.5/14.5. | 13.5 |

| 12.6 | Reach northern junction (elev. 5,500 feet) with Westside Trail, which leads 0.9 mile west to rejoin the A.T. at mile 14.1/11.9 and bypasses the Mt. Washington summit to the west. | 13.4 |

| 13.1 | At this point (elev. 5,925 feet), the Great Gulf Trail leads 4.8 miles east into the Great Gulf Wilderness and rejoins the A.T at mile 4.0/22.0. | 12.9 |

| 13.2 | Cross **Mt. Washington Cog Railway** tracks. | 12.8 |

SECTION HIGHLIGHTS

Trinity Heights Connector→

This trail was created to allow the A.T. to make a loop over the summit of Mt. Washington; formerly, the true summit was a side trip from the A.T.

Mt. Washington →

Mt. Washington, the highest point east of the Mississippi River and north of the Carolinas, is named in honor of George Washington, first president of the United States. Although, of course, native Americans had seen it from land for thousands of years, the mountain reportedly was first seen from the ocean in 1524 by Giovanni da Verrazano, on a ship off the coast near today's Portsmouth, New Hampshire. The first recorded ascent of the mountain occurred in 1642, when colonist Darby Field—one of whose descendants went on to chair the Appalachian Trail Conservancy and work as a volunteer A.T. maintainer in Maine for more than 50 years—climbed to its summit accompanied by native-American guides. The summit today is home to broadcast towers for television and radio stations, the weather station and scientific research facility of the Mt. Washington Observatory, and Mt. Washington State Park facilities (see page 38). Mt. Washington is considered by some to be the home of the world's worst weather, due to its combination of cold temperatures, heavy snows, dense fog, frequent icing, and high winds. Mt. Washington is the most visited of the Presidential peaks, thanks to its road and railroad, which bring about 200,000 people to its summit each summer. An estimated 50,000 hikers also ascend the mountain each year. The mountain's harsh weather, steep slopes, and popularity have proven a deadly combination for dozens of individuals who have tragically perished here. No overnight lodging for the public is available on the summit.

Tuckerman Ravine Trail→

Leads 1.2 miles east to Hermit Lake Shelters and 2.4 miles beyond to Pinkham Notch.

N-S

TRAIL DESCRIPTION

Mt. Washington

13.3 Reach junction with **Trinity Heights Connector** (elev.   **12.7**
6,100 feet). ■ SOUTHBOUND hikers turn left on Trinity
Heights Connector to the summit of **Mt. Washington**. ■
NORTHBOUND hikers turn right on Gulfside Trail.

13.5 Reach summit of **Mt. Washington** at junction with the   **12.5**
Tuckerman Ravine Trail (elev. 6,288 feet). ■ SOUTHBOUND
hikers descend from summit on the Crawford Path. ■
NORTHBOUND hikers descend from the summit on the
Trinity Heights Connector to the Gulfside Trail.

13.7 Gulfside Trail leaves to the west to rejoin the A.T at mile   **12.3**
13.3/12.7. To the east is the old Glen House horse corral
(elev. 6,150 feet).

S-N

SECTION HIGHLIGHTS

Davis Path →

Leads 14.4 miles east, following Montalban Ridge to U.S. 302. The Davis Path, completed by Nathaniel T.P. Davis in 1845, was the third (and longest) bridle path constructed to the summit of Mt. Washington.

Tuckerman Crossover →

Leads 0.8 mile east, crossing over Bigelow Lawn to Tuckerman Junction. Bigelow Lawn, the largest of the level grassy areas in the Presidentials, was named for a 19th-century New England botanist, Dr. Jacob Bigelow. From Tuckerman Junction, the Tuckerman Ravine Trail descends 1.2 miles east, steeply and treacherously, to Hermit Lake Shelters and Tentsites and 2.4 miles beyond them to AMC's Pinkham Notch Visitors Center, where it rejoins the A.T at the northern end of this section. This route, eliminating the northern Presidential Range, is recommended in bad weather but should be approached with caution, too. AMC maintains and operates the USFS Hermit Lake Shelters and Tentsites under a special-use permit, with a caretaker and fee. Eight shelters and three tent platforms accommodate 86. In the summer, potable water from a hand-pump and flush toilets are available. In the winter, a privy is available, and untreated water may be available from the Cutler River. Dogs are not permitted overnight.

Dry River Trail →

Leads 9.6 miles east down the headwall of Oakes Gulf and into the Presidential Range–Dry River Wilderness to U.S. 302.

Lakes of the Clouds Hut →

Above treeline, this is the highest and most popular hut in the AMC chain. Backpacker rates are available for the six-person refuge room (cellar) known as "The Dungeon." The refuge room can be used for emergency shelter when hut is closed but *must not be used as a backcountry destination*. The hut itself, with solar and wind power for energy, is full-service only in season (late spring/summer); reservations recommended; fee. Accommodates 90. The resident staff

N-S

TRAIL DESCRIPTION

14.1 Reach southern junction with the Westside
5,625 feet), which leads west 0.9 mile and rej
at mile 12.6/13.4. South 35 yards on the A.T. is
tion with the **Davis Path**.

14.8 Junction with **Tuckerman Crossover** and the Camel Trail   **11.2**
(elev. 5,125 feet), which leads 0.7 mile east to the Davis
Path.

14.9 Pass junction with **Dry River Trail**. Thirty yards to the south   **11.1**
is **Lakes of the Clouds Hut** (elev. 5,012 feet). At the south
corner of the hut is the **Ammonoosuc Ravine Trail**.

Ammonoosuc Ravine Trail

members have with trail information and weather reports, and the hut has a small retail store with safety items, snacks, and water.

Ammonoosuc Ravine Trail→

Descends 3.1 miles west to a parking lot on the Base Road (AMC hiker-shuttle stop), passing near Marshfield Station, the base station of the Mt. Washington Cog Railway. *Ammonoosuc* is Abenaki for "fish place."

Mt. Monroe →

Mt. Monroe (elev. 5,372 feet) was named in honor of James Monroe, the fifth president of the United States.

Mt. Franklin →

Mt. Franklin (elev. 5,001 feet) is named in honor of Benjamin Franklin, one of the most important founding fathers of the United States, a leading author, political theorist, politician, printer, scientist, inventor, civic activist, and diplomat.

Mt. Eisenhower Trail→

Descends 2.7 miles east into Oakes Gulf and the Presidential Range–Dry River Wilderness to the Dry River Trail.

Mt. Eisenhower →

Mt. Eisenhower (elev. 4,671 feet) was named in 1972 in honor of Dwight D. Eisenhower, the five-star general who was the thirty-fourth U.S. president. Previously, this mountain was known as Mt. Pleasant, or Pleasant Dome, a reference to the rounded appearance of its summit area. The native-American presence in the White Mountains is memorialized here by Abenaki Brook, Abenaki Ravine, and Sokokis Brook, all on Mt. Eisenhower's western flank.

N-S

<table>
<tr><td colspan="3" align="center">TRAIL DESCRIPTION</td></tr>
</table>

N-S		S-N
15.0	Reach northern junction (elev. 5,075 feet) of Mt. Monroe Loop, which leads 0.4 mile west to the summit of **Mt. Monroe** and rejoins the A.T. at mile 15.7/10.3.	**11.0**
15.7	Southern junction (elev. 5,075 feet) of Mt. Monroe Loop, which leads 0.4 mile west to summit of **Mt. Monroe** and rejoins the A.T. above in 0.4 mile farther.	**10.3**
16.0	Unmarked path leads 130 yards east to the summit of **Mt. Franklin**.	**10.0**
16.4	Pass west of the summit of **Mt. Franklin**.	**9.6**
16.9	Junction with Mt. Eisenhower Trail (elev. 4,475 feet).	**9.1**
17.1	Reach northern junction of the Mt. Eisenhower Loop (elev. 4,475 feet), which leads 0.4 mile west to the summit of **Mt. Eisenhower** and rejoins the A.T. at mile 17.6/8.4. The Edmands Path, 50 yards to the west of this junction, descends 2.9 miles west to Mt. Clinton Road.	**8.9**
17.6	Pass the southern junction with the Mt. Eisenhower Loop (elev. 4,425 feet), which leads west 0.4 mile to summit of Mt. Eisenhower and rejoins the A.T at mile 17.1/8.9. ■ SOUTHBOUND hikers leave the alpine zone. ■ NORTHBOUND hikers enter the alpine zone.	**8.4**
18.0	Cross small stream in col.	**8.0**

S-N

SECTION HIGHLIGHTS

Webster Cliff Trail →

This trail coincides with the A.T. for 7.3 miles from here to U.S. 302 (AMC hiker-shuttle stop) at the southern end of the section.

Crawford Path →

Coincides with the northbound A.T. for 5.2 miles. Here, it leads 2.9 miles west to U.S. 302 at AMC's Highland Center (see southern end of section). The Crawford Path is one of the oldest hiking trails in the country, originally built during the 1800s and used as a horse trail from the "Crawford House" (now AMC's Highland Center) to the summit of Mt. Washington. *Caution: Parts of this trail are dangerous in bad weather.*

Mt. Pierce (Mt. Clinton) →

Mt. Pierce honors the only U.S. president to hail from the Granite State (New Hampshire), Franklin Pierce, the fourteenth chief executive (1853–1857). The mountain was given the name of Pierce in 1913. The name "Mt. Clinton" is still commonly associated with it, however, since it bore that name for many years in honor of DeWitt Clinton, "Father of the Erie Canal," who served nine years as governor of New York in the early 1800s after 10 years in split terms as mayor of New York City.

N-S

TRAIL DESCRIPTION

Junction of Webster Cliff Trail and Crawford Path

18.7 | Join or leave the **Webster Cliff Trail** or the **Crawford Path** | **7.3**
(elev. 4,250 feet) ■ SOUTHBOUND hikers turn left on the
Webster Cliff Trail. ■ NORTHBOUND hikers turn right on
the Crawford Path and follow ridge.

18.8 | Cross summit of **Mt. Pierce**, also called **Mt. Clinton** (elev. | **7.2**
4,312 feet). *The A.T. is mostly above treeline for the next
12.7 miles north and should be attempted only in favorable weather.*

S-N

SECTION HIGHLIGHTS

Mizpah Spring Hut →

Mizpah means "pillar in the wilderness," and the hut overlooks the Montalban Range, the Dry River Wilderness, and Crawford Notch. Full-service in season (late spring/summer), self-service earlier in the year; reservations recommended; fee. Accommodates 60. The resident staff members can provide trail information and weather reports. The solar-powered hut, with solar preheating of water, includes a small retail store with safety items, snacks, and water. Clivus composting toilets.

Nauman Tentsite →

Built and maintained by AMC, with a caretaker; fee. Five single and three double tent platforms accommodate 30. Composting privy; bear box. The water source is the stream. Next shelter or campsite: south, 8.2 miles (Dry River); north, 11.2 (The Perch).

Mt. Clinton Trail →

Descends 3.0 miles east into Oakes Gulf and the Presidential Range–Dry River Wilderness to the Dry River Trail.

Mizpah Cutoff→

Descends 0.6 mile west to the Crawford Path, which leads 1.7 miles from that point to U.S. 302 at the AMC's Highland Center.

Mt. Jackson →

Mt. Jackson is named for Charles T. Jackson, who once served as New Hampshire's state geologist, and not for President Andrew Jackson.

Jackson Branch→

Descends 1.2 miles west to the Webster–Jackson Trail and continues 1.3 miles to U.S. 302 at Saco Lake, 0.2 mile east of AMC's Highland Center.

N-S

TRAIL DESCR.

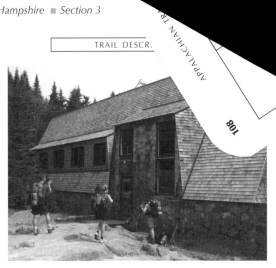

Mizpah Spring Hut

19.6	Reach **Mizpah Spring Hut** and **Nauman Tentsite** and junction with the **Mt. Clinton Trail** (elev. 3,800 feet).	**6.4**
19.7	The **Mizpah Cutoff** enters from the west (elev. 3,862 feet).	**6.3**
21.3	Reach **Mt. Jackson** summit (elev. 4,052 feet) and **Jackson Branch** of Webster–Jackson Trail.	**4.7**

S-N

Webster Branch →

Descends 1.0 mile west to the Webster–Jackson Trail and continues 1.3 miles to U.S. 302 at Saco Lake, 0.2 mile east of AMC's Highland Center (see below).

Presidential Range–Dry River Wilderness →

Congress designated the Presidential Range–Dry River Wilderness in 1975. It now has a total of 27,380 acres and is managed by the USFS.

Mt. Webster →

Mt. Webster honors American statesman Daniel Webster. In 1835, a 3,300-acre parcel of mountain land above Crawford Notch, now in the WMNF, was granted to Charles Bean of Maine.

Saco River Trail →

The northern junction leads 1.6 miles east to the Dry River Trail. The southern junction (mile 25.8/0.2) leads 1.2 miles west to U.S. 302, across from the seasonal Crawford Notch State Park Visitors Center.

Saco River →

The headwaters begin at Saco Lake in Crawford Notch, and the river flows southeast for 134 miles, passing through several hydro-electric stations before reaching the Atlantic Ocean.

N-S   ┌─────────────────────────────┐
                       │   TRAIL DESCRIPTION   │
                       └─────────────────────────────┘

22.6 Junction of **Webster Branch** of Webster–Jackson Trail   **3.4**
          (elev. 3,840 feet). ■ SOUTHBOUND hikers enter **Presidential
          Range–Dry River Wilderness**. ■ NORTHBOUND hikers leave
          Presidential Range–Dry River Wilderness.

22.7 Reach summit of Mt. Webster (elev. 3,910 feet), honoring   **3.3**
          statesman Daniel Webster.

23.6 View available from ledge, straight down to state-park   **2.4**
          buildings.

24.2 View from Webster Cliffs (elev. 3,025 feet). ■ Southbound   **1.8**
          hikers enter Crawford Notch State Park. ■ Northbound
          hikers leave Crawford Notch State Park.

25.7 Reach northern junction with the **Saco River Trail** (elev. **0.3**
          1,400 feet). ■ SOUTHBOUND hikers leave **Presidential
          Range–Dry River Wilderness**. ■ NORTHBOUND hikers enter
          Presidential Range–Dry River Wilderness.

25.8 Pass southern junction with the Saco River Trail (elev.   **0.2**
          1,350 feet).

25.9 Cross the **Saco River** on a new (2008) footbridge (elev.   **0.1**
          1,300 feet).

SECTION HIGHLIGHTS

Southern end of section →

The Trail crosses U.S. 302 in Crawford Notch opposite the Willey House Station Road (AMC hiker-shuttle stop). A hiker parking area is 0.3 mile south, on the Trail, at the end of the Willey House Station Road. Theft and vandalism have been reported; do not leave valuables in vehicles. On U.S. 302, it is 1.8 miles east to the Dry River Campground, operated and maintained by the New Hampshire Division of Parks in Crawford Notch State Park, with 24 tentsites and ample water. Next shelter or campsite: south, 4.7 miles (Ethan Pond); north, 8.2 miles (Nauman). It is 3 miles east to Crawford Notch Campground and General Store (telephones, campground, bunkhouse hostel, and groceries). It is 13 miles east to Bartlett (ZIP Code 03812), with telephones, lodging, meals, and groceries. It is 25 miles east by way of N.H. 16 to North Conway (ZIP Code 03860), with lodging, restaurants, groceries, coin laundry, outfitters, cobbler, and bus stop. The Willey House (telephone, snacks) is 1 mile west. It is 3.7 miles west to the AMC's Highland Center at Crawford Notch (AMC hiker-shuttle stop). The center is open year-round; reservations strongly recommended. Its lodge accommodates 122 in private, family, or shared rooms; the Shapleigh bunkhouse accommodates 16. Breakfast and lunch service is buffet-style, while dinner is served family-style. Twin Mountain (ZIP Code 03595) is 10 miles west, with motels, restaurants, and groceries. Service from here to and from Boston is available through Concord Coach Lines; (800) 639-3317; <www.concordcoachlines.com>. Greyhound, <www.greyhound.com>, also has service in New Hampshire.

N-S

TRAIL DESCRIPTION

26.0 Reach U.S. 302 at Crawford Notch (elev. 1,275 feet), the   **0.0**
southern end of section. ▪ SOUTHBOUND hikers cross U.S.
302 and ascend on Willey House Station Road (see New
Hampshire Section Four). ▪ NORTHBOUND hikers enter
hardwood forest on the **Webster Cliff Trail**.

> *Regulations*—Camping and wood fires are prohib-
> ited, except at designated areas, within one-quarter
> mile of Madison Springs Hut, The Perch Shelter,
> Gray Knob Cabin, Crag Camp Cabin, Lakes of the
> Clouds Hut, and Mizpah Spring Hut; above
> treeline, which includes virtually all of the A.T. from
> Mt. Madison to Mt. Pierce; in the Cutler River
> Drainage (including the 1.9-mile section of Trail
> between Pinkham Notch and the Mt. Washington
> Auto Road); or within one-quarter mile of N.H. 16.
> In the Great Gulf Wilderness, no wood fires are
> allowed, and no camping is permitted within 200
> feet of any trail, except at designated sites. Between
> the Auto Road and Osgood Tentsite, camping is
> prohibited within 200 feet of the Trail. This section
> also falls under the following forest-protection-area
> regulations: no camping or fires at Glen Ellis Falls
> or along U.S. 302 from Bartlett to Bethlehem or on
> the Valley Way from the Scar Trail to Madison Hut.
> Campfire permits are required for open fires outside
> WMNF lands. Permits can be obtained at Pinkham
> Notch Visitors Center, in Crawford Notch State Park
> at the Willey House, and from other cooperators
> (inquire locally).
>
>   The southern end lies within Crawford Notch
> State Park, where camping and fires are not permit-
> ted except at Dry River Campground. The rest of
> the Trail passes through the WMNF.

S-N

Crawford Notch (U.S. 302) to Franconia Notch (U.S. 3)

27.7 MILES

Crossing the Willey Range and Zealand, Garfield, and Franconia ridges, this is the longest section of uninterrupted footpath on the A.T. in New Hampshire or Vermont. The Trail traces a route partly through dense hardwood and coniferous forests and partly across high ridges and summits. Hiking here is extremely strenuous…and rewarding.

Most of the Trail lies along the edges of the Pemigewasset Wilderness. Beginning on Ethan Pond Trail, the A.T. climbs steeply from the floor of Crawford Notch, crosses a low point on the Willey Range, passes Ethan Pond and Thoreau Falls, and follows an old logging-railroad bed through Zealand Notch. Ascending Zealand Ridge, north of the Pemigewasset Wilderness on the Twinway Trail, it continues, always high on the ridge, on the northern, then western, sides of the Pemigewasset on the Garfield Ridge Trail and the Franconia Ridge Trail. For two miles, on sometimes

continued on page 56

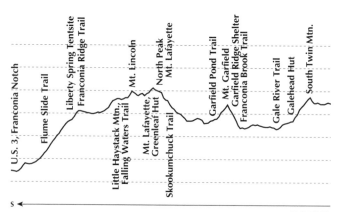

S ←

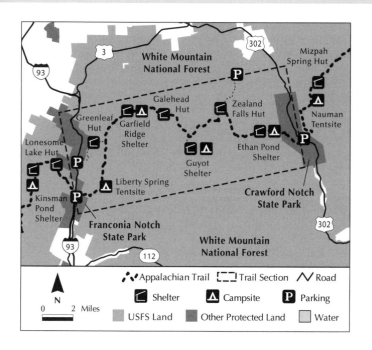

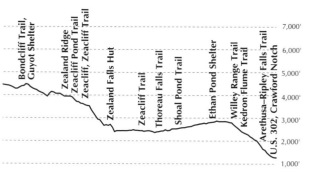

narrow and precipitous Franconia Ridge, the Trail passes above treeline, providing a vista from the summit of Mt. Lafayette, the highest peak in this section. The Trail route descends from Franconia Ridge on Liberty Spring Trail into Franconia Notch State Park on U.S. 3. Water is scarce on the ridgecrests.

Franconia Ridge is exposed to the full force of storms, which rise rapidly and violently, with winds of hurricane force and freezing conditions, even in summer. Carry extra clothing. If the weather becomes threatening, promptly descend to shelter by the shortest route.

Many steep ascents and descents are encountered at the section ends and on a number of peaks. The Trail in this section passes over seven major peaks, which are, from north to south: Mt. Guyot, 4,580 feet; South Twin Mountain, 4,902 feet; Mt. Garfield, 4,500 feet; Mt. Lafayette, 5,260 feet; Mt. Lincoln, 5,089 feet; Little Haystack Mountain, 4,780 feet; and (by way of a short side trail) Mt. Liberty, 4,450 feet.

The elevation at U.S. 302 in Crawford Notch is 1,275 feet; on U.S. 3 in Franconia Notch, 1,450 feet. The highest elevation is on the summit of Mt. Lafayette.

Road Approaches—Both ends are accessible by vehicle. Concord Coach Lines, <www.concordcoachlines.com>, and Greyhound, <www.greyhound.com>, both provide bus service in New Hampshire.

Maps—For route navigation, refer to Map Three with this guide; AMC Map 2 (Franconia–Pemigewasset); the White Mountain National Forest map (1:250,000); or the Franconia Notch State Park hiking map. For area detail but not current trail routes, refer to the USGS 15-minute topographic quadrangle for Crawford Notch, New Hampshire, or these USGS 7½-minute quadrangles: South Twin Mountain, Franconia, and Lincoln, New Hampshire.

Shelters and Campsites—This section has three campsites with shelters: Ethan Pond Campsite and Shelter (mile 2.9/24.8), Guyot Campsite and Shelter (mile 11.9/15.8), and Garfield Ridge Campsite and Shelter (mile 17.4/10.3). It also has two tentsites: 13 Falls (mile 16.9/10.8) and Liberty Spring (mile 25.1/2.6). Crawford Notch State Park's Dry River

Campground is 1.8 miles from the northern end of the section, and Franconia Notch State Park's Lafayette Place Campground is 2.5 miles from the southern end of the section.

The section also is home to three seasonal AMC mountain huts: Zealand Falls Hut (mile 7.7/20.0), Galehead Hut (mile 14.7/13.0), and Greenleaf Hut (mile 21.3/6.4).

Summit of Mt. Garfield

SECTION HIGHLIGHTS

Northern end of section →

The Trail crosses U.S. 302 in Crawford Notch opposite the Willey House Station Road (AMC hiker-shuttle stop). A hiker parking area is 0.3 mile south, on the Trail, at the end of the Willey House Station Road. Theft and vandalism have been reported; do not leave valuables in vehicles. On U.S. 302, it is 1.8 miles east to the Dry River Campground, operated and maintained by the New Hampshire Division of Parks in Crawford Notch State Park, with 24 tentsites and ample water. Next shelter or campsite: south, 4.7 miles (Ethan Pond); north, 8.2 miles (Nauman). It is 3 miles east to Crawford Notch Campground and General Store (telephones, campground, bunkhouse hostel, and groceries). It is 25 miles east by way of N.H. 16 to North Conway (ZIP Code 03860), with lodging, restaurants, groceries, coin laundry, outfitters, cobbler, and bus stop. The Willey House (telephone, snacks) is 1 mile west. It is 3.7 miles west to the AMC's Highland Center at Crawford Notch (AMC hiker-shuttle stop). The center is open year-round; reservations strongly recommended. Its lodge accommodates 122 in private, family, or shared rooms; the Shapleigh bunkhouse accommodates 16. Breakfast and lunch service is buffet-style, while dinner is served family-style. Twin Mountain (ZIP Code 03595) is 10 miles west, with motels, restaurants, and groceries.

Ethan Pond Trail →

This trail, coaligned with the A.T. for 7.2 miles, begins at the Willey House Station site and ends at the junction of the Zealand Trail and the Twinway (mile 7.5/20.2), below Zealand Falls Hut.

Willey House →

The Willey House historic site, formerly a small inn and residence in Crawford Notch, is the location of a landslide that claimed nine lives in August 1826. Although the surrounding area was strewn with boulders and debris, the Willey House stood unharmed. The family, however, perished in the landslide, becoming part of the legend of Willey House.

N-S

TRAIL DESCRIPTION

0.0   U.S. 302 at Crawford Notch (elev. 1,275 feet) is the   **27.7**
          northern end of section. ■ SOUTHBOUND hikers cross
          U.S. 302 and ascend on paved Willey House Station
          Road. ■ NORTHBOUND hikers cross U.S. 302 and enter
          woods on the Webster Cliff Trail (see New Hampshire
          Section Three).

0.3   Pass **Willey House** site parking area (elev. 1,440 feet). ■   **27.4**
          SOUTHBOUND hikers cross railroad tracks and ascend on
          old logging road to **Ethan Pond Trail**. ■ NORTHBOUND
          hikers descend on paved Willey House Station Road to
          U.S. 302.

S-N

Arethusa–Ripley Falls Trail →

Leads east 0.3 mile to Ripley Falls, 2.5 miles to Arethusa Falls, and 1.5 miles beyond to U.S. 302. Arethusa Falls at 200 feet high are the highest in New Hampshire. Ripley Falls are 100 feet high.

Kedron Flume Trail →

Decends very steeply 1.3 miles west to Willey House on U.S. 302 (telephones, snacks).

Willey Range Trail →

Leads west across Kedron Brook and ascends 1.1 miles to Mt. Willey, 2.5 miles to Mt. Field, and beyond to the A-Z Trail and the Avalon Trail.

Ethan Pond Campsite and Shelter →

Around 1830, Ethan Allen Crawford discovered this pond while on one of his trapping trips, and it was named for him. The shelter was built in the 1970s and is maintained by AMC with a caretaker; fee. Accommodates 10 at the shelter and 20 on three single and two double tent platforms. Composting privy; bear box. Water source is a brook near the site. Next shelter or campsite: south, 9.8 miles (Guyot); north, 4.7 miles (Dry River).

Shoal Pond Trail →

Leads 0.7 mile east on railroad grade to Shoal Pond and continues 3.3 miles to Stillwater Junction in the Pemigewasset Wilderness (see page 41).

Thoreau Falls Trail →

Leads east, passes the 80-foot falls, and continues 5.1 miles to the Wilderness Trail, which leads 6.3 miles to the Kancamagus Highway, a 34-mile-long, two-lane road that was formerly the bed of the Lincoln and East Branch Railroad. Completed in 1959, the "Kank" crosses the rugged terrain of the WMNF from the Pemigewasset River in Lincoln to Conway, New Hampshire. This is a busy New Hampshire road during "leaf-peeping" season; also referred to as N.H. 112, closed in winter.

N-S

TRAIL DESCRIPTION

0.5	Reach junction with **Arethusa–Ripley Falls Trail** (elev. 1,600 feet). ■ SOUTHBOUND hikers ascend steeply for the next 0.5 mile, then gradually. ■ NORTHBOUND hikers descend, crossing railroad tracks to parking area.	**27.2**
1.6	Pass **Kedron Flume Trail** junction (elev. 2,450 feet).	**26.1**
1.9	Pass **Willey Range Trail** (elev. 2,680 feet). ■ SOUTHBOUND hikers turn left and ascend, following **Ethan Pond Trail**. ■ NORTHBOUND hikers turn right and follow Ethan Pond Trail.	**25.8**
2.4	Reach height of land (elev. 2,900 feet). ■ SOUTHBOUND hikers leave Crawford Notch State Park and enter WNMF. ■ NORTHBOUND hikers enter Crawford Notch State Park and leave WNMF.	**25.3**
2.9	Side trail leads 250 yards west to **Ethan Pond Campsite and Shelter** (elev. 2,860 feet).	**24.8**
4.7	Cross a brook (elev. 2,520 feet). ■ SOUTHBOUND hikers merge with old Zealand Valley Railroad bed. ■ NORTHBOUND hikers leave railroad grade.	**23.0**
4.9	Pass **Shoal Pond Trail** (elev. 2,500 feet).	**22.8**
5.2	Cross North Fork on wooden bridge (elev. 2,490 feet).	**22.5**
5.4	Reach junction with the **Thoreau Falls Trail** (elev. 2,460 feet). *Camping is prohibited at the falls.*	**22.3**

S-N

SECTION HIGHLIGHTS

Zealand Notch→

This steep-walled, U-shaped notch lies between Whitewall Mountain, Zeacliff, and Zealand Mountain. Here reportedly once stood the most beautiful, longest-standing virgin forest in New Hampshire before it was ravaged by fire and attracted 19th-century lumber baron James Everett Henry.

Zeacliff Trail→

Leads 1.4 miles east across a brook and climbs very steeply.

Twinway→

Coaligned with the A.T. for its entire length, 7.2 miles north from Galehead Hut (mile 14.7/13.0) to this junction with the Zealand Trail and the Ethan Pond Trail.

Zealand Trail→

Descends gradually 2.3 miles west to a gate on Zealand Road/ FR 16 (closed in winter but an AMC hiker-shuttle stop in season), 3.5 miles from U.S. 302 at Zealand Campground and 2.3 miles east of Twin Mountain. The A-Z Trail intersects the Zealand Trail in 0.2 mile and leads 3.7 miles east to the Avalon Trail, which leads 1.3 miles to U.S. 302 at AMC's Highland Center at northern end of section.

Zealand Falls Hut→

A popular family destination because of its relatively easy access, waterfalls, and views of the Pemigewasset Wilderness. Full-service in season (late spring/summer); self-service the rest of the year; reservations recommended; fee. Accommodates 36. Clivus composting toilets. Resident staff members have trail information and weather reports, and the hut—using solar, wind, and hydropower— has a small retail store with safety items and snacks.

Lend-a-Hand→

Leads west 2.7 miles to the summit of Mt. Hale (elev. 4,054 feet). From the summit, the Hale Brook Trail descends 2.2 miles to Zealand Road/FR 16 (closed in winter; AMC hiker-shuttle stop in season), which leads 2.5 miles to U.S. 302.

N-S

TRAIL DESCRIPTION

5.9　Pass to the east of the slide-scarred slopes (elev. 2,450 **21.8**
feet) of Whitewall Mountain, with sweeping views of
Zealand Notch.

6.2　Reach northern junction (elev. 2,448 feet) with the **Zea-** **21.5**
cliff Trail, which rejoins the A.T. on the **Twinway** at mile
9.0/18.7.

7.5　Pass **Zealand Trail** junction (elev. 2,460 feet). ■ SOUTH- **20.2**
BOUND hikers turn left, follow the **Twinway**, cross outlet
of Zealand Pond, and ascend steeply on rock steps. ■
NORTHBOUND hikers turn right and follow the Ethan Pond
Trail along an old railroad grade (badly washed out in
places, but it improves).

7.6　Spur trail on east (elev. 2,600 feet) leads to view of Zea- **20.1**
land Falls.

7.7　Reach **Zealand Falls Hut** (elev. 2,630 feet). **20.0**

7.8　Reach junction with **Lend-a-Hand** (elev. 2,730 feet). South **19.9**
on A.T. 200 yards, Whitewall Brook is crossed twice.

8.9　At crest of rise (elev. 3,670 feet), a 100-yard side loop **18.8**
swings east to a spectacular lookout at edge of Zeacliff.

9.0　Reach southern junction of the **Zeacliff Trail** (elev. 3,700 **18.7**
feet), which rejoins the A.T./Ethan Pond Trail at mile
6.2/21.5.

9.4　Spur trail descends 0.1 mile east to Zeacliff Pond (elev. **18.3**
3,800 feet).

S-N

Mt. Guyot→

Named for 19th-century geographer Arnold Henry Guyot, who wrote many papers on the Appalachian Mountains and also has a mountain along the A.T. in Great Smoky Mountains National Park named for him. He proved that Mt. Washington was not the highest summit in the eastern United States, that Mt. Mitchell should carry this distinction. Myron H. Avery, ATC's formative leader in the 1930s and 1940s, unearthed Guyot's papers from the National Archives and gave them considerable circulation.

Bondcliff Trail →

Leads 0.6 mile east to Guyot Spur Trail, which leads 0.2 mile west to Guyot Campsite and Shelter. The Bondcliff Trail continues past the spur 1.2 miles to Mt. Bond, 1.2 miles more to Bondcliff, 4.4 miles to the Wilderness Trail at the site of Camp 16, and 4.7 miles to the Kancamagus Highway.

Guyot Campsite and Shelter→

Shelter rebuilt in 1977 and maintained by AMC with a caretaker; fee. Accommodates 12 at the shelter and 18 on four single and two double tent platforms. Composting privy. Water source is a spring at the site. Next shelter or campsite: south, 8.0 miles (13 Falls); north, 9.8 miles (Ethan Pond).

N-S

TRAIL DESCRIPTION

10.6   At height of land (elev. 4,250 feet), spur trail leads very   **17.1**
gradually 0.1 mile west to summit of Zealand Mountain.

11.9   Reach open summit of **Mt. Guyot** (elev. 4,580 feet). One   **15.8**
hundred yards south is the junction with the **Bondcliff Trail** leading 0.8 mile east to **Guyot Campsite and Shelter**. ■ SOUTHBOUNDERS turn right on the Twinway. ■
NORTHBOUNDERS turn left on the Twinway.

13.0   Cross ledgy hump (elev. 4,550 feet) with views to the   **14.7**
south of South Twin Mountain and to the north of mounts
Guyot and Carrigain.

Mt. Guyot

S-N

SECTION HIGHLIGHTS

North Twin Spur →

Leads 1.3 miles west to the summit of North Twin (elev. 4,761 feet). From there, the North Twin Trail descends 6.8 miles to U.S. 3, 2.3 miles west of Twin Mountain.

Garfield Ridge Trail →

This 6.6-mile trail, coinciding with the A.T., runs to the summit of Mt. Lafayette (mile 21.3/6.4).

Galehead Hut →

Originally built in 1931 from native trees, this hut survived the hurricane of 1938 that broke up the A.T. a year after it was originally completed. In 2000, the hut was completely rebuilt. Full-service in season (late spring/summer); self-service in spring; reservations recommended; fee. Accommodates 38. Clivus composting toilets. Resident staff members have trail information and weather reports; small retail store has safety items and snacks. Hut employs solar and wind power.

Gale River Trail →

Descends 4.0 miles west to Gale River Loop Road (FR 92), an AMC hiker-shuttle stop 1.6 miles from U.S. 3 at "Five Corners," opposite Trudeau Road.

Franconia Brook Trail →

Descends 3.0 miles past the tentsite to the Wilderness Trail, which leads 3.3 additional miles through the Pemigewasset Wilderness to the Kancamagus Highway.

13 Falls Tentsite →

Maintained by AMC with a caretaker; fee. Nine tent pads accommodate 36. Bear box. Water on site. Next shelter or campsite: south, 2.8 miles (Garfield Ridge); north, 8.0 miles (Guyot).

N-S

TRAIL DESCRIPTION

View of Mt. Garfield from Galehead Hut

13.9	Reach summit of South Twin Mountain (elev. 4,902 feet) and junction with **North Twin Spur**. ■ SOUTHBOUND hikers turn left and descend steeply over rocky slope. ■ NORTHBOUND hikers turn right and follow ridge southeasterly.	**13.8**
14.7	Join **Garfield Ridge Trail**. Frost Trail leads 40 yards east to **Galehead Hut** (elev. 3,780 feet). ■ SOUTHBOUND hikers continue on **Garfield Ridge Trail**. ■ NORTHBOUND hikers follow the **Twinway** (A.T.) and ascend South Twin Mountain.	**13.0**
15.3	Pass **Gale River Trail** (elev. 3,390 feet).	**12.4**
15.6	Viewpoint on ledgy knob (elev. 3,590 feet) toward Owl's Head Mountain.	**12.1**
16.9	**Franconia Brook Trail** (elev. 3,420 feet) leads 2.2 miles east to **13 Falls Tentsite**.	**10.8**

S-N

SECTION HIGHLIGHTS

Garfield Ridge Campsite and Shelter →

Shelter built in 1970 and maintained by AMC with caretaker; fee. Accommodates 12 at shelter and 28 on two single and five double tent platforms. Water source is brook at side-trail junction with A.T. Next shelter or campsite: south, 7.8 miles (Liberty Spring); north, 2.8 miles (13 Falls).

Garfield Trail →

Descends 4.8 miles west, along the old access road to the former Mt. Garfield fire tower, to Gale River Loop Road (FR 92) and then 1.2 miles to U.S. 3 at the Gale River.

Mt. Garfield →

Named in honor of James A. Garfield, 20th president of the United States. Only the cement foundation of the Mt. Garfield fire tower, which went into operation in 1940 and burned in 1950, remains on the summit.

Skookumchuck Trail →

Descends west 4.3 miles to a parking lot that also serves the northern end of the Franconia Notch Bike Path, located 0.3 mile south of the junction of U.S. 3 and N.H. 141 and just north of the point where U.S. 3 divides at its northern junction with I-93 and the Franconia Notch Parkway. *Skookumchuck* is a word in the Chinook jargon. *Skookum* means "strong" or "powerful," and *chuck* means "water."

N-S

TRAIL DESCRIPTION

17.1   Cross small brook (elev. 3,590 feet). ■ SOUTHBOUND hikers   **10.6**
ascend tricky, steep, wet ledge.

17.4   Spur trail leads 0.1 mile west to **Garfield Ridge Campsite**   **10.3**
and Shelter. Water source is a small brook at this junction
(elev. 3,900 feet). ■ NORTHBOUND hikers descend tricky,
steep, wet ledge.

17.6   Pass **Garfield Trail** (elev. 4,180 feet).   **10.1**

17.8   Mt. Garfield Spur leads 60 yards east to summit of **Mt.**   **9.9**
Garfield (elev. 4,500 feet).

18.3   Pass east of Garfield Pond (elev. 3,860 feet).   **9.4**

20.5   Reach treeline on Franconia Ridge (see page 41) and   **7.2**
junction with the **Skookumchuck Trail** (elev. 4,680 feet).
*Because of the sharpness, narrowness, and complete
exposure to weather, the next 2.5 miles south along
the ridgecrest should only be hiked in favorable weather.
Particular care should be taken if electrical storms
threaten.* ■ SOUTHBOUND hikers enter alpine zone.
■ NORTHBOUND hikers leave alpine zone.

20.9   Cross North Peak of Mt. Lafayette (elev. 5,000 feet).   **6.8**

S-N

SECTION HIGHLIGHTS

Mt. Lafayette→

Once known as Great Haystack, this is the highest peak in the Franconia Range and named after the French statesman and American Revolutionary War hero, the Marquis de Lafayette. A summit house once provided shelter for early climbers on the peak, but only its foundation remains, just below summit to the west.

Greenleaf Trail →

Descends 300 yards west to a spring, 1.1 miles to Greenleaf Hut, and 2.7 miles to the Cannon Mountain Tramway parking lot on the west side of the Franconia Notch Parkway.

Greenleaf Hut →

Perched at treeline at 4,200 feet on the shoulder of Mt. Lafayette. Full-service in season (late spring/summer); self-service earlier; reservations recommended; fee. Accommodates 48. Clivus composting toilets, with solar and wind power supplying the hut. Resident staff members provide trail information and weather reports. A small retail store has safety items and snacks. From Greenleaf Hut, the Old Bridle Path, which once served as a pony trail from Franconia Notch to the summit house on Mt. Lafayette, descends 2.9 miles to the Lafayette Place parking lots (located on each side of the Franconia Notch Parkway; AMC hiker-shuttle stop), across from Lafayette Place Campground at the southern end of the section.

Mt. Lincoln →

Mt. Lincoln honors Abraham Lincoln, the 16th U.S. president.

Little Haystack →

Early settlers referred to mounts Liberty, Flume, Lafayette, and this peak as haystacks because of their shape.

Falling Waters Trail →

Descends 3.2 miles west to the Lafayette Place parking lots (located on each side of the Franconia Notch Parkway; AMC hiker-shuttle stop), across from Lafayette Place Campground at the southern end of the section.

N-S

TRAIL DESCRIPTION

21.3   Reach summit of **Mt. Lafayette** (elev. 5,260 feet) and   **6.4**
           northern junction of coaligned Franconia Ridge Trail. The
           Greenleaf Trail leads 1.1 mile west to **Greenleaf Hut**.
           ■ SOUTHBOUND hikers descend from summit on the Fran-
           conia Ridge Trail. ■ NORTHBOUND hikers continue on the
           coaligned Garfield Ridge Trail.

21.8   Cross prominent, unnamed hump (elev. 5,020 feet).   **5.9**

22.3   Reach summit of **Mt. Lincoln** (elev. 5,089 feet).   **5.4**

23.0   Reach summit of **Little Haystack** and junction with the   **4.7**
           Falling Waters Trail (elev. 5,089 feet). *Because of the*
           sharpness, narrowness, and complete exposure to
           weather, the next 2.5 miles north along the ridgecrest
           should only be hiked in favorable weather. Particular care
           should be taken if electrical storms threaten.

Little Haystack

S-N

SECTION HIGHLIGHTS

Franconia Ridge Trail →

From Mt. Lafayette to the Liberty Spring Trail, this trail is part of the A.T. At this point, the Franconia Ridge Trail continues south 0.3 mile to the summit of Mt. Liberty (elev. 4,459 feet), another 1.2 miles to the summit of Mt. Flume (elev. 4,328 feet), and 0.1 mile beyond that to the Flume Slide Trail. There, the Osseo Trail begins and descends south along the ridge 5.5 miles to the Kancamagus Highway east of Lincoln, New Hampshire.

Liberty Spring Tentsite →

Built and maintained by AMC with caretaker; fee. Seven single and three double tent platforms accommodate 44. Composting privy. Water from spring. Next shelter or campsite: south, 5.1 miles (Lafayette Place); north, 7.8 miles (Garfield Ridge).

Flume Slide Trail →

Leads 3.3 miles east to the Franconia Ridge Trail and 0.1 mile beyond that to the summit of Mt. Flume.

N-S   TRAIL DESCRIPTION

24.8   Reach junction with Liberty Spring Trail (elev. 4,260 feet).   **2.9**
           ■ SOUTHBOUND hikers turn right and descend onto Liberty
           Spring Trail, leaving an alpine zone. ■ NORTHBOUND hik-
           ers turn left onto **Franconia Ridge Trail**, enter an alpine
           zone, and follow ridge, ascending steeply on ledges to
           Little Haystack.

25.1   Pass **Liberty Spring Tentsite**. Spring is 10 yards east (elev.   **2.6**
           3,870 feet). ■ SOUTHBOUND hikers continue steep descent
           across ledges. ■ NORTHBOUND hikers: This is your last sure
           water on the Trail until Garfield Pond, mile 18.3/9.4.

25.5   Reach the bottom of a gap (elev. 3,310 feet). ■ SOUTH-   **2.2**
           BOUND hikers make a sharp turn left at end of steep de-
           scent. ■ NORTHBOUND hikers turn sharply right and climb
           steeply on rough footing.

26.3   Northern junction with an old logging road (elev. 2,350   **1.4**
           feet). ■ SOUTHBOUND hikers turn sharply right onto
           old road. ■ NORTHBOUND hikers turn sharply left off old
           logging road.

26.6   Cross large brook (elev. 2,050 feet).   **1.1**

27.1   Pass **Flume Slide Trail** (elev. 1,800 feet).   **0.6**

27.3   Southern junction with old logging road (elev. 1,680 feet).   **0.4**
           ■ SOUTHBOUND hikers turn sharply left off old main logging
           road from former Whitehouse Mill, enter Franconia Notch
           State Park, leave WMNF, and cross two small brooks.
           ■ NORTHBOUND hikers turn sharply right, joining old main
           logging road, entering WMNF and leaving Franconia
           Notch State Park.

S-N

SECTION HIGHLIGHTS

Southern end of section →

The A.T. crosses under U.S. 3 at the site of the former Whitehouse Bridge (where parking is no longer available). On U.S. 3, a large hiker parking lot is available (AMC hiker-shuttle stop) 0.2 mile north of the Flume Visitors Center. From that hiker parking lot, the Whitehouse Trail leads 0.7 mile compass-north to the Liberty Spring Trail–Cascade Brook Trail intersection. From the end of the section, it is 0.8 mile east to the Flume Visitors Center (telephones, snacks). It is 5.8 miles east to North Woodstock, New Hampshire (ZIP Code 03262), with telephones, motels, restaurants, groceries, and a coin laundry. Lincoln, New Hampshire (ZIP Code 03251), is 6.8 miles east, with telephones, motels, restaurants, groceries, outfitters, a hostel, the Linwood Medical Center, and a bus stop. It is 2.5 miles west on the Franconia Notch Bike Path to Lafayette Place Campground, operated and maintained by the New Hampshire Division of Parks in Franconia Notch State Park; fee. Tentsites accommdoate 97. Limited provisions; showers; telephones; ample water; AMC hiker-shuttle stop. Next shelter or campsite: south, 4.8 miles (Kinsman); north, 2.6 miles (Liberty Spring). Franconia Notch State Park headquarters is 4.9 miles west, with an aerial tramway, telephones, snacks, and souvenirs. Franconia, New Hampshire (ZIP Code 03580), is 10.2 miles west, with telephones, motels, restaurants, groceries, and a bus stop. From the Trailhead, it is 20.0 miles west to Littleton, New Hampshire (ZIP Code 03561), a full-service town with a cobbler, hospital, and bus stop. Concord Coach Lines, (800) 639-3317, <www.concordcoachlines.com>, serves this area, to and from Boston. Greyhound, <www.greyhound.com>, also has service in New Hampshire.

N-S

TRAIL DESCRIPTION

27.7   The **southern end of section** is in Franconia Notch State   0.0
        Park where the paved Franconia Notch Bike Path inter-
        sects Liberty Spring Trail (elev. 1,450 feet). ■ SOUTHBOUND
        hikers turn left onto the bike trail, cross a steel bridge over
        Pemigewasset River, and turn right under U.S. 3 onto
        Cascade Brook Trail (see New Hampshire Section Five).
        ■ NORTHBOUND hikers, from intersection of Bike Path and
        Liberty Spring Trail, enter woods, cross two small brooks,
        and soon follow logging road.

> *Regulations—This section is within the White
> Mountain National Forest (WMNF), except for the
> northern end, within Crawford Notch State Park,
> and the southern end, part of Franconia Notch State
> Park. Camping and fires are prohibited in those
> parks except at the two campgrounds. WMNF
> regulations apply throughout the section: Camping
> and fires are permitted only below treeline (where
> trees are 8 feet tall or less); 0.25 mile from any hut,
> shelter, tent platform, cabin, picnic area, or camp-
> ground; and at any trailhead, except at designated
> sites. This section also falls under these forest-pro-
> tection-area regulations: no camping within 0.25
> mile of Thoreau Falls and Zealand Road (FR 16),
> and no camping or wood fires within 200 feet of
> the Liberty Spring Trail and Old Bridle Path. Camp-
> ing and wood fires are prohibited within 0.25 mile
> of Ethan Pond Campsite and Shelter, Zealand Falls
> Hut, Mt. Guyot Campsite and Shelter, Galehead
> Hut, 13 Falls Tentsite, Garfield Ridge Campsite and
> Shelter, Greenleaf Hut, or Liberty Spring Tentsite,
> except at designated areas. Camping and wood
> fires are prohibited within 200 feet of the A.T. from
> Galehead Hut to Liberty Spring Tentsite.*

S-N

Franconia Notch (U.S. 3) to Kinsman Notch (N.H. 112)

16.3 MILES

Most of the Trail in this section traverses the northeast-to-southwest Kinsman Ridge through heavily wooded country past mountain ponds and cascades. Hiking here is extremely strenuous, due to the change in elevation from both ends and the often wet and rugged footway.

From Franconia Notch State Park, the Trail climbs on the Cascade Brook Trail. At Lonesome Lake, a high mountain pond on the shoulder of Cannon Mountain, it ascends on the wet and at times steep Fishin' Jimmy Trail. Reaching Kinsman Pond, the Trail ascends on the Kinsman Ridge Trail to the northern and southern peaks of Kinsman Mountain. It descends past Harrington Pond and the cascades of Eliza Brook and then follows a wooded ridge to Kinsman Notch. The elevation at U.S. 3 is 1,450 feet; at N.H. 112, 1,870 feet. The highest elevation is on North Kinsman Peak, at 4,293 feet.

Road Approaches—Both ends are accessible by vehicle. Concord Coach Lines, <www.concordcoachlines.com>, and Greyhound, <www.greyhound.com>, provide bus service in New Hampshire.

Maps—For route navigation, refer to Map Three with this guide; AMC Map 2 (Franconia–Pemigewasset); the White Mountain National Forest map (1:250,000); or Franconia Notch State Park hiking-trails map. For area detail, refer to these USGS 7½-minute topographic quadrangles: Lincoln, Mt. Moosilauke, and Franconia, New Hampshire.

Shelters and Campsites—This section has one campsite with a shelter, Kinsman Pond Campsite and Shelter (mile 4.8/11.5); one shelter, Eliza Brook (mile 8.8/7.5); and one public campground, Lafayette Place Campground, 1.8 miles from the northern end of the section. There also is one AMC mountain hut, Lonesome Lake Hut (mile 2.9/13.4).

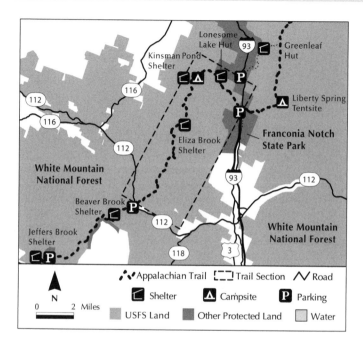

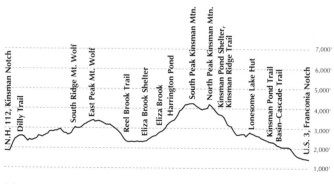

16.3 MILES

Northern end of section →

The A.T. crosses under U.S. 3 at the site of the former Whitehouse Bridge (where parking is no longer available). On U.S. 3, a large hiker parking lot is available (AMC hiker-shuttle stop) 0.2 mile north of the Flume Visitors Center. From that hiker parking lot, the Whitehouse Trail leads 0.7 mile compass-north to the Liberty Spring Trail–Cascade Brook Trail intersection. From the end of the section, it is 0.8 mile east to the Flume Visitors Center (telephones, snacks). Visitors can tour, for a fee, the Flume Gorge, a natural chasm featuring an 800-foot-long gorge with sheer 90-foot walls, scenic pools, glacial boulders, and mountain views. It is 5.8 miles east to North Woodstock, New Hampshire (ZIP Code 03262), with telephones, motels, restaurants, groceries, and a coin laundry. Lincoln, New Hampshire (ZIP Code 03251), is 6.8 miles east, with telephones, motels, restaurants, groceries, outfitters, a hostel, the Linwood Medical Center, and a bus stop. It is 2.5 miles west on the Franconia Notch Bike Path to Lafayette Place Campground, operated and maintained by the New Hampshire Division of Parks in Franconia Notch State Park; fee. Tentsites accommdoate 97. Limited provisions; showers; telephones; ample water; AMC hiker-shuttle stop. Next shelter or campsite: south, 7.4 miles (Kinsman); north, 2.6 miles (Liberty Spring). Franconia Notch State Park headquarters is 4.9 miles west, with an aerial tramway, telephones, snacks, and souvenirs. Franconia, New Hampshire (ZIP Code 03580), is 10.2 miles west, with telephones, motels, restaurants, groceries, and a bus stop. From the Trailhead, it is 20.0 miles west to Littleton, New Hampshire (ZIP Code 03561), a full-service town with a cobbler, hospital, and bus stop. Concord Coach Lines, (800) 639-3317, <www.concord-coachlines.com>, serves this area, to and from Boston, as does Greyhound, <www.greyhound.com>.

Franconia Notch Bike Path →

Leads west to Profile Lake and east to The Flume, a total distance of 6.9 miles.

N-S

TRAIL DESCRIPTION

0.0   The **northern end of the section** is near U.S. 3 in Fran-   **16.3**
conia Notch State Park, where the paved **Franconia Notch
Bike Path** intersects the Liberty Spring Trail (elev. 1,400
feet). ■ SOUTHBOUND hikers turn left onto the bike trail,
cross a steel bridge over the Pemigewasset River, and turn
west under U.S. 3 onto the **Cascade Brook Trail**, ascending into woods on an old logging road. ■ NORTHBOUND
hikers reach the paved bike path, bear right over a steel
bridge to the Liberty Spring Trail, and enter the woods
(see New Hampshire Section Four).

S-N

SECTION HIGHLIGHTS

Cascade Brook Trail →

Coincides with the A.T. from the Franconia Notch Bike Path to Lonesome Lake (mile 2.8/13.5). At the lake, it continues 0.3 mile along the western shore to Lonesome Lake Trail, which leads 1.1 miles east to the Kinsman Ridge Trail and 1.2 miles west through Lafayette Place Campground to U.S. 3.

Pemi Trail →

Leads 2.7 miles west to Lafayette Place Campground (mile 0.0/16.3) and another 2.0 miles to a parking area on the west side of Franconia Notch Parkway near Profile Lake.

Basin–Cascade Trail →

Descends 1.0 mile west, past Kinsman Falls, to The Basin, a large glacial pothole along U.S. 3.

Kinsman Pond Trail →

Ascends 2.4 miles east to Kinsman Pond Campsite and Shelter (see mile 4.8/11.5) and 2.5 miles more to Kinsman Junction, where it rejoins the A.T.

Fishin' Jimmy Trail →

A part of the A.T. for 2 miles from Lonesome Lake to the Kinsman Ridge Trail at Kinsman Junction, near Kinsman Pond (mile 4.8/11.5). "Fishin' Jimmy" was the nickname for James Whitcher from Franconia, who loved to fish in the brooks of the White Mountains and was immortalized in a 1921 book of the same name by Annie Trumbull Slosson.

N-S	TRAIL DESCRIPTION	
0.1	Pass under U.S. 3 (elev. 1,450 feet).	**16.2**
0.2	Pass junction with **Pemi Trail** (elev. 1,520 feet).	**16.1**
0.4	Cross Whitehouse Brook on rocks (elev.1,610 feet).	**15.9**
1.5	Reach junction with **Basin–Cascade Trail**, and cross Cascade Brook on footbridge (elev. 2,084 feet).	**14.8**
2.0	Pass northern junction (elev. 2,294 feet) with the **Kinsman Pond Trail**, which connects with the A.T. again at mile 4.8/11.5.	**14.3**
2.8	Reach southern edge of Lonesome Lake (elev. 2,740 feet) and junction with the **Fishin' Jimmy Trail**. *No camping.* ■ Southbound hikers turn left and ascend on Fishin' Jimmy Trail, crossing Lonesome Lake outlet brook. ■ Northbound hikers turn right and descend on **Cascade Brook Trail** parallel to Lonesome Lake outlet brook.	**13.5**

SECTION HIGHLIGHTS

Lonesome Lake Hut→

Leased from the state of New Hampshire and operated by AMC. Full-service in season only (late spring/summer); self-service the rest of the year; reservations recommended; fee. Accommodates 44. Clivus composting toilets. Resident staff members can provide trail information and weather reports. The hut, which employs solar and wind power, also has a small retail store with safety items and snacks.

Around-Lonesome Lake Trail→

Leads 0.3 mile west to the Lonesome Lake Trail, which then leads 0.9 mile east to the Kinsman Ridge Trail or 1.4 miles west through Lafayette Place Campground to U.S. 3.

Kinsman Ridge Trail →

Coincides with the A.T. from Kinsman Junction to the southern end of the section at N.H. 112. At mile 4.8/11.5, it leads west over the Cannon Balls to Cannon Mountain and from there descends in 5.4 miles to the parking lot of the Cannon Mountain aerial-tramway base station on U.S. 3. From there, across Franconia Notch Parkway, the Greenleaf Trail ascends 3.8 miles to the summit of Mt. Lafayette, rejoining the A.T. (see New Hampshire Section Four).

Kinsman Pond Campsite and Shelter→

The shelter was rebuilt in 2007 and is maintained by AMC with a caretaker; fee. The shelter accommodates 15, and two single and two double tent platforms accommodate 15. Bear box; composting privy. The water source is the pond (should be boiled or treated); better water can be found 1.9 mile north on the A.T. Next shelter or campsite: south, 4.1 miles (Eliza Brook); north, 7.4 miles (Lafayette Place).

Mt. Kinsman Trail→

Descends 3.7 miles west, past Bald Peak and Kinsman Flume, to N.H. 116.

N-S

TRAIL DESCRIPTION

Kinsman Pond Shelter

2.9 Reach **Lonesome Lake Hut** and junction of the **Around-**   **13.4**
        Lonesome Lake Trail (elev. 2,760 feet).

4.8 Reach Kinsman Junction (elev. 3,750 feet). The **Kinsman**   **11.5**
        Pond Trail, a loop, leads 0.1 mile east to **Kinsman Pond**
        Campsite and Shelter and rejoins the A.T. at mile
        2.0/14.3. Also reach the northern junction with the **Kins-**
        man Ridge Trail. ■ SOUTHBOUND hikers continue straight
        ahead on the Kinsman Ridge Trail, ascending North Kins-
        man. ■ NORTHBOUNDERS continue straight ahead on the
        Fishin' Jimmy Trail to Lonesome Lake.

5.0 Pass junction of **Mt. Kinsman Trail** (elev. 3,900 feet).   **11.3**

S-N

North Kinsman Mountain→

Near the summit, a spur trail leads 70 yards east to a cliff overlooking Kinsman Pond. Asa Kinsman was a pioneer settler of Easton, and it is for him that the two mountains and notch are named.

Harrington Pond→

Good view of the shoulder of South Kinsman Mountain.

Eliza Brook Shelter →

Built in 1993 and maintained by AMC. Shelter accommodates 8, and four tent pads accommodate another 8; also one group site. Bear box; composting privy. Water source is the brook. Next shelter or campsite: south, 9.1 miles (Beaver Brook Shelter); north, 4.1 miles (Kinsman Pond).

N-S	TRAIL DESCRIPTION	

5.4 Cross summit of **North Kinsman Mountain** (elev. 4,293 feet). **10.9**

5.8 Pass through col (elev. 4,050 feet) between South and North Kinsman mountains; water may be found to the west. **10.5**

6.3 Pass 15 yards west of the north knob of South Kinsman Mountain (elev. 4,358 feet). ■ SOUTHBOUND hikers begin a very steep, rough, exposed descent, requiring rock scrambling and extra time. **10.0**

6.4 Reach very exposed south knob of South Kinsman Mountain (elev. 4,300 feet). **9.9**

7.3 Cross a brook (elev. 3,425 feet). ■ NORTHBOUND hikers begin a very steep, rough, exposed ascent, requiring rock scrambling and extra time. **9.0**

7.4 Pass to the east of **Harrington Pond** on log bridges (elev. 3,400 feet). **8.9**

7.7 On marshy, rough footway, cross the headwaters of Eliza Brook (elev. 2,880 feet). **8.6**

8.3 Pass cascades to west (elev. 2,760 feet). **8.0**

8.5 Junction with grass-over-gravel logging road (elev. 2,650 feet). ■ SOUTHBOUND hikers turn right onto road. ■ NORTHBOUND hikers turn left off road. **7.8**

8.8 ■ SOUTHBOUND hikers turn right off logging road, cross Eliza Brook, and reach short side trail to **Eliza Brook Shelter** (elev. 2,400 feet). ■ NORTHBOUND hikers reach Eliza Brook Shelter spur trail, cross Eliza Brook, and turn to left, upstream, onto old logging road. **7.5**

S-N

SECTION HIGHLIGHTS

Reel Brook Trail →

Descends west 2.9 miles to a gravel road that leads 0.6 mile to N.H. 116 near Easton.

Gordon Pond Trail →

Descends 0.3 mile east to Gordon Pond, 1.1 miles to Gordon Falls, and 5 miles to N.H. 112.

Dilly Trail →

Trail is open only during the hours and seasons (summer and fall, daytime) when Lost River Gorge and Boulder Caves is open. Closed to the public at all other times.

Lost River Gorge and Boulder Caves →

Located 0.3 mile east of the Trail crossing on N.H. 112, this 157-acre geological curiosity and surrounding area was preserved by the Society for Protection of New Hampshire Forest in 1912 as the Lost River Reservation and operates seasonally today as the Lost River Gorge and Boulder Caves; fee. Souvenirs and vending machines are on site, but no accommodations. Lost River was accidentally "discovered" in 1852, when Lyman Jackman (who was fishing with his brother, Royal, at the time) slipped through a moss-covered hole and dropped 15 feet into what is now known as the Shadow Cave. Lost River is so named because the brook draining the southern part of Kinsman Notch disappears below the surface in the narrow, steep-walled glacial gorge. Trails, boardwalks, and ladders access the caves, glacial potholes, and waterfalls. Self-guided tours of the gorge, ecology trail, and nature garden are available.

N-S	TRAIL DESCRIPTION	
9.3	Pass under power line (elev. 2,625 feet).	**7.0**
9.8	Pass junction with **Reel Brook Trail** (elev. 2,600 feet).	**6.5**
10.9	Spur trail (elev. 3,200 feet) descends 20 yards east to the edge of a bog known as Falling Water Pond, with views of South Kinsman Mountain.	**5.4**
11.7	Cross East Peak of Mt. Wolf (elev. 3,478 feet); spur trail leads 60 yards east to outlook.	**4.6**
11.8	Reach western summit of Mt. Wolf (elev. 3,360 feet).	**4.5**
12.4	Cross reliable small brook (elev. 3,100 feet).	**3.9**
13.0	Pass junction with **Gordon Pond Trail** (elev. 2,700 feet).	**3.3**
15.4	Cross summit of wooded knob (elev. 2,750 feet).	**0.9**
15.7	Reach junction with **Dilly Trail** (elev. 2,650 feet), which descends steeply 0.5 mile over rough terrain to **Lost River Gorge and Boulder Caves** on N.H. 112.	**0.6**

SECTION HIGHLIGHTS

Southern end of section →

The Trail crosses N.H. 112 at the height of land in Kinsman Notch, near a large WMNF trailhead parking area (fee) to the east. It is 4.8 miles west to Bungay Corner (junction of N.H. 112 and N.H. 116). North Woodstock, New Hampshire (ZIP Code 03262), is 6.2 miles east, with telephones, motels, restaurants, groceries, and coin laundry. Lincoln, New Hampshire (ZIP Code 03251), is 7.7 miles east, with telephones, motels, restaurants, groceries, outfitters, hostel, coin laundry, Linwood Medical Center, and bus service. The WMNF Wildwood Campground and Picnic Area (26 sites; self-service) is 2 miles west. It is 12.0 miles west to Swiftwater (groceries, restaurant) and 15.4 miles west to Bath (ZIP Code 03740), with telephones and groceries. By way of U.S. 302, it is 17.8 miles west to Woodsville (ZIP Code 03785), near I-91, with telephones, motels, a restaurant, and groceries. Concord Coach Lines, (800) 639-3317, <www.concordcoachlines.com>, and Greyhound, <www.greyhound.com>, have bus service in New Hampshire and points east and south.

N-S

TRAIL DESCRIPTION

16.3   N.H. 112 in Kinsman Notch is the **southern end of**   **0.0**
            section (elev. 1,870 feet). ■ SOUTHBOUND hikers cross
            N.H. 112 diagonally left and enter woods on the Beaver
            Brook Trail (see New Hampshire Section Six). ■ NORTH-
            BOUND hikers cross N.H. 112 diagonally left and begin
            steep ascent on Kinsman Ridge Trail.

> ***Regulations***—*The northern mile of the section and
> the area around Lonesome Lake (including the hut)
> lie in Franconia Notch State Park. Camping and
> fires are prohibited in Franconia Notch State Park,
> except at Lafayette Place Campground on U.S. 3.
> The rest of the Trail in this section lies within the
> White Mountain National Forest (WMNF), where
> camping and fires are restricted to sites 200 feet or
> more off the Trail. WMNF regulations apply
> throughout the section: Namely, camping and fires
> are permitted only below treeline and 0.25 mile
> from any campsite, hut, cabin, or shelter. This sec-
> tion also falls under the following forest-protection-
> area regulations: no camping within 0.25 mile of
> N.H. 112 (Kinsman Notch Road) between Lincoln
> and Bath. The southern end is part of the Lost
> River Reservation.*

Kinsman Notch (N.H. 112) to Glencliff (N.H. 25)

9.5 MILES

The Trail in this section traverses the massive, bald Mt. Moosilauke, "the gentle giant," an area of 30 square miles towering over the southwestern corner of the White Mountains, including 100 acres of alpine tundra. From Kinsman Notch, the Trail follows the Beaver Brook Trail, steeply ascending past cascades on rock steps, on wooden steps bolted into ledges, and over hand rungs of "rebar" (steel reinforcing bars) to the summit. From the summit, the A.T. follows large rock cairns along the Moosilauke Carriage Road for a mile, turning onto the Glencliff Trail and descending steeply on the western slope to a road walk along High Street and Long Pond Road, where the Trail joins the Town Line Trail to N.H. 25. This section can usually be hiked in a day, and water is abundant. The elevation at Kinsman Notch is 1,870 feet; at N.H. 25, 1,000 feet. The highest point is on Mt. Moosilauke, at 4,082 feet. *Use caution* on the steep, cliffside section of the Beaver Brook Trail and on Mt. Moosilauke, which is above treeline and subject to the full force of violent storms.

Road Approaches—Both the northern and southern ends of the section are accessible from major highways. Road access is also available at High Street, mile 7.7/1.8, and at Long Pond Road, mile 8.2/1.3.

Maps—For route navigation, refer to Map Four with this guide; AMC Map 4 (Moosilauke–Kinsman); Dartmouth Outing Club (DOC) Mt. Moosilauke Map; or DOC Trail Map. For area detail but not current trail routes, refer to the USGS 15-minute topographic quadrangle for Rumney, New Hampshire, or the USGS 7½-minute quadrangles for Mt. Moosilauke, Mt. Kineo, and Warren, New Hampshire.

Shelters and Campsites—Two shelters are available in this section: Beaver Brook (mile 1.5/8.0) and Jeffers Brook (mile 8.4/1.1).

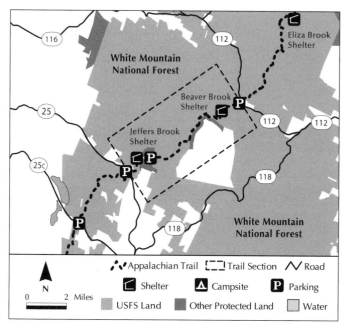

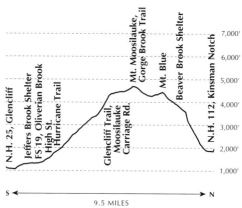

Northern end of section →

The Trail crosses N.H. 112 at the height of land in Kinsman Notch, near a large WMNF trailhead parking area (fee) to the east. It is 4.8 miles west to Bungay Corner (junction of N.H. 112 and N.H. 116). North Woodstock, New Hampshire (ZIP Code 03262), is 6.2 miles east, with telephones, motels, restaurants, groceries, and coin laundry. Lincoln, New Hampshire (ZIP Code 03251), is 7.7 miles east, with telephones, motels, restaurants, groceries, outfitters, hostel, coin laundry, Linwood Medical Center, and bus service. The WMNF Wildwood Campground and Picnic Area (26 sites; self-service) is 2 miles west. It is 12.0 miles west to Swiftwater (groceries, restaurant) and 15.4 miles west to Bath (ZIP Code 03740), with telephones and groceries. By way of U.S. 302, it is 17.8 miles west to Woodsville (ZIP Code 03785), near I-91, with telephones, motels, a restaurant, and groceries. Concord Coach Lines, (800) 639-3317, <www.concordcoachlines.com>, and Greyhound, <www.greyhound.com>, have bus service in New Hampshire.

Beaver Brook Trail →

Coincides with the A.T. from N.H. 112 to the summit of Mt. Moosilauke, a distance of 3.8 miles.

Beaver Brook Cascades →

Many rock steps, wooden steps, and hand rungs. This section of Trail is extremely steep and rough and, in icy conditions, may be dangerous.

Beaver Brook Shelter →

Built in 1993 and maintained by DOC; views of Franconia Range. Accommodates 8 at shelter and 8 on two tent platforms. Composting privy. Water source is Beaver Brook. Next shelter or campsite: south, 6.8 miles (Jeffers Brook); north, 9.1 miles (Eliza Brook).

N-S	TRAIL DESCRIPTION	
0.0	The **northern end of section** (elev. 1,870 feet) is at N.H. 112 in Kinsman Notch. ■ SOUTHBOUND hikers cross N.H. 112 diagonally left and enter the woods on the **Beaver Brook Trail**. ■ NORTHBOUND hikers cross N.H. 112 diagonally left, enter the woods, and ascend steeply on the Kinsman Ridge Trail (see New Hampshire Section Five).	**9.5**
0.1	Cross Beaver Brook on footbridge (elev. 1,880 feet).	**9.4**
0.2	Cross Beaver Brook on bridge (elev. 1,890 feet).	**9.3**
1.1	Pass **Beaver Brook Cascades** (elev. 3,000 feet).	**8.4**
1.5	Side trail leads west 80 yards to **Beaver Brook Shelter** (elev. 3,750 feet).	**8.0**

Beaver Brook

S-N

SECTION HIGHLIGHTS

Asquam Ridge Trail→
Descends 3.9 miles east over summit of Mt. Jim to Ravine Lodge.

Jobildunk Ravine→
A deep, bowl-shaped cirque cut into the eastern side of Mt. Moosilauke and the southern side of Mt. Blue by the last glaciers.

Benton Trail→
Leads west 3.1 miles to Tunnel Brook Road (FR 700), leading north to Benton.

Mt. Moosilauke →
See page 43.

Ravine Lodge →
At the eastern base of Mt. Moosilauke; accessible from the Trail by the Hurricane Trail (5.1 miles), Moosilauke Carriage Road/Snapper Trail (2.3 miles), Gorge Brook Trail (3.6 miles), or Asquam-Ridge Trail (3.9 miles). Telephones, family-style meals, bunk rooms, snacks, first aid. Reservations recommended, (603) 764-5858; fee. Open mid-May to mid-October. Ravine Lodge Road is off N.H. 118, 7.3 miles from Warren. See "For More Information," page 349.

South Peak →
Spur trail to the east, on the Glencliff Trail, within a few feet of the Moosilauke Carriage Road, leads 0.2 mile to the summit of South Peak (elev. 4,523 feet), with excellent views into Tunnel Ravine, a deep cleft between Mt. Moosilauke and Mt. Clough.

Moosilauke Carriage Road →
Descends 4.2 miles on gravel bed to Breezy Point, a large clearing with good views, the site of the former Moosilauke Inn. The road up to Breezy Point leaves N.H. 118 2.5 miles north of its junction with N.H. 25 (1 mile north of Warren village). The Moosilauke Carriage Road was once traveled by the elegant guests of the summer hotel on the summit, but both the hotel and a DOC cabin are long gone, and the road is now a hiking trail.

N-S | TRAIL DESCRIPTION |

1.9 Reach junction with **Asquam Ridge Trail** (elev. 4,050   **7.6**
feet). The A.T. continues on Beaver Brook Trail in col near
edge of **Jobildunk Ravine**.

2.4 Pass spring dripping from ledge (elev. 4,200 feet).   **7.1**

3.4 Reach junction with **Benton Trail** (elev. 4,550 feet). This **6.1**
trail coincides with Beaver Brook Trail for 0.4 mile to sum-
mit of Mt. Moosilauke. Continue on Beaver Brook Trail.

3.8 Reach summit of **Mt. Moosilauke** (elev. 4,802 feet) and   **5.7**
junction with the Gorge Brook Trail, which descends east
2.6 miles to Dartmouth College's Moosilauke **Ravine
Lodge**. ■ SOUTHBOUND hikers follow Moosilauke Carriage
Road Trail, marked with prominent rock cairns. ■ NORTH-
BOUND hikers follow Beaver Brook Trail/Benton Trail away
from summit.

4.0 Reach treeline on Mt. Moosilauke (elev. 4,600 feet).   **5.5**

4.4 Pass over Middle Peak (elev. 4,500 feet). Side trail to the **5.1**
east 50 feet offers views of the ravine.

4.7 Reach junction with Glencliff Trail (elev. 4,460 feet) and   **4.8**
spur trail to **South Peak**. ■ SOUTHBOUND hikers turn right
on the Glencliff Trail. ■ NORTHBOUND hikers turn left on
the **Moosilauke Carriage Road**.

6.7 Cross a stream (elev. 2,000 feet).   **2.8**

SECTION HIGHLIGHTS

Hurricane Trail→

Passes east over Hurricane Mountain to DOC's Ravine Lodge in 5.1 miles.

High Street→

The Trailhead is 1.2 miles from its junction with N.H. 25 in Glencliff village. The parking area is a short distance uphill, to the east, past the trail sign.

Sanitarium →

The current Glencliff Home for the Elderly was formerly the Glencliff Sanitarium, which opened in the summer of 1909 for New Hampshire residents infected with tuberculosis, seeking respite and a cure in the mountain air.

Town Line Trail→

This 1.3-mile trail was constructed mainly to eliminate a road walk for A.T. hikers. *In high-water conditions, to avoid a dangerous crossing of Oliverian Brook, hikers should follow High Street to N.H. 25 rather than take the Town Line Trail/A.T.*

Jeffers Brook Shelter →

Built in the 1970s and maintained by DOC. Accommodates 8. Water source is Jeffers Brook. Next shelter or campsite: south, 8.6 miles (Ore Hill); north, 6.8 miles (Beaver Brook).

Oliverian Notch →

Westernmost of the major passes through the White Mountains.

| | TRAIL DESCRIPTION | |

7.3	Reach junction with the **Hurricane Trail** at the edge of a clearing (elev. 1,680 feet).	2.2
7.4	Cross a brook (elev. 1,500 feet).	2.1
7.7	Reach **High Street** (formerly **Sanitarium** Road) (elev. 1,480 feet). ■ SOUTHBOUND hikers turn left on paved road. ■ NORTHBOUND hikers turn right and enter woods on Glencliff Trail.	1.8
8.0	Reach junction of Long Pond Road/FS 19 (formerly North and South Road) and High Street (formerly Sanitarium Road). ■ SOUTHBOUND hikers turn right onto gravel Long Pond Road. *In high-water conditions, to avoid dangerous crossing of Oliverian Brook, continue 0.9 mile on High Street to N.H. 25, turn compass-north, and follow it 0.6 mile to Trail crossing.* ■ NORTHBOUND hikers turn left onto paved High Street.	1.5
8.2	Reach junction of Long Pond Road and **Town Line Trail** (elev. 1,330 feet). ■ SOUTHBOUND hikers turn left off road and enter woods on Town Line Trail. ■ NORTHBOUND hikers turn right onto gravel Long Pond Road/FS 19 (formerly North and South Road).	1.3
8.4	Pass northern junction (elev. 1,350 feet) of loop trail to **Jeffers Brook Shelter**, 70 yards to west.	1.1
8.5	Side path leads east 40 yards to cascades on Jeffers Brook in **Oliverian Notch.**	1.0
8.6	Cross Jeffers Brook on a bridge. Ninety yards north on the Trail is the southern junction of a loop trail that leads 0.1 mile west to **Jeffers Brook Shelter**.	0.9

Oliverian Brook →

The 13.1-mile-long Oliverian Brook is a tributary of the Connecticut River. *In high-water conditions, to avoid a dangerous crossing, hikers should follow N.H. 25 to High Street rather than follow the Town Line Trail/A.T.*

Southern end of section →

The Trailhead on N.H. 25 is 4.4 miles west of the junction of N.H. 25 and N.H. 118 and 0.5 mile east of the Glencliff post office, just southeast of the Warren–Benton town line. Parking is 100 yards southeast on the southwest side of N.H. 25 or at the hostel in Glencliff. From the Trail crossing at N.H. 25, it is 0.5 mile east to Glencliff (ZIP Code 03238), with telephones and hostel, and 5.0 miles to Warren, New Hampshire (ZIP Code 03279), with telephones, B&B, restaurant, groceries, coin laundry, and campground.

N-S

TRAIL DESCRIPTION

9.5 Ford **Oliverian Brook** to reach N.H. 25 (elev. 1, 000 feet)   **0.0**
at **southern end of section**. ■ SOUTHBOUND hikers cross
N.H. 25, walk through parking area 150 yards compass-
south to an old woods road, cross an old railroad grade,
and continue on Wachipauka Pond Trail (see New Hampshire Section Seven). ■ NORTHBOUND hikers descend a
steep bank to ford Oliverian Brook and continue on **Town
Line Trail**.

> ***Regulations**—From Kinsman Notch to the Hurri-
> cane Trail junction near Glencliff, the A.T. passes
> across WMNF, state, and private lands. The north-
> ern end is part of Lost River Reservation. The sum-
> mit of Mt. Moosilauke, from the Asquam Ridge Trail
> junction to the Carriage Road–Glencliff Trail junc-
> tion, including the Gorge Brook and upper Baker
> River drainages, is owned by Dartmouth College.
> The southern end of the Glencliff Trail is within
> Benton State Forest.*
>
> *WMNF regulations apply throughout the sec-
> tion: Camping and fires are permitted only below
> treeline and 0.25 mile from any campsite, hut,
> cabin, or shelter. This section also falls under the
> following forest-protection-area regulations: no
> camping within 0.25 mile of N.H. 112 (Kinsman
> Notch Road) between Lincoln and Bath; no camp-
> ing within 0.25 mile of the former site of the Beaver
> Brook Shelter; and no camping within 200 feet of
> the entire A.T. from N.H. 25A to Kinsman Notch.
> No camping or fires are permitted on Dartmouth
> College land except at Beaver Brook Shelter.*

S-N

Glencliff (N.H. 25) to N.H. 25A

9.7 MILES

The Trail in this section passes through lowcountry hardwood forests. Ascending on the Wachipauka Pond Trail to Wyatt Hill, passing to the west of Wachipauka Pond and east of Webster Slide Mountain, it climbs Mt. Mist—at 2,220 feet, the highest point in the section—to N.H. 25C. From there, the Trail ascends on the Ore Hill Trail to Ore Hill (1,866 feet), joins the Atwell Hill Trail, and reaches N.H. 25A. The elevation at Glencliff (N.H. 25) is 1,000 feet; at N.H. 25A, 900 feet.

Road Approaches— Both the northern and southern ends of the section are accessible from major highways. Road access is also available at N.H. 25C (mile 5.0 below). Concord Coach Lines, <www.concordcoachlines.com>, and Greyhound, <www.greyhound.com>, provide bus service in New Hampshire.

Maps—For route navigation, refer to Map Four with this guide; AMC Map 4 (Moosilauke–Kinsman); or the Dartmouth Outing Club (DOC) Trail Map. For area detail but not current trail routes, consult the USGS 15-minute topographic quadrangles for Rumney and Mt. Cube, New Hampshire, or the USGS 7½-minute quadrangle for Warren, New Hampshire.

Shelters and Campsites—This section has one shelter: Ore Hill Shelter (mile 7.5/2.2). The segment of the Trail between Glencliff (N.H. 25) and the northern summit of Ore Hill lies within the White Mountain National Forest (WMNF), where camping and fires are permitted only at sites 200 feet or more from the Trail. From the northern summit of Ore Hill to N.H. 25A, the Trail passes through Forest Service-managed lands on which camping and fires are prohibited, except at Ore Hill Shelter. Just south of Ore Hill Shelter, the Trail enters Sentinel Mountain State Forest land for a short distance and then WMNF jurisdiction resumes to N.H. 25A.

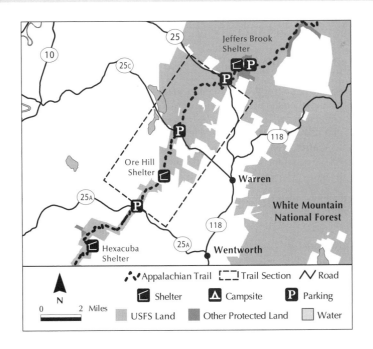

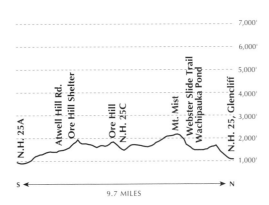

SECTION HIGHLIGHTS

Northern end of section →

The Trailhead on N.H. 25 is 4.4 miles west of the junction of N.H. 25 and N.H. 118 and 0.5 mile east of the Glencliff post office, just southeast of the Warren–Benton town line. Parking is 100 yards southeast on the southwest side of N.H. 25 or at the hostel in Glencliff. From the Trail crossing at N.H. 25, it is 0.5 mile east to Glencliff (ZIP Code 03238), with telephones and hostel, and 5.0 miles to Warren, New Hampshire (ZIP Code 03279), with telephones, B&B, restaurant, groceries, coin laundry, and campground.

Wachipauka Pond Trail →

Coincides with the A.T. from N.H. 25 to N.H. 25C, a distance of 4.9 miles.

Wachipauka Pond →

This remote, 22-acre pond has a depth of 37 feet and is stocked annually with fingerling brook trout.

Webster Slide Trail →

Ascends steeply 0.7 mile west to a spectacular outlook from the eastern ledges on Webster Slide Mountain (elev. 2,184 feet); views straight down onto Wachipauka Pond. Descends 0.2 mile east to a clearing on the northwest corner of Wachipauka Pond.

N-S

| TRAIL DESCRIPTION |

0.0 The **northern end of section** is at N.H. 25 (elev. 1,000 **9.7**
feet). ■ SOUTHBOUND hikers cross N.H. 25, walk compass-
south through a parking area for 150 yards to an old woods
road, cross an old railroad grade, and continue on the
Wachipauka Pond Trail. ■ NORTHBOUND hikers cross N.H.
25, walk 150 yards compass-north, enter the woods, and
ford Oliverian Brook (see New Hampshire Section Six).

0.4 Ascend/descend steadily (elev. 1,200 feet). **9.3**

1.1 Pass north of summit of Wyatt Hill (elev. 1,700 feet). **8.6**

1.9 Skirt northern and western shores of **Wachipauka Pond** **7.8**
(elev. 1,493 feet).

2.0 Pass Hairy Root Spring (elev. 1,600 feet). **7.7**

2.2 Reach junction with **Webster Slide Trail** (elev. 1,650 **7.5**
feet).

2.3 Pass vista to east (elev. 2,000 feet) overlooking **Wa- 7.4**
chipauka Pond**.

View from Webster Slide Mountain

SECTION HIGHLIGHTS

N.H. 25C →

The Trail crosses N.H. 25C; limited parking along the gravel shoulder. It is 4 miles east to Warren, New Hampshire (ZIP Code 03279), with telephones, B&B, restaurant, groceries, coin laundry, and campgrounds. It is 10 miles west to Piermont (ZIP Code 03779), with groceries.

Ore Hill Brook →

Water near Ore Hill Brook should be treated with caution. The former Ore Hill Mine has had its effects on Ore Hill Brook through the discharge of acidic water with high metal content.

Ore Hill Trail →

Coincides with the A.T. from N.H. 25C to Cape Moonshine Road, a distance of 3.2 miles.

Ore Hill →

A 48-foot-wide vein was discovered by the landowner, True Merrill, in 1834. The ore deposit was worked by various companies from 1834 to 1915 for lead, copper, zinc, and silver. When the mine was abandoned in 1915, several piles of tailings and a pile of waste rock were left on the site. A small drainage with poor water quality ran through the site and affected water quality and aquatic species downstream in Ore Hill Brook. In 1937, the federal government acquired most of the site to be part of the White Mountain National Forest. In 1962, the Forest Service planted red pine on the site, but few survived. In 1979, the National Park Service acquired the rest of the site for the Appalachian Trail corridor. The A.T., which had traversed the unsightly three acres, was rerouted several hundred feet to the west, and the mine site was closed to the public. In late 2006 and into 2007, the soil was excavated, cleaned of heavy metals (arsenic, cadmium, copper, iron, lead, mercury, and zinc), and then reseeded with a wildflower mix.

N-S

	TRAIL DESCRIPTION	

2.4   Cross summit of Mt. Mist (elev. 2,220 feet).   **7.3**

4.9   Reach **N.H. 25C** (elev. 1,550 feet). ■ SOUTHBOUND hikers   **4.8**
cross **Ore Hill Brook**, turn right at road, walk 100 feet,
cross under power line, enter woods on left, and follow
the **Ore Hill Trail**. ■ NORTHBOUND hikers turn right at road,
pass under power line, enter woods on left in 100 feet,
and follow the **Wachipauka Pond Trail**, crossing Ore Hill
Brook.

5.2   Reach high point on **Ore Hill** in fine stand of sugar maples   **4.5**
(elev. 1,850 feet).

5.9   Pass a beaver pond to the east (elev. 1,650 feet).   **3.8**

6.2   Cross a small stream.   **3.5**

6.6   Cross a woods road.   **3.1**

6.9   Pass side trail to spring on east (elev. 1,800 feet).   **2.8**

7.2   Reach height of land on Sentinel Mountain (elev. 1,925   **2.5**
feet).

S-N

Ore Hill Shelter→

Built in 1999 and maintained by DOC. Accommodates 10. Privy; two primitive tent pads. The water source is a small spring 150 yards south of the shelter. Next shelter or campsite: south, 7.6 miles (Hexacuba); north, 8.6 miles (Jeffers Brook).

Atwell Hill Trail →

Coincides with the A.T. from Cape Moonshine Road to N.H. 25A, a distance of 1.6 miles.

Southern end of section →

The Trail crosses N.H. 25A between Upper and Lower Baker ponds. Limited parking is possible along the southern shoulder of N.H. 25A. Wentworth (ZIP Code 03282) is 4.3 miles east, with telephones, B&B, and a limited selection of groceries. It is 20.2 miles east to I-93 and Plymouth, New Hampshire (ZIP Code 03264), with telephones, motels, restaurants, supermarket, and coin laundry. To the west, it is 1.9 miles to the Mt. Cube Sugar House (seasonal fruit, maple syrup, and other items during the summer); 10.8 miles to Orford (ZIP Code 03777) on N.H. 10, with telephones, limited selection of groceries; and 11.2 miles to I-91 at Fairlee, Vermont (ZIP Code 05045), with motels and groceries.

N-S

TRAIL DESCRIPTION

7.5   Side trail to **Ore Hill Shelter** leads 100 yards to east (elev. 1,720 feet).   **2.2**

8.1   Cross gravel Cape Moonshine Road (elev. 1,400 feet). ■ SOUTHBOUND hikers cross road and enter woods on **Atwell Hill Trail**. ■ NORTHBOUND hikers cross road and follow **Ore Hill Trail** uphill.   **1.6**

9.6   Southern edge of a swampy area with many stepping stones (elev. 1,200 feet). ■ NORTHBOUND hikers ascend through pine, birches, and fir.   **0.1**

9.7   Reach N.H. 25A (elev. 900 feet) and **southern end of section**. ■ SOUTHBOUND hikers turn right for 100 yards, cross highway bridge, and enter woods on left on Mt. Cube Trail (see New Hampshire Section Eight). ■ NORTHBOUND hikers turn right, cross highway bridge, road walk for 100 yards, and enter woods on left on **Atwell Hill Trail,** passing through swampy area.   **0.0**

S-N

N.H. 25A to Lyme–Dorchester Road (Dartmouth Skiway)

16.0 MILES

The Trail in this section crosses two outstanding features—Mt. Cube, elevation 2,909 feet, and Smarts Mountain, 3,240 feet. Going south from N.H. 25A (coinciding with the Mt. Cube Trail), the Trail enters woods, ascends gently over old logging roads past stone walls and cellar holes, passes several brooks, crosses Brackett Brook, and then rises more steeply on switchbacks to ascend Mt. Cube, with views of the Connecticut River Valley below and Smarts Mountain and Mt. Ascutney high above. The Trail continues along a ridge on the Kodak Trail, descending to Jacobs Brook before ascending on the J Trail to Smarts Mountain. From there, the Trail descends on the Lambert Ridge Trail. The elevation at N.H. 25A is 900 feet; at Lyme–Dorchester Road (Dartmouth Skiway), 880 feet. The highest point is Smarts Mountain.

Road Approaches—Both the northern and southern ends of the section are accessible from major highways.

Maps—For route navigation, refer to Map Four with this guide and the Dartmouth Outing Club (DOC) Trail Map. For area detail but not current trail routes, consult the USGS 15-minute topographic quadrangle for Mt. Cube, New Hampshire.

Shelters and Campsites—This section has a shelter, a tentsite, and a cabin: Hexacuba Shelter (mile 4.9/11.1), the Firewarden's Cabin (mile 10.2/5.8), and Smarts Mountain Tentsite (mile 10.3/5.7). Part of this section south of N.H. 25A is still on, or surrounded by, private land, and camping and fires are permitted only at official campsites. On the narrow A.T. corridor, camping is permitted but not within 200 feet of the A.T. itself, except at the designated campsites.

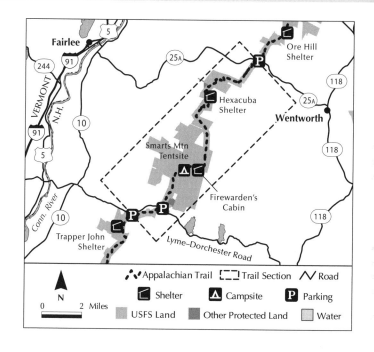

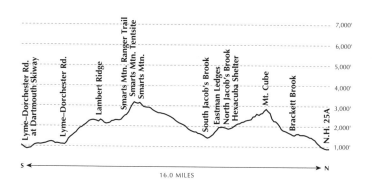

16.0 MILES

Northern end of section →

The Trail crosses N.H. 25A between Upper and Lower Baker ponds. Limited parking is possible along the southern shoulder of N.H. 25A. Wentworth (ZIP Code 03282) is 4.3 miles east, with telephones, B&B, and a limited selection of groceries. It is 20.2 miles east to I-93 and Plymouth, New Hampshire (ZIP Code 03264), with telephones, motels, restaurants, supermarket, and coin laundry. To the west, it is 1.9 miles to the Mt. Cube Sugar House (seasonal fruit, maple syrup, and other items during the summer); 10.8 miles to Orford (ZIP Code 03777) on N.H. 10, with telephones, limited selection of groceries; and 11.2 miles to I-91 at Fairlee, Vermont (ZIP Code 05045), with motels and groceries.

Mt. Cube Section →

A side trail that descends west 1.5 miles to Baker Farm Road, 1.5 miles from N.H. 25A. This is a former route of the A.T.

South Mt. Cube →

Smarts Mountain and Mt. Ascutney dominate a view that covers much of the Upper Valley of the Connecticut River.

Kodak Trail →

Coincides with the A.T. from the summit of Mt. Cube south to a logging road intersection at South Jacobs Brook, where it splits from the A.T., leading 1.5 mile west, through a gate, to Quinttown.

Hexacuba Shelter →

Built in 1989 (Penta-style) and maintained by DOC; elev. 1,980 feet. Accommodates 8. Privy. Water source (unreliable) is the brook at the junction of the A.T. and the spur path. Next shelter or campsite: south, 5.6 miles (Firewarden's Cabin); north, 7.6 miles (Ore Hill).

N-S

TRAIL DESCRIPTION

0.0 The **northern end of section** is at N.H. 25A (elev. 900   **16.0**
feet). ■ Southbound hikers enter the woods on the **Mt. Cube Trail** (coincides with the A.T. to South Cube), cross a small swamp, and follow an abandoned logging road. ■ Northbound hikers turn right for 100 yards, cross a highway bridge, and enter the woods to the left on the Atwell Hill Trail (see New Hampshire Section Seven).

0.5 Cross a gravel logging road.   **15.5**

1.5 ■ Southbound hikers turn left onto an old logging road,   **14.5**
follow it for 50 yards, and then turn right into the woods. ■ Northbound hikers turn left onto an old logging road, follow it 50 yards, and then turn right into the woods.

1.8 Ford Brackett Brook.   **14.2**

2.5 Pass a stone chair on the west.   **13.5**

3.3 Pass 0.3-mile side trail west to open **North Mt. Cube** in **12.7**
saddle between North and South summits, with fine views of Mt. Moosilauke.

3.5 At summit of **South Mt. Cube** (elev. 2,909 feet), reach   **12.5**
junction with **Mt. Cube Section** and **Mt. Cube trails**. ■ Southbound hikers descend on the **Kodak Trail**. ■ Northbound hikers turn east and descend on the **Mt. Cube Trail** (coincides with the A.T. to N.H. 25A).

4.9 Cross a branch of North Jacobs Brook (elev. 1,450 feet).   **11.1**
Just to south is a side trail leading 0.3 mile east to **Hexacuba Shelter**.

5.2 Cross an old logging road and North Branch of Jacobs   **10.8**
Brook.

S-N

Eastman Ledges

Afford a fine view of Smarts Mountain. The naming of the ledges and the (Eastman) Kodak Trail stemmed from trail-builders' attempts to celebrate the number of "Kodak moments" along this stretch.

J Trail →

Named after the J-shaped ridge it follows, coinciding with the A.T. to Smarts Mountain. Here, the Kodak Trail leads 1.5 mile west, through a gate, to Quinttown.

Smarts Mountain Fire Tower →

On the summit (elev. 3,240 feet) and in use from 1915 to 1973, this restored steel firetower may be the only New Hampshire fire tower preserved by legislative action. "Smarts" has a boreal feel about it, similar to the higher White Mountain peaks farther north.

Firewarden's Cabin →

Built by the N.H. Forest Service, maintained by DOC. Accommodates 8. Privy. Water source is Mike Murphy Spring, located 0.2 mile north on blue-blazed Daniel Doan Trail, which leads 3.5 miles along Mousley Brook to Mousley Brook Road to Quinttown, four miles from Orfordville off N.H. 25A. Next shelter or campsite: south, 0.2 mile (Smarts Mountain); north, 5.6 miles (Hexacuba).

Smarts Mountain Tentsite →

Maintained by DOC; cleared area for three tents. Privy. Water source is Mike Murphy Spring (see previous entry). Next shelter or campsite: south, 6.9 miles (Trapper John Shelter); north, 0.2 mile (Firewarden's Cabin).

Smarts Mountain Ranger Trail →

This old firewarden's trail to the tower on Smarts Mountain leads 3.0 miles to Lyme–Dorchester Road.

Lambert Ridge Trail →

Coincides with the A.T. from the summit of Smarts Mountain to the Lyme–Dorchester Road parking lot.

N-S | TRAIL DESCRIPTION |

5.7	Traverse the rocky **Eastman Ledges**.	10.3
6.3	Cross South Jacobs Brook logging road at intersection of J Trail and Kodak Trail. ■ SOUTHBOUND hikers ascend on the **J Trail**. ■ NORTHBOUND hikers continue on the Kodak Trail.	9.7
6.4	Cross South Jacobs Brook on rocks.	9.6
10.0	Pass junction on the east with abandoned DOC Clark Pond Loop.	6.0
10.2	Reach southern end of J Trail (elev. 3,230 feet). **Smarts Mountain Fire tower** and **Firewarden's Cabin** are 50 yards west. ■ SOUTHBOUND hikers descend from the summit on the **Lambert Ridge Trail**. ■ NORTHBOUND hikers follow the J Trail.	5.8
10.3	Side trail (elev. 3,200 feet) leads 500 feet east to **Smarts Mountain Tentsite**. Intermittent spring is north on Trail (unreliable).	5.7
10.8	**Smarts Mountain Ranger Trail** (elev. 2,600 feet) leads to east. ■ SOUTHBOUND hikers turn right onto **Lambert Ridge Trail** and descend steeply. ■ NORTHBOUND hikers continue on Lambert RidgeTrail/Smarts Mountain Ranger Trail, ascending steeply to summit.	5.2
11.7	Cross stream. ■ NORTHBOUND hikers begin ascent of Smarts Mountain.	4.3
12.2	North end of Lambert Ridge, with view of summit.	3.8

Lyme–Dorchester Road parking lot →

Road leads 5.1 miles west to N.H. 10 in Lyme (see below). Informational kiosk stands at limited parking area. This is the trailhead for both the Lambert Ridge Trail (A.T.) and Smarts Mountain Ranger Trail, which leads east from the parking lot 3.6 miles to the summit of Smarts Mountain. The area near the bottom of the trails is used for bear research by Benjamin Killam, author of *Among the Bears*; signs request that his radio-collared bears not be shot.

Southern end of section →

The Trail crosses Lyme–Dorchester Road at the fork leading to the Dartmouth Skiway. Ample parking can be found 0.1 mile beyond the right fork, at the Dartmouth Skiway. The left fork may be followed as far north as the Smarts Ranger Trail junction (limited parking). It is 1.2 miles west to Lyme Center (ZIP Code 03769), and 3.2 miles west to N.H. 10 in Lyme (ZIP Code 03768), with telephones, a limited selection of groceries, B&Bs, lodges with cottages, meals, and the ATC New England regional office on the common. It is 5.0 miles west to East Thetford, Vermont.

N-S

TRAIL DESCRIPTION

13.2 Pass numerous, open, quartzite-ledge outcrops along Lambert Ridge, passing in and out of woods, with good views.   **2.8**

14.0 Reach **Lyme–Dorchester Road parking lot** (elev. 1,110 feet). ■ SOUTHBOUND hikers bear left across road bridge, immediately turn right, and, in 50 feet, turn right again onto old road. ■ NORTHBOUND hikers bear left across bridge and parking lot and begin ascent on **Lambert Ridge Trail**.   **2.0**

14.1 Cross Grant Brook.   **1.9**

14.3 Reach junction with old road at granite A.T. marker.   **1.7**

14.7 Skirting northwest side of Winslow Ledge (Dartmouth Skiway), cross stream in shallow gorge.   **1.3**

15.8 The edge of an overgrown field is marked by a blazed post; cross a snowmobile trail.   **0.2**

16.0 The **southern end of section** is at Lyme–Dorchester Road/ Dartmouth Skiway (elev. 880 feet). ■ SOUTHBOUND hikers enter woods and ascend on Holts Ledge Trail (see New Hampshire Section Nine). ■ NORTHBOUND hikers turn right at left fork in Lyme–Dorchester Road into field (at blazed post) near snowmaking pond.   **0.0**

S-N

Lyme–Dorchester Road (Dartmouth Skiway) to Connecticut River (N.H.–Vt. State Line)

18.1 MILES

This section follows the southwestern end of the White Mountain foothills between Mt. Moosilauke and the Connecticut River, following woods roads and footpaths through pastures, fields, and forest and coinciding with the following Dartmouth Outing Club (DOC) trails: Holts Ledge, Moose Mountain, Hanover Center, and Velvet Rocks. The ATC New England regional office is located in the village of Lyme near the northern end of the section. Except for the ascents of Holts Ledge and Moose Mountain, the terrain here is easy to hike. Passing through Hanover, home of Dartmouth College, the Trail descends to the Connecticut River, the southern end of the New Hampshire A.T. The elevation at Lyme–Dorchester Road is 880 feet; at the Connecticut River, 400 feet. The highest point is the summit of Moose Mountain, at 2,300 feet.

Road Approaches—Both ends are accessible by vehicle. Road access is also available at Goose Pond Road (mile 3.4/14.7), Three-Mile Road (mile 9.2/8.9), Etna–Hanover Center Road (mile 11.7/6.4), and Trescott Road (mile 13.1/5.0). Concord Coach Lines and Greyhound provide bus service in New Hampshire. The southern end also is served by Vermont Transit Bus, (800) 552-8737, <www.vermonttransit.com>, and Amtrak, (800) USA-RAIL, <www.amtrak.com>.

Maps—For route navigation, see Map Five with this guide or DOC Trail Map. For detail but not current trail routes, consult the USGS 15-minute topographic quadrangles for Mt. Cube and Mascoma, New Hampshire, and the USGS 7½-minute quadrangle for Hanover.

Shelters—This section has three shelters: Trapper John (mile 0.9/17.2), Moose Mountain (mile 6.6/11.5), and Velvet Rocks (mile 16.1/2.0).

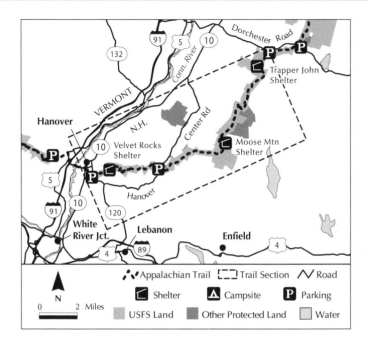

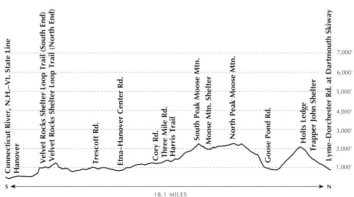

SECTION HIGHLIGHTS

Northern end of section →

The Trail crosses Lyme–Dorchester Road at the fork leading to Dartmouth Skiway. Ample parking can be found 0.1 mile beyond the right fork at Dartmouth Skiway. The left fork may be followed as far north as the Smarts Ranger Trail junction (limited parking). It is 1.2 miles west to Lyme Center (ZIP Code 03769) and 3.2 miles west to N.H. 10 in Lyme (ZIP Code 03768), with telephones, limited selection of groceries, B&Bs, lodges with cottages, meals, and the ATC New England regional office on the southeastern corner of the town common. For Trail information and assistance, visit the office or call (603) 795-4935. From the Trailhead, it is 5.0 miles west to East Thetford, Vermont.

Trapper John Shelter →

Named after televison's "M*A*S*H" character, a fictional Dartmouth graduate. Built in the 1990s and maintained by the DOC. Accommodates 8. Privy. Ample water from a brook 15 yards to the left of the shelter. Next shelter or campsite: south, 5.9 miles (Moose Mountain); north, 6.9 miles (Smarts Mountain).

Holts Ledge →

Holts Ledge is a precipitous cliff with fine views to the east. The cliff edge is fenced off, not only to protect unaware hikers on foggy days, but also the peregrine falcons that nest on the cliff. Before being protected by the Endangered Species Act, peregrines were driven out of New England by the ravages of DDT, which caused the eggs to break before the chicks were mature enough to survive. Holts Ledge was one of the first sites in New Hampshire where peregrines were successfully reintroduced (in 1987) through a cooperative program of ATC, DOC, New Hampshire Audubon, the state Fish and Game Commission, and the U.S. Fish and Wildlife Service.

Dartmouth Skiway →

The Dartmouth Skiway opened in 1957 and is now one of two college-owned ski areas in the Northeast, along with the Middlebury College's Snow Bowl.

N-S

| TRAIL DESCRIPTION |

0.0	The **northern end of section** is at the Lyme–Dorchester Road/Dartmouth Skiway (elev. 880 feet). ■ Southbounders enter woods on Holts Ledge Trail. ■ Northbounders, at left fork of Lyme–Dorchester Road, turn right off road into field (at blazed post), near Dartmouth Skiway snowmaking pond (see New Hampshire Section Eight).	**18.1**
0.7	Cross ski-area access road.	**17.4**
0.9	Side trail leads 0.2 mile west to **Trapper John Shelter** (elev. 1,345 feet).	**17.2**
1.1	Cross small, intermittent brook.	**17.0**
1.4	Side trail (elev. 1,930 feet) leads 0.1 mile east to **Holts Ledge** viewpoint and **Dartmouth Skiway**. *Please heed carefully the fences and obey the signs during the peregrine-falcon nesting season.*	**16.7**
1.7	Reach height of land on Holts Ledge (elev. 2,100 feet).	**16.4**

Peregrine falcon chick

S-N

SECTION HIGHLIGHTS

Moose Mountain Shelter →

Log shelter built in 2004 entirely with hand tools by DOC; maintained by DOC. Accommodates 8 in the shelter and 8 at two tentsites. Privy. Water is at the north end of the loop trail. Next shelter or campsite: south, 9.9 miles (Velvet Rocks); north, 5.9 miles (Trapper John).

Old Wolfeboro Road →

In 1772, to attend Dartmouth's first commencement, New Hampshire Governor Benning Wentworth had a road cut to connect Portsmouth with Hanover. Known locally as the Wolfeboro Road, the now-abandoned DOC Clark Pond Loop followed this historic road as it passed through Moose Mountain Col.

South Peak of Moose Mountain →

In 1968, a Northeast Airlines plane crashed on the south ridge below the summit. As part of the rescue effort, a bulldozer drove up and cleared the summit for a helicopter landing area. Subsequently, a caterpillar infestation killed much of the remaining timber, creating an open view from this otherwise forested summit.

Fred Harris Trail →

A two-rut woods road and obscure in places, this trail leads 4.6 miles west to rejoin the A.T. at Goose Pond Road (mile 3.4/14.7). Dartmouth student Fred Harris in 1909 proposed forming the DOC, now the oldest and largest collegiate outing club in the United States, to "stimulate interest in out-of-door winter sports." The club soon grew to encompass the college's year-round outdoor-recreation program.

N-S	TRAIL DESCRIPTION	
2.5	Cross former logging road, now a snowmobile trail.	**15.6**
3.1	Cross beaver-pond dam.	**15.0**
3.4	Reach **Goose Pond Road** (elev. 952 feet), which leads 3.3 miles west to N.H. 10. ■ SOUTHBOUND hikers turn left for 50 feet, then turn right, and reenter woods. ■ NORTHBOUND hikers turn left for 50 feet, then turn right on a narrow road through old log landing.	**14.7**
3.8	Cross branch of Hewes Brook.	**14.3**
5.4	Cross **North Peak of Moose Mountain** (elev. 2,300 feet), with southwest views from quartzite ledges to west.	**12.7**
6.5	Northern junction of loop trail leading 100 yards east to **Moose Mountain Shelter**. North 50 yards on A.T., cross a brook.	**11.6**
6.6	Southern junction (elev. 1,850 feet) of loop trail leading 75 yards east to **Moose Mountain Shelter**.	**11.5**
6.8	Cross woods road, **Old Wolfeboro Road** (Province Road), at junction with abandoned DOC Clark Pond Loop (elev. 2,000 feet).	**11.3**
7.4	Cross **South Peak of Moose Mountain** (elev. 2,290 feet).	**10.7**
8.8	Cross woods road at junction with the **Fred Harris Trail**.	**9.3**
9.0	Cross Mink Brook.	**9.1**

SECTION HIGHLIGHTS

Three-Mile Road→

The Trailhead is 1.3 miles east of Ruddsboro Road, which leads 1.5 miles to Etna–Hanover Center Road 0.5 mile east of Etna (see below) and 7.3 miles east of Hanover (see below). Limited parking space is available on the southern side of the road.

Etna–Hanover Center Road →

The Trailhead is 0.7 mile east of Etna (see below) and 4.7 miles east of Hanover (see below). Limited parking space is available on the southern side of the road.

Trescott Road →

Leads 0.9 mile east to Etna–Hanover Road, 0.2 mile west of Etna (ZIP Code 03750), with limited groceries and deli, and 4.0 miles east of Hanover (see below). A small hiker parking lot is located 50 yards west, on the eastern side of the road. Numerous stone walls can be found within the mature woods in this area.

Trescott Road Spur Trail →

Leads 0.4 mile west to Trescott Road, 0.3 mile east of Grasse Road. A former A.T. route, it is poorly cleared and blazed in the scrub at the top but becomes more obvious in the hardwoods.

N-S	TRAIL DESCRIPTION	

9.2	Reach unpaved **Three-Mile Road** (elev. 1,400 feet). ■ Southbound hikers turn left, then right through small parking lot, and reenter woods. ■ Northbound hikers turn left through small parking lot, then right to renter woods.	8.9
9.7	Cross Cory Road (woods road).	8.4
11.1	Cross a large field with view southwest.	7.0
11.7	Cross **Etna–Hanover Center Road** (elev. 845 feet).	6.4
11.8	Pass a cemetery to the west.	6.3
11.9	Cross a brook.	6.2
12.0	Cross a brook.	6.1
12.4	■ Southbound hikers bear left onto old road, follow it for 90 yards, then bear right off road. ■ Northbound hikers bear left onto old road, follow it for 90 yards, then bear right off road.	5.7
13.1	Cross **Trescott Road** (elev. 915 feet).	5.0
13.4	Pass through conifer plantation.	4.7
13.7	Cross bridge just south of dam over cattail marsh and large beaver pond.	4.4
14.1	■ Southbound hikers turn sharply left on old logging road. ■ Northbound hikers leave old logging road and switch-back down.	4.1
14.8	Reach high point on Velvet Rocks ridge (elev. 1,243 feet).	3.3
15.0	Pass junction with unsigned, blue-blazed **Trescott Road Spur Trail**.	3.1

SECTION HIGHLIGHTS

Velvet Rocks Shelter Loop Trail →

Joins the Ledyard Spring Trail and leads 0.2 mile west to Ledyard Spring and 0.4 mile to the shelter. Total length is 0.6 mile.

Ledyard Spring Trail →

Leads 0.5 mile west to Trescott Road in Hanover. The spring at 0.2 mile, inside a corrugated metal ring, is unreliable in dry seasons.

Velvet Rocks Shelter →

Built in 1980s and renovated in 2006; maintained by DOC. Accommodates 4. Composting privy. Water might be found 0.2 mile east on northern Velvet Rocks Loop/Ledyard Spring Trail. Next shelter or campsite: south, 7.8 miles (Happy Hill); north, 9.9 miles (Moose Mountain).

Hanover, New Hampshire →

The educational and cultural facilities of Dartmouth College, as well as the largest shopping area directly on the Trail in New Hampshire and Vermont, are in Hanover (ZIP Code 03755), with telephones, supermarket, specialty backpacking stores, bookstore, restaurants, an expensive inn, the Dartmouth-Hitchcock Medical Center, and local and regional bus service to Boston. Two motels on N.H. 10, one 2.0 miles north and the other 2.0 miles south, are served by a local bus: Advance Transit, (802) 295-1824, <www.advancetransit.com>.

Dartmouth College →

The ninth-oldest U.S. college and one of the most prestigious liberal-arts colleges. On December 13, 1769, George III of England approved a charter prepared by Governor John Wentworth of New Hampshire, establishing an institution "for the education and instruction of Youth of the Indian Tribes in this Land in reading, writing and all parts of Learning which shall appear necessary and expedient for civilizing and Christianizing Children of Pagans as well as in all liberal Arts and Sciences and also of English Youth and any others." Wentworth decided to name the college after the Earl of Dartmouth, the school's sponsor and benefactor. The Rev. Eleazar

N-S

TRAIL DESCRIPTION

15.6   Pass northern junction of loop trail that leads 0.4 mile   **2.5**
west to **Velvet Rocks Shelter**, passing Ledyard Spring
halfway on **Ledyard Spring Trail**.

16.1   Pass southern junction (elev. 1,040 feet) of loop trail that   **2.0**
leads 0.2 mile to **Velvet Rocks Shelter** and 0.2 mile be-
yond that to Ledyard Spring.

16.4   Pass spring on east (unreliable).   **1.7**

16.7   Reach northern edge of DOC Chase Field (soccer field).   **1.4**

16.9   Reach N.H. 120 at service station in **Hanover, New**   **1.2**
Hampshire. ■ SOUTHBOUND hikers turn right, follow Park
Street 150 feet to crosswalk, cross there, pass through
small bank-building parking lot to Lebanon Street, turn
right, follow Lebanon Street to South Main Street (N.H.
10), turn right at light, and pass through downtown Hanover. ■ NORTHBOUND hikers cross Park Street across from
Hanover Food Co-op, turn right, go 150 feet to service
station, turn left, and follow southern edge of soccer field
to reenter woods.

S-N

SECTION HIGHLIGHTS

Wheelock struck off into the New Hampshire wilderness in 1770 and built a single log hut, the beginning of Dartmouth. It was there that the first class, all four students, graduated in 1771. Today, the Ivy League school also has graduate schools of medicine, engineering, and business.

Dartmouth Outing Club →

The offices of the Dartmouth Outing Club (DOC) are in Robinson Hall, Room 113, second building on the left to the west (or ahead) on Main Street. Hikers and visitors are welcome. A stop here will provide you with all the local-services information you need.

Connecticut River →

The river's name is the French corruption of the Algonquian word *quinetucket* and means "long tidal river." The Connecticut is the longest river in New England, flowing south 407 miles from the Connecticut Lakes in northern New Hampshire, along the border between New Hampshire and Vermont, through western Massachusetts and central Connecticut, into Long Island Sound.

Southern end of section →

The Trail crosses the Connecticut River 0.2 mile compass-east of U.S. 5/I-91 in Vermont. Along N.H. 10 and Lebanon Street, parking is metered and difficult to find. No parking is permitted along N.H. 120. Parking may be available in Dartmouth parking lot "A," east of the campus, for visitors and hikers. Call parking operations, (603) 646-2204, to make arrangements. On the Trail 1.0 mile south is Norwich, Vermont (ZIP Code 05055), with lodging, meals, and groceries. Four miles south of Hanover, the larger towns of White River Junction, Vermont (ZIP Code 05001), with lodging, hostel, restaurants, supermarkets, bus stop, and Amtrak; and West Lebanon, New Hampshire, with lodging, restaurants, supermarkets, coin laundry, and outfitter, provide services over a wide price range. Both are served by Vermont Transit Bus, (800) 552-8737, <www.vermont-transit.com>, and Amtrak, (800) USA-RAIL, <www.amtrak.com>.

N-S

TRAIL DESCRIPTION

17.6   Reach the intersection of North Main and East Wheelock   **0.5**
streets, directly across the green at **Dartmouth College**
and a half-block from the **Dartmouth Outing Club**. ■
Southbound hikers turn left and descend to the **Connecticut River** on West Wheelock Street. ■ Northbound
hikers turn right on South Main Street (N.H. 10), pass
through downtown Hanover, turn left at traffic light at
Lebanon Street, follow Lebanon Street to just before
N.H. 120 intersection, and pass left through parking lot of
bank building, using pedestrian crosswalk to Park Street.

18.1   The **southern end of section** is on the west bank of the   **0.0**
Connecticut River at the New Hampshire/Vermont state
line (elev. 400 feet). ■ Southbound hikers continue to
road walk along Vt. 10A, pass under I-91, and reach U.S.
5N in Norwich, Vermont. (see Vermont Section One).
■ Northbound hikers follow West Wheelock Street uphill
into Hanover proper.

***Regulations**—Camping and fires are prohibited in
this section, except at the shelters. The corridor in
this section is very narrow and surrounded by
private lands. In the A.T. corridor, camping is permitted but not within 200 feet of the A.T. itself,
except at the shelters. South of Goose Pond Road,
the Trail passes through Goodwin Forest, a Hanover
town forest.*

S-N

Vermont

The terrain of the northern part of the Trail in Vermont, from the Connecticut River Valley south to Sherburne Pass, does not follow a continuous ridgecrest but crosses a series of short, steep, and strenuous hills running east to west—mostly through lowland hardwood country and across wooded hills dotted with fields, pastures, and abandoned roads

and farms of an earlier era. Stone walls and cellar holes are frequently found. In the southern part, from Sherburne Pass (U.S. 4 between Rutland and Killington) to the Massachusetts border, the Trail follows the central spine of the Green Mountains, coinciding for 105 miles with its older sister, the Long Trail, passing several mountain ponds and approaching treeline on Killington and Stratton mountains. Everywhere are indications of the area's history and its gradual reversion to forest after intensive settlement, farming, and logging.

View from Bromley Mountain

Connecticut River (N.H.–Vt. Line) to White River (Vt. 14 at West Hartford)

9.3 MILES

The Trail in this section traverses the partly forested, partly cleared mountains between the Connecticut River and the White River in Vermont. After following hard-surfaced roads on both the northern and southern ends, the Trail enters woods where the climbs are moderate through white pines and overgrown pastures and along woods roads. The elevation at the Connecticut River and the White River is 400 feet. The highest point is on Griggs Mountain, at 1,570 feet.

Road Approaches—Both ends are accessible by vehicle. Road access is also available at Elm Street, mile 1.8/7.5, and the northern junction with Podunk Road, mile 7.9/1.4.

Maps—For route navigation, refer to Map Five with this guide; the *Long Trail Guide* Appalachian Trail Map 2; or the DOC Trail Map. For area detail but not current trail routes, refer to these USGS 7½-minute topographic quadrangles: Hanover, New Hampshire–Vermont, and Quechee, Vermont.

Shelters and Campsites—This section has one shelter, Happy Hill Shelter (mile 5.3/4.0). Camping and fires are prohibited elsewhere.

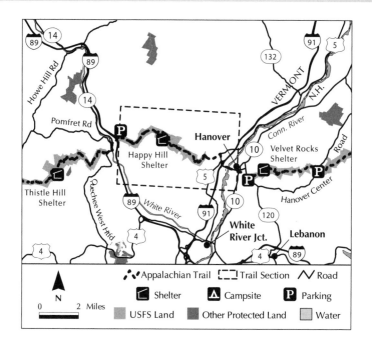

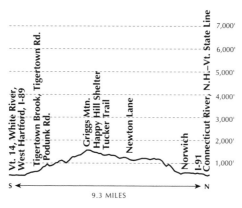

SECTION HIGHLIGHTS

Northern end of section →

The Connecticut River at Norwich, Vermont, and Hanover, New Hampshire, is reached from the north and south by I-89 and I-91, U.S. 5, and N.H. 10; from the west, by U.S. 4 and Vt. 14; and, from the east, by U.S. 4. Vehicles can be left at the Trailhead on Elm Street in Norwich (mile 1.8/7.5). Hanover (ZIP Code 03755) is north on the Trail 0.5 mile, with telephone, supermarkets, specialty backpacking stores, bookstores, restaurants, an inn, the Dartmouth-Hitchcock Medical Center, and local and Vermont Transit bus service. For more information on Hanover, refer to New Hampshire Section Nine. Norwich (ZIP Code 05055) is south 1.0 mile on the Trail, with telephone, lodging, restaurants, groceries, and an extensive hardware store. Four miles compass-south of Hanover are the larger towns of White River Junction, Vermont (ZIP Code 05001), with motels, a hostel, restaurants, supermarkets, a Vermont Transit bus stop, and Amtrak service; and West Lebanon, New Hampshire, with motels, restaurants, a supermarket, a coin laundry, and an outfitter). Vermont Transit Bus can be contacted at (800) 552-8737 or <www.vermont-transit.com>; Amtrak, (800) USA-RAIL, <www.amtrak.com>.

Norwich →

The town was named after Norwich, Connecticut, from which the first settlers originated. Norwich was the original home of Norwich University, which moved to Northfield in 1866 after a fire devastated the campus.

Elm Street →

Trailhead is located 0.8 mile south of U.S. 5 in Norwich, with information kiosk. Spaces for two vehicles.

Power line →

Right-of-way provides view, 15 yards east, of Wilder Dam on the Connecticut River.

N-S

TRAIL DESCRIPTION

0.0 The **northern end of section** is at the west bank of the **9.3**
Connecticut River on the New Hampshire/Vermont state
line (elev. 400 feet). ■ SOUTHBOUND hikers continue to
road-walk on Vt. 10A, pass under I-91, and, at traffic light,
reach U.S. 5N, following it into Norwich, Vermont.
■ NORTHBOUND hikers follow West Wheelock Street uphill
into Hanover (see New Hampshire Section Nine).

1.0 Reach junction of Elm Street and U.S. 5 opposite the **8.3**
gazebo on the **Norwich** village green (elev. 537 feet).
■ SOUTHBOUND hikers turn left onto Elm Street. ■ NORTH-
BOUND hikers turn right onto U.S. 5 and follow highway
compass-south; at traffic light, continue straight on
Vt. 10A, pass under I-91, and descend to river bridge.

1.3 Cross over Bloody Brook. **8.0**

1.5 Cross Hopson Road. **7.8**

1.8 Reach **Elm Street** Trailhead (elev. 750 feet). ■ SOUTHBOUND **7.5**
hikers turn left 50 yards south of Hopson Road, enter
woods, and cross a small stream. ■ NORTHBOUND hikers
turn right and descend steadily on Elm Street, soon crossing Hopson Road.

2.3 Cross small stream. **7.0**

2.4 Cross under **power line**. **6.9**

2.8 Skirt east of Mosley Hill (elev. 1,180 feet). **6.5**

3.7 Cross Newton Lane (1,120 feet). **5.6**

S-N

SECTION HIGHLIGHTS

William Tucker Trail →

Descends 0.8 mile to the east to a gate on gravel Happy Hill Road, which leads downhill to Bragg Hill Road, Meadow Brook Road, and Main Street (U.S. 5) in Norwich in 3.1 miles. An alternate route to the A.T. from Norwich and Happy Hill Shelter, it is mostly on roads. This trail honors the Rev. William Jewett Tucker, ninth president of Dartmouth College (1893–1909).

Happy Hill Shelter →

The oldest A.T. shelter (built in 1918, before the A.T.) was torn down and burned on-site when it was nearly 80 years old; the debris was carried out. In 1998, a new stone shelter, maintained by DOC, was built 0.2 mile north of the original site. Accommodates 8 in the shelter and 10 at tentsites. Privy. Water source (unreliable) is the brook. The shelter also is reached from the north by the Tucker Trail. Next shelter or campsite: south, 9.0 miles (Thistle Hill Shelter); north, 7.4 miles (Velvet Rocks Shelter).

Podunk Brook →

Podunk is a Nipmuc word for "where you sink in mire," a boggy place. The Nipmuc were the original inhabitants of central New England and became part of the "Eastern Woodlands" or Algonquin native-American alliance in eastern North America.

Podunk Road →

This Trailhead on a gravel road is 0.8 mile north of the Tigertown–Poduck Road junction (mile 8.7/0.6). Limited parking is available on the shoulder.

Tigertown Road →

In nineteenth-century slang, a "tiger" was a rough or hard-fighting man, so it is presumed that Tigertown was at one time an uncivil neighborhood.

N-S

	TRAIL DESCRIPTION	

5.1	Reach junction with **William Tucker Trail** (elev. 1,320 feet). ■ SOUTHBOUND hikers turn left onto abandoned road and ascend. ■ NORTHBOUND hikers turn right off old road and descend.	**4.2**
5.3	Side trail leads 0.1 mile east to **Happy Hill Shelter** (elev. 1,460 feet).	**4.0**
5.4	Cross overgrown clearing.	**3.9**
5.5	Cross small stream (seasonal).	**3.8**
5.8	Pass over wooded shoulder of Griggs Mountain (elev. 1,570 feet).	**3.5**
6.2	In overgrown field, cross snowmobile trail.	**3.1**
6.9	Cross a logging road.	**2.4**
7.0	Cross East Fork of Podunk Brook and logging road.	**2.3**
7.3	Cross well-used logging road.	**2.0**
7.6	Cross logging road.	**1.7**
7.8	Cross **Podunk Brook** (elev. 860 feet).	**1.5**
7.9	Reach northern junction with **Podunk Road**.	**1.4**
8.7	Reach southern junction with Podunk Road at **Tigertown Road**. ■ SOUTHBOUND hikers bear right on Podunk Road to Tigertown Road, turn left, and walk under I-89. ■ NORTHBOUND hikers turn right on Podunk Road and enter woods on left.	**0.6**

S-N

SECTION HIGHLIGHTS

Patriots Bridge →

In 2006, an old iron bridge over the White River was torn down and replaced by this more modern span, named in honor of three soldiers from Hartford who died while serving the United States.

Southern end of section →

The White River bridge on Vt. 14 in West Hartford is eight miles west of the junction of I-89 and I-91 near White River Junction along the New Hampshire–Vermont line and seven miles compass-north of the junction of U.S. 4 and U.S. 5 in White River Junction. It is five miles south of Sharon on Vt. 14 (exit 2 on I-89). Limited parking is available at the Tigertown and Podunk roads junction (mile 8.7/0.6) and at the northern junction with Podunk Road (mile 7.9/1.4). The Trail passes through the village of West Hartford (ZIP Code 05084), with telephone, groceries, and a café. It is 9 miles east to West Lebanon, New Hampshire, with motels, restaurants, a supermarket, coin laundry, and an outfitter, just beyond White River Junction (ZIP Code 05001), which has motels, a hostel, restaurants, a supermarket, and long-term parking. White River Junction is served by Vermont Transit Bus, (800) 552-8737, <www.vermont-transit.com>, and Amtrak, (800) USA-RAIL, <www.amtrak.com>.

N-S

TRAIL DESCRIPTION

8.8 Stetson Road joins on east. ■ SOUTHBOUND hikers continue descending on Tigertown Road, crossing railroad tracks. ■ NORTHBOUND hikers continue on Tigertown Road under I-89. **0.5**

8.9 Reach junction of Vt. 14 and Tigertown Road. ■ SOUTHBOUND hikers turn left on Vt. 14 and follow highway south into village of West Hartford. ■ NORTHBOUND hikers turn right, uphill, on Tigertown Road, crossing railroad tracks. **0.4**

9.3 The eastern end of **Patriots Bridge** (Quechee–West Hartford Road) over the White River is the **southern end of section** (elev. 400 feet). ■ SOUTHBOUND hikers turn right, cross bridge, and continue on the Quechee–West Hartford Road (see Vermont Section Two). ■ NORTHBOUND hikers turn left onto Vt. 14, passing through village of West Hartford. **0.0**

S-N

White River (Vt. 14 at West Hartford) to Vt. 12

12.6 MILES

The Trail in this section rolls across a patchwork of wooded and cleared hills, ridges, and valleys. Evidence of the extensive farming that once covered the area—old cellar holes, stone walls, open hilltops, and abandoned woods roads—can be found around every turn. The elevation at the White River in West Hartford is 400 feet; at Vt. 12, 882 feet. The highest point is Thistle Hill, with an elevation of 1,800 feet.

Road Approaches—Both ends are accessible by vehicle. Road access is also available at Cloudland Road (mile 7.1/5.5), Pomfret–South Pomfret Road (mile 8.9/3.7), and Woodstock Stage Road (mile 11.1/1.5).

Maps—For route navigation, refer to Map Five with this guide, the *Long Trail Guide* Appalachian Trail Map 2, or the DOC Trail Map. For area detail but not current trail routes, refer to the USGS 7½-minute topographic quadrangles for Quechee and Woodstock North, Vermont.

Shelters and Campsites—This section has one shelter: Thistle Hill (mile 4.8/7.8). Camping and fires are prohibited throughout the section, except at Thistle Hill Shelter.

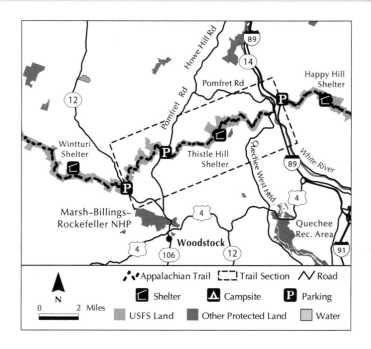

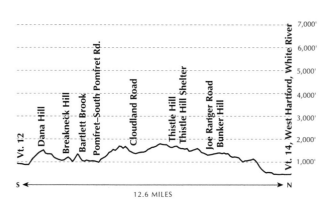

SECTION HIGHLIGHTS

Northern end of section →

The White River bridge on Vt. 14 in West Hartford is eight miles west of the junction of I-89 and I-91 near White River Junction along the New Hampshire–Vermont line and seven miles compass-north of the junction of U.S. 4 and U.S. 5 in White River Junction. It is five miles south of Sharon on Vt. 14 (exit 2 on I-89). Limited parking is available at the Tigertown and Podunk roads junction (mile 8.7/0.6) and at the northern junction with Podunk Road (mile 7.9/1.4). The Trail passes through the village of West Hartford (ZIP Code 05084), with telephone, groceries, and a café. It is 9 miles east to West Lebanon, New Hampshire, with motels, restaurants, a supermarket, coin laundry, and an outfitter, just beyond White River Junction (ZIP Code 05001), which has motels, a hostel, restaurants, a supermarket, and long-term parking. White River Junction is served by Vermont Transit Bus, (800) 552-8737, <www.vermont-transit.com>, and Amtrak, (800) USA-RAIL, <www.amtrak.com>.

White River →

This 56-mile river, a tributary of the Connecticut, rises at Skylight Pond, south of Breadloaf Mountain on the Long Trail, and flows east to Hartford.

Quechee–West Hartford Road →

Connects the towns of Quechee and West Hartford in a distance of 6 miles.

Red-pine plantation →

Also known as the Norway pine, this evergreen tree is used commercially for timber, paper pulp, and landscaping.

Bunker Hill →

This hill in Pomfret got its name from the fact that Revolutionary War veterans set up residence here. The nearby cemetery to the north is their final resting place.

N-S	TRAIL DESCRIPTION	

0.0	The **northern end of section** is the eastern end of Patriots Bridge over the White River (on Quechee-West Hartford Road) at Vt. 14 (elev. 400 feet). ■ SOUTHBOUND hikers turn right, cross bridge, and continue on Quechee–West Hartford Road. ■ NORTHBOUND hikers cross over bridge and turn left onto Vt. 14, passing through village of West Hartford (see Vermont Section One).	**12.6**
0.1	Pass junction with Pomfret Road on the western bank of the **White River**.	**12.5**
0.3	Reach southern junction with **Quechee–West Hartford Road**. ■ SOUTHBOUND hikers turn right, enter woods, cross swampy area on puncheon, and ascend through open hardwoods. ■ NORTHBOUND hikers descend through open hardwoods, cross swampy area on puncheon, and turn left on road.	**12.3**
1.0	Cross hilltop field with outstanding views of the White River Valley.	**11.6**
1.8	Pass through **red-pine plantation**.	**10.8**
2.3	Cross old farm road.	**10.3**
2.4	Pass through hilltop pastures with views to the southeast.	**10.2**
2.6	Cross old town road by a cemetery.	**10.0**
2.7	Reach wooded summit of **Bunker Hill** (elev. 1,520 feet).	**9.9**

SECTION HIGHLIGHTS

Joe Ranger Road →

Born in 1875, Joe Ranger was known locally as an eccentric old hermit who claimed to be able to communicate with the beavers in the ponds next to his shack near the Pomfret–Hartford line.

Arms Hill →

Etching artist John Taylor Arms is associated with this hill and the town of Pomfret.

Thistle Hill Shelter →

Built in 1995 and maintained by DOC. Accommodates 8. Privy. Water available from two nearby streams. Next shelter or campsite: south, 11.9 miles (Winturri); north, 9.0 miles (Happy Hill).

Cloudland Road →

Trailhead is 4.0 miles north of Woodstock. *Do not block gate; this is an active farmland property*.

DuPuis Hill →

A bald summit with panoramic views. Mt. Ascutney stands alone to the south.

N-S	TRAIL DESCRIPTION	
3.3	Cross unpaved **Joe Ranger Road** by a small pond with a stone dam (elev. 1,280 feet).	**9.3**
3.5	Cross open field with views to the north.	**9.1**
4.0	Reach open field atop **Arms Hill**, with views to the south.	**8.6**
4.2	Cross small brook.	**8.4**
4.8	Spur trail leads 0.1 mile east to **Thistle Hill Shelter** (elev. 1,480 feet).	**7.8**
5.1	Cross a woods road (snowmobile trail) and top of wooded Thistle Hill (elev. 1,800 feet).	**7.5**
6.3	Cross under power line.	**6.3**
7.1	Reach gravel **Cloudland Road** (elev. 1,370 feet). ■ SOUTH-BOUND hikers reach open field (active), turn left, follow edge of field to Cloudland Road at gate (red house to the east), turn right on the road for 200 feet, enter field on left, and ascend switchbacks through pasture. ■ NORTH-BOUND hikers descend on switchbacks through open pasture, turn right on road for 200 feet, turn left off road at gate (red house to the east), stay to the right of the open field (watch for electric-fence lines and livestock), and enter woods to the right at gap in stone wall.	**5.5**
7.6	Reach summit of **DuPuis Hill** at cairn (elev. 1,730 feet).	**5.0**
8.0	Blue-blazed spur to east leads 50 feet uphill to a small spring (unreliable).	**4.6**
8.1	Follow old town road with stone wall on east.	**4.5**
8.2	Pass old four-way junction.	**4.4**

S-N

SECTION HIGHLIGHTS

Old Kings Highway →
A major eighteenth-century thoroughfare through Pomfret. The Trail crosses another section of this old road near Bunker Hill (mile 2.7/9.9).

Pomfret–South Pomfret Road →
The A.T. crosses this road 1.3 miles compass-north of South Pomfret and 4.5 miles compass-north of Woodstock. Parking is available at a small pull-off on the compass-south side of the road.

Breakneck Hill →
The springs in this area create a very wet, grassy area to traverse.

Woodstock Stage Road →
The A.T. crosses this road 0.9 mile compass-north of South Pomfret and 4.1 miles north of Woodstock. Parking area is on the north side of the road. It is 0.9 mile east to South Pomfret (ZIP Code 05067), with groceries.

Southern end of section →
The Trail crosses Vt. 12 4.4 miles compass-north of Woodstock and 12.2 miles compass-south of Vt. 107 in Bethel. A hiker parking lot and information kiosk are on the compass-west side of the highway. It is 4.4 miles east to Woodstock (ZIP Code 05091), with telephone, motels, inns, restaurants, a supermarket, a coin laundry, a pharmacy, a bank, a doctor, and a dentist. It is 14 miles to White River Junction and 16 miles to West Lebanon, New Hampshire (see northern end of section).

N-S

TRAIL DESCRIPTION

8.4 Reach hilltop field with views to south and west. ■ SOUTH-BOUND hikers bear right into open field and descend steeply through mixed woods. ■ NORTHBOUND hikers turn left at edge of field and follow a woods road, a remnant of the **Old Kings Highway**. **4.2**

8.9 Reach **Pomfret–South Pomfret Road** and Pomfret Brook (elev. 980 feet). ■ SOUTHBOUND hikers cross road, cross brook, turn right, ascend, then turn left, and follow old fencerow through woods and fields. ■ NORTHBOUND hikers cross brook, cross road, and ascend steeply through mixed hardwoods. **3.7**

9.6 Reach gravel Bartlett Brook Road and creek (elev. 980 feet). ■ SOUTHBOUND hikers cross the road, ascend through a field, and turn left. ■ NORTHBOUND hikers cross the road, cross the creek, and follow an old fence row through woods and fields. **3.0**

10.3 Cross Town Highway 38 (a narrow, dirt road). **2.3**

10.4 Cross brook. **2.2**

10.6 Cross notch between Totman Hill and **Breakneck Hill**. **2.0**

11.1 Cross paved **Woodstock Stage Road** at footbridge over Barnard Creek (elev. 820 feet). **1.5**

11.9 Reach tree-covered Dana Hill (elev. 1,530 feet). **0.7**

12.3 Cross the corner of a hilltop field on a stile. **0.3**

12.6 The **southern end of section** is at Vt. 12 (elev. 882 feet). ■ SOUTHBOUND hikers cross Vt. 12 and pass through an A.T. parking lot to the bridge over the Gulf Stream (see Vermont Section Three). ■ NORTHBOUND hikers leave the A.T. parking lot, cross Vt. 12, cross a small field, and climb steeply. **0.0**

S-N

Vt. 12 to U.S. 4

23.7 MILES

The Trail in this section turns from its usual north–south orientation to a strongly east–west orientation between the Connecticut River Valley on its eastern side and the range of the Green Mountains on its western side. It follows many ridges, and the terrain is rugged, with steep ascents and descents involving considerable exertion. A portion of the footpath follows old logging roads, often rough and overgrown. The autumn foliage in this section is outstanding. The A.T. coincides with the Long Trail at Maine Junction in Willard Gap (mile 22.0/1.7), 1.0 mile north of U.S. 4 (mile 23.0/0.7), for 105.2 miles south to the Massachusetts–Vermont State line. The Trail passes through Gifford Woods State Park, which has a virgin hardwood forest. The elevation at Vt. 12 is 882 feet; at U.S. 4, 1,880 feet. The highest point is Lakota Lake Lookout, at 2,640 feet.

Road Approaches—Both ends are accessible by vehicle. Road access may be available at (seasonal) Chateauguay Road (mile 9.0/14.7) and at (seasonal) Stony Brook Road (mile 12.9/10.8), River Road (mile 18.0/5.7),

continued on page 204

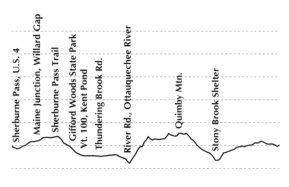

S ←——————————————————————

23.7 MILES

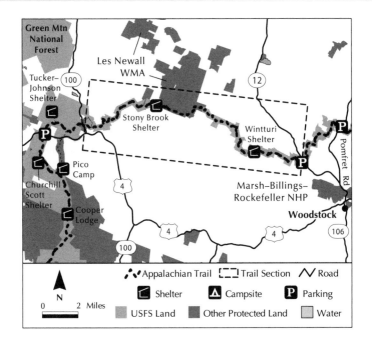

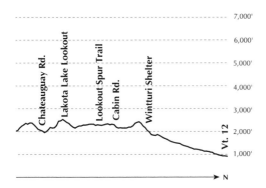

Thundering Brook Road (mile 18.5/5.2 and 19.7/4.0), and Vt. 100 (mile 20.4/3.3).

Maps—For route navigation, refer to Map Six with this guide or the Green Mountain Club's *Long Trail Guide* Appalachian Trail Map 1. For area detail but not current trail routes, refer to these USGS 7½-minute topographic quadrangles: Woodstock North, Delectable Mountain, and Pico Peak, Vermont.

Shelters and Campsites—Three shelters are available in this section: Wintturi Shelter (mile 3.8/19.9), Stony Brook Shelter (mile 12.9/10.8), and Tucker–Johnson Shelter (mile 22.7/1.0). The one public campground is at Gifford Woods State Park (mile 20.7/3.0). Camping and fires are prohibited, except at those shelters and the campground.

Boardwalk over Ottauquechee floodplain

SECTION HIGHLIGHTS

Northern end of section →

The Trail crosses Vt. 12 4.4 miles compass-north of Woodstock and 12.2 miles compass-south of Vt. 107 in Bethel. A hiker parking lot and information kiosk are on the compass-west side of the highway. It is 4.4 miles east to Woodstock (ZIP Code 05091), with telephone, motels, inns, restaurants, a supermarket, a coin laundry, a pharmacy, a bank, a doctor, and a dentist. It is 14 miles to White River Junction and 16 miles to West Lebanon, New Hampshire.

Mt. Ascutney →

With an elevation of 3,144 feet, this is the state's only monadnock. *Ascutney* is an Abenaki word for "at the end of the river fork."

Wintturi Shelter→

Replacing an older structure by the same name, in honor of longtime Trail-maintainer Mauri Wintturi, this frame shelter was built by Erik and Laurel Tobiason and friends in 1994. Maintained by GMC. Accommodates 6. Privy. Water source is a spring 100 yards compass-north of the shelter. Next shelter or campsite: south, 10.1 miles (Stony Brook); north, 11.9 miles (Thistle Hill).

N-S

TRAIL DESCRIPTION

0.0 The **northern end of the section** is at Vt. 12 (elev. 882 **23.7**
feet). ■ SOUTHBOUND hikers cross Vt. 12, pass through the
A.T. parking lot to the bridge over the Gulf Stream, turn
right, pass through a lower pasture, and ascend two more
pastures, crossing fences on wooden stiles. ■ NORTHBOUND
hikers cross the Gulf Stream on a foot bridge, turn right
at the kiosk in the parking lot, and reach Vt. 12 (see
Vermont Section Two).

0.2 Reach edge of hillside clearing where wooden stile **23.5**
crosses electric fence. ■ SOUTHBOUND hikers enter woods.
■ NORTHBOUND hikers descend through two more fields
that provide pastoral views of valley and hills beyond,
crossing fences on stiles.

1.2 Reach bald hilltop with panoramic views. ■ NORTHBOUND **22.5**
hikers reenter woods, make an abrupt left turn, and descend through open area.

1.4 Reach open ridge with views to the southeast of **Mt.** **22.3**
Ascutney.

2.2 Cross old woods road. **21.5**

2.8 On the crest of a low ridge, a spur trail leads east to a **20.9**
view of North Bridgewater.

3.0 Cross an old woods road. **20.7**

3.8 Spur trail (elev. 1,900 feet) leads 0.2 mile west to **19.9**
Wintturi Shelter.

4.4 Reach height of land on Sawyer Hill. **19.3**

4.5 Southwestern view of Killington and Pico peaks from **19.2**
Don's Rock on The Pinnacle.

S-N

Lookout Farm Road →

This old farm road leads 0.3 mile west to Green Gate Road, which leads 1.2 miles east to School House Road, then 0.5 mile west to Lakota Road, and east 0.1 mile to Vt. 12—at a point 3.5 miles compass-south of Barnard and 5.4 miles compass-north of Woodstock.

The Lookout →

Old woods road leads 0.1 mile west to a private cabin on property outside the A.T. corridor. The owners permit its use *as a viewpoint* for hikers. Please respect this property.

Chateauguay Road →

Pronounced "Shat-a-gee." From the Trailhead, it is 3.2 miles west to Vt. 12 at a point 3.8 miles compass-south of the junctions of Vt. 107 and Vt.12 and 2.1 miles compass-north of Barnard. Parking is available for three vehicles on the north side of road. *Caution: This is an active logging road.*

Les Newell Wildlife Management Area→

A tract of 7,988 acres owned by the state of Vermont and managed by the Vermont Fish and Wildlife Department. Surrounded by privately owned timber-company land, the LNWMA is a part of an undeveloped 50,000 acres.

"Continental Divide" →

The water flowing to the west of here eventually reaches Lake Champlain; to the east, the Connecticut River.

N-S	TRAIL DESCRIPTION	
5.1	Pass northern junction with King Cabin Road. ■ SOUTH-BOUND hikers turn right onto King Cabin Road. ■ NORTH-BOUND hikers turn left off old road.	**18.6**
5.3	Reach southern junction with King Cabin Road southern junction. ■ SOUTHBOUND hikers turn left off road. ■ NORTH-BOUND hikers turn right onto King Cabin Road.	**18.4**
5.4	Reach junction with **Lookout Farm Road**.	**18.3**
6.2	Pass junction with trail to **The Lookout** (elev. 2,320 feet).	**17.5**
7.9	Reach Lakota Lake Lookout (elev. 2,640 feet), with a view of Lakota Lake below and the White Mountains in the distance.	**15.8**
8.1	Cross intermittent brook.	**15.6**
8.6	Cross brook.	**15.1**
9.0	Cross gravel **Chateauguay Road** (elev. 2,000 feet) and, 200 feet to the north, Locust Creek. For the next nearly four miles south, you are in Vermont's **Les Newell Wildlife Management Area**.	**14.7**
9.5	Cross logging road.	**14.2**
9.7	Pass west of Bull Hill.	**14.0**
10.5	Cross intermittent brook.	**13.2**
10.6	Cross logging road.	**13.1**
11.0	Pass a small pond and a sag known locally as the "**Continental Divide**."	**12.7**
11.1	Reach height of land (elev. 2,260 feet).	**12.6**

Stony Brook Road →

From the Trailhead, it is 5.2 miles west to Vt. 107 at a point 5.2 miles compass-east of Pittsfield on Vt. 100 and 4.4 miles compass-west of the junctions of Vt. 107 and Vt. 12. Parking for two cars is available on the north side of road. More off-road parking can be found 0.3 mile west. *Caution: This is an active logging road.*

Stony Brook Shelter →

This frame shelter was built in 1997 by Erik and Laurel Tobiason and friends and GMC Ottaquechee Section volunteers. It honors section volunteers who relocated the A.T. between Vt. 100 and Vt. 12 from 1980 to 1990. Maintained by GMC. Accommodates 6. Privy. The water source is the brook 300 feet north on A.T. Next shelter or campsite: south, 6.0 miles (Gifford Woods State Park); north, 10.1 miles (Wintturi).

Quimby Mountain →

On Quimby Mountain, the watershed divides between the Ottauquechee River and Stony Brook.

Ottauquechee River Valley →

The Ottauquechee (pronounced "AWT-ah-KWEE-che"), an Abenaki word for "swift mountain stream," is a 40-mile tributary of the Connecticut River. The headwaters rise in Killington and flow easterly toward Hartland.

N-S

TRAIL DESCRIPTION

12.9	One after another, cross Mink Brook (elev. 1,360 feet) and Stony Brook (or *vice versa*), with Notown Clearing to the east, and end (or start) at **Stony Brook Road**. From Stony Brook Road to near Chateauguay Road to the north, you are in Vermont's **Les Newell Wildlife Management Area**. ■ SOUTHBOUND hikers turn left uphill, cross the road, reenter woods on right, and begin ascent. ■ NORTHBOUND hikers turn left downhill, cross the road, then turn right to cross Stony Brook on bridge.	**10.8**
13.5	Reach ladder on steep ledge.	**10.2**
13.7	Spur trail (elev. 1,760 feet) leads 250 feet east to **Stony Brook Shelter**. The brook crossing is 300 feet north on the A.T.	**10.0**
14.8	Reach height of land on northern shoulder of **Quimby Mountain** (elev. 2,550 feet).	**8.9**
15.6	Cross unnamed summit (elev. 2,600 feet).	**8.1**
15.9	Cross a woods road.	**7.8**
16.2	Cross a power-line clearing.	**7.5**
16.7	Reach summit of unnamed hill (elev. 2,523 feet).	**7.0**
17.2	Pass vista with late-fall and early-spring views of the **Ottauquechee River Valley** and the Coolidge Range to the south.	**6.5**

S-N

River Road →

From the Trailhead, it is 1.4 miles east to U.S. 4 at a point 2.0 miles compass-east of the junctions of Vt. 100 and U.S. 4 in Killington. It is 2.3 miles west to Vt. 100 at a point 2 miles compass-north of Gifford Woods State Park and 6 miles compass-south of Pittsfield. Limited roadside parking is available near the boardwalk. Killington town offices and recreation fields are 0.2 mile east.

Boardwalk over Ottauquechee floodplain →

This relocation of the Trail, a 30-year effort, opened in the fall of 2007. It replaced a road walk on Thundering Brook Road and features an 850-foot, wheelchair-accessible, composite-deck boardwalk from River Road through the Ottauquechee River floodplain to one of Vermont's highest waterfalls.

Thundering Falls →

Wheelchair-accessible spur trail leads to 140-foot waterfalls.

Thundering Brook Road northern junction →

This road crossing is 0.5 mile east of River Road (see above) and 1.4 miles west of U.S. 4. Parking for five vehicles can be found 50 feet west on the north side of the road.

Thundering Brook Road southern junction →

Mountain Meadows Lodge (lodging, meals) is 200 feet east, and U.S. 4 is 0.3 mile to the east.

Vt. 100 →

The Trail crosses Vt. 100 about 400 yards compass-south of the entrance to Gifford Woods State Park and 0.6 mile compass-north of the intersection of U.S. 4 and Vt. 100, at the entrance to the Vermont Fish and Wildlife Department's parking area for the Kent Pond fishing access. Parking also is available at the Kent Pond boat launch. From here, it is 0.6 mile east on U.S. 4 to Killington (ZIP Code 05751), with motels, a deli, groceries, and a local bus stop at Bill's Country Store. On the Killington Access Road, it is 2.4 miles to groceries, a deli, and a local bus stop at the Killington Market.

N-S

TRAIL DESCRIPTION

18.0 Cross **River Road** (elev. 1,214 feet). ■ Southbound hikers cross the road and reach the northern end of a **boardwalk over the Ottauquechee floodplain**. ■ Northbound hikers cross the road, reenter the woods, and gently ascend through mixed hardwoods, on and off old logging roads. **5.7**

18.1 Views east and west from **boardwalk over Ottauquechee floodplain**. **5.6**

18.3 Spur trail leads 200 feet west to **Thundering Falls**. **5.4**

18.5 Reach northern junction with **Thundering Brook Road**. ■ Southbound hikers cross the road and reenter the woods on stone steps. ■ Northbound hikers cross the road, reenter the woods, and turn right on initially raised, crushed-stone footpath, descending through hemlock forest to Thundering Falls. **5.2**

19.7 Reach southern junction with gravel **Thundering Brook Road**. One hundred yards to the south, the Trail crosses an open field and passes the swimming area at Kent Pond. **4.0**

20.2 Reach shore of Kent Pond. **3.5**

20.3 Cross a footbridge over Kent Brook (elev. 1,580 feet). **3.4**

20.4 Reach **Vt. 100** (elev. 1,580 feet). ■ Southbound hikers turn right onto Vt. 100 for 300 feet, bear left across the highway, and enter woods on a path that leads to Gifford Woods State Park. ■ Northbound hikers turn right onto Vt. 100, follow it for 300 feet, bear left and cross road to Kent Pond fishing access, cross the entry drive for the parking lot, and reenter the woods. **3.3**

S-N

Gifford Woods State Park →

This seasonal park was created in 1931 to preserve one of the few remaining undisturbed northern-hardwood forests in New England. Within its 114 acres is a seven-acre plot of virgin forest dominated by sugar maples, Vermont's state tree. Many other species of trees, including an eastern hemlock more than four hundred years old, are scattered over the park. Operated and maintained by the Vermont Department of Forests, Parks, and Recreation; fee. Accommodates 22 at tent and RV sites, 21 in lean-tos, and 4 in cabins. Showers; ample water. Next shelter or campsite: south, 2.4 miles (Tucker–Johnson, on the Long Trail); north, 6.0 miles (Stony Brook).

Sherburne Pass Trail →

This trail extends north and south of U.S. 4 and is the historic route of the A.T./Long Trail, abandoned as such after negotiations with the ski areas to the south to better protect the footpath. From the northern junction here, it is 0.5 mile east to the Inn at Long Trail; it then crosses U.S. 4 and continues south to rejoin the A.T. at "Jungle Junction" in 3.4 miles (see Vermont Section Four).

Deer Leap Trail→

This 1.3-mile trail leads to a ledge overlooking U.S. 4 and the Coolidge Range. From the southern junction, it leads 1.1 miles east over Deer Leap Mountain to Deer Leap Overlook by way of the Overlook spur trail. From the northern junction, at mile 21.8/1.9, it is 0.6 mile east to Deer Leap Overlook by way of the spur trail.

Maine Junction→

Here, the southbound A.T. and northbound Long Trail separate. To Trail-west, the Long Trail leads north 166.8 miles to Canada, passing Tucker–Johnson Shelter along the way. Both trails are blazed in white, so be careful that you're on the trail you want!

N-S

TRAIL DESCRIPTION

20.7 Reach upper camping area of **Gifford Woods State Park** (elev. 1,660 feet). ■ SOUTHBOUND hikers turn left from gravel road onto a trail through picnic areas, rejoin gravel road, turn left, and pass road on left leading to stone building (toilets and showers). ■ NORTHBOUND hikers pass road on right to stone building (toilets and showers), turn left off gravel road (to left is caretaker's house, where shelters and tentsites may be rented), pass through picnic area, turn right onto gravel road, and turn left off road onto footpath. **3.0**

21.5 Spur trail leads 50 feet east to views of Killington and Pico peaks. **2.2**

21.8 Pass northern junction with the **Sherburne Pass Trail**, which rejoins the A.T. at "Jungle Junction" (see Vermont Section Four). Seventy yards south on the A.T. is the northern junction of the **Deer Leap Trail**, which also intersects at mile 22.6/1.1 (elev. 2,290 feet). ■ SOUTHBOUND hikers turn right, slabbing the east side of Deer Leap Mountain. ■ NORTHBOUND hikers turn left and climb a low ridge. **1.9**

22.6 Pass southern junction of **Deer Leap Trail,** which rejoins the A.T at mile 21.8/1.9 (elev. 2,290 feet). **1.1**

S-N

Tucker–Johnson Shelter →

Built in 1969 by the Long Trail Patrol, Louis Stare, and members of the Killington Section of GMC and named for Fred H. Tucker of Boston, a long-time member of GMC, and Otto Johnson of Proctor, Vermont. Maintained by GMC. Accommodates 8. Privy. Water source is a nearby stream. Next shelter or campsite: south, 3.4 (Churchill Scott); north, 2.4 miles (Gifford Woods State Park).

Southern end of section →

The Trail crosses U.S. 4 0.9 mile west of the crest of Sherburne Pass (ample parking), 2.4 miles west of Killington, and 8.6 miles east of U.S. 7 in Rutland. A large, well-marked hiker parking lot is on the south side of the highway, but it is not always plowed in the winter. Another area 0.3 mile east at Pico Ski Area is always plowed. Theft and vandalism have been reported; do not leave valuables in vehicles. Long-term parking is not recommended. The Inn at Long Trail is 0.9 mile east at the top of the pass (lodging, meals, local bus stop); it will hold parcels marked "Hold for Appalachian Trail Hiker," if sent by way of United Parcel Service to Inn at Long Trail, Sherburne Pass, 709 U.S. 4, Killington, VT 05751. It is 2.4 miles to Killington (ZIP Code 05751), with motels, a deli, groceries, and a local bus stop. Passing several motels and restaurants along the way, it is 8.6 miles west on U.S. 4 to Rutland (ZIP Code 05701), with all services, plus Amtrak (800-USA-RAIL, <www.amtrak.com>), local bus service, an airport, and the Rutland Regional Medical Center, (802) 775-7111. Marble Valley Regional Transit community bus, (802) 773-3244, serves the U.S. 7 corridor from Manchester to Rutland and U.S. 4 to Killington.

N-S

TRAIL DESCRIPTION

22.7 Reach **Maine Junction** at Willard Gap. The Long Trail **1.0**
leads 0.4 mile west to **Tucker–Johnson Shelter** (elev.
2,250 feet). ▪ SOUTHBOUND hikers bear left on the A.T.,
gently descending to U.S. 4. ▪ NORTHBOUND hikers bear
right on the A.T. to Katahdin.

23.6 Blue-blazed Catamount Trail diverges to west. Vermont's **0.1**
300-mile-long, backcountry ski trail extends from the
Massachusetts line to the Canadian border; for more information, visit <www.catamounttrail.org>.

23.7 The road crossing at U.S. 4 is the **southern end of section** **0.0**
(elev. 1,880 feet). *Use caution when crossing U.S. 4;
traffic moves at high speeds.* ▪ SOUTHBOUND hikers cross
U.S. 4 and enter woods (see Vermont Section Four).
▪ NORTHBOUND hikers, from the north side of U.S. 4, cross
wet area on raised footpath and gently ascend.

S-N

U.S. 4 to Vt. 103

17.4 MILES

In this section, the A.T. traverses its highest elevations in Vermont, along the Coolidge Range of the Green Mountains, and descends into foothills, winding through pastures, fields, open woods, and thick, second-growth conifers. Mostly in dense hardwood and evergreen forests, the treadway is often rocky and muddy. A spur trail leads to Killington Peak, at 4,235 feet the second-highest mountain in Vermont. The A.T. and the Long Trail coincide throughout this section. The elevation at U.S. 4 is 1,880 feet; at Vt. 103, 860 feet. The highest elevation is at the junction with the Killington spur trail, 3,900 feet.

Road Approaches—Both ends are accessible by vehicle. Road access is also available at Upper Cold River Road, mile 12.0 /5.4; Cold River Road (Lower), mile 13.5/3.9; Keiffer Road, mile 13.8/3.6; and Lottery Road, mile 15.5/1.9.

Maps—For route navigation, refer to Map Six with this guide; GMC's *Long Trail Guide* Long Trail Map 5; or "Vermont's Long Trail Waterproof Hiking Map (revised third edition)," from the Wilderness Map Company. For area detail but not current trail routes, refer to these USGS 7½-minute topographic quadrangles: Pico Peak, Killington Peak, and Rutland, Vermont.

Shelters and Campsites—This section has five shelters: Churchill Scott Shelter (mile 1.9/15.5), Pico Camp (mile 3.8/13.6), Cooper Lodge (mile 6.3/11.1), Governor Clement Shelter (mile 10.6/6.8), and Clarendon Shelter (mile 16.4/1.0). Camping is limited to the shelters. Small wood fires, although discouraged, are permitted at the shelters' established fire rings, with the exception of Cooper Lodge, due to its sensitive high-elevation location, and Churchill Scott Shelter, because of permit guidelines designed to protect the Rutland watershed in which it sits.

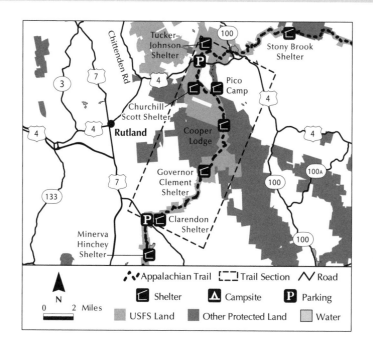

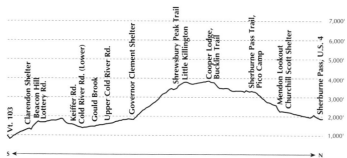

SECTION HIGHLIGHTS

Northern end of section →

The Trail crosses U.S. 4 0.9 mile west of the crest of Sherburne Pass (ample parking), 2.4 miles west of Killington, and 8.6 miles east of U.S. 7 in Rutland. A large, well-marked hiker parking lot is on the south side of the highway, but it is not always plowed in the winter. Another area 0.3 mile east at Pico Ski Area is always plowed. Theft and vandalism have been reported; do not leave valuables in vehicles. Long-term parking is not recommended. The Inn at Long Trail is 0.9 mile east at the top of the pass (lodging, meals, local bus stop); it will hold parcels marked "Hold for Appalachian Trail Hiker, "if sent by way of United Parcel Service to Inn at Long Trail, Sherburne Pass, 709 U.S. 4, Killington, VT 05751. It is 2.4 miles to Killington (ZIP Code 05751), with motels, a deli, groceries, and a local bus stop. Passing several motels and restaurants along the way, it is 8.6 miles west on U.S. 4 to Rutland (ZIP Code 05701), with all services, plus Amtrak (800-USA-RAIL, <www.amtrak.com>), local bus service, an airport, and the Rutland Regional Medical Center, (802) 775-7111. Marble Valley Regional Transit community bus, (802) 773-3244, serves the U.S. 7 corridor from Manchester to Rutland and U.S. 4 to Killington.

Churchill Scott Shelter →

This post-and-beam structure was built by Erik and Laurel Tobiason, the GMC Killington Section, and other GMC volunteers in 2002. It is named in honor of a long-time Killington Section leader and maintainer and dedicated to the memory of Alice H. Ferrence, an Appalachian Trail long-distance hiker who drowned attempting to ford Maine's Kennebec River in 1985. Maintained by the GMC. Accommodates 8. Also has a tent platform. Handicap-accessible, composting privy. Water source is a spring downhill behind the shelter. Because this location is within the Rutland city watershed, *no fires are permitted*. A GMC caretaker may be present and an overnight fee charged. Next shelter or campsite: south, 2.5 miles (Pico Camp by way of Sherburne Pass Trail); north, 3.4 miles (Tucker–Johnson on the Long Trail).

N-S

TRAIL DESCRIPTION

Bunchberry

0.0   The road crossing at U.S. 4 (elev. 1,880 feet), below the   **17.4**
peak of Sherburne Pass, is the **northern end of section**.
*Use caution when crossing U.S.4; traffic moves at high
speeds.* ■ SOUTHBOUND hikers, from the south side of U.S.
4, enter woods, cross a bridge over a brook, turn left off
an old woods road, and ascend gradually. ■ NORTHBOUND
hikers cross U.S. 4 and enter woods (see Vermont Section
Three).

1.8   Cross brook.   **15.6**

1.9   Spur trail (elev. 2,560 feet) leads 0.1 mile east to **Churchill**   **15.5**
Scott Shelter.

2.2   Reach Mendon Lookout (elev. 2,890 feet).   **15.2**

S-N

SECTION HIGHLIGHTS

"Jungle Junction" →

The name originated after a 1938 hurricane (which essentially "broke" the A.T. a year after it became a 2,000-mile continuous footpath) left behind a "jungle" of blowdowns at the A.T./Long Trail's then junction with Pico Peak's abandoned West Side Trail.

Sherburne Pass Trail →

This trail extends north and south of U.S. 4 and is the historic route of the A.T./Long Trail (until this century). From the southern junction, it is 0.5 mile east to the Pico Camp. It continues beyond to U.S. 4 at the Inn at Long Trail and then north to rejoin the A.T. in 3.4 miles (see Vermont Section Three), east of Maine Junction.

Pico Camp →

Closed, frame cabin built by the Long Trail Patrol in 1959. Maintained by GMC. Accommodates 12. Composting privy. Water can be found 100 feet east on the spur trail. A GMC caretaker may be present and an overnight fee charged. Next shelter or campsite: south, 3.0 miles (Cooper Lodge); north, 2.5 miles (Churchill Scott Shelter).

Pico Link →

Behind Pico Camp, a spur trail leads 0.4 mile to the summit of Pico Peak (elev. 3,957 feet).

Bucklin Trail→

Descends 3.3 miles to Wheelerville Road at Brewers Corners, 4 miles east of U.S. 4.

Killington Carriage Road→

In 1861, a rustic cabin was built 300 feet below Killington Peak. Nineteen years later, it was replaced by the "Killington House" hotel, accessed by this carriage path ascending from Wheelerville.

N-S

TRAIL DESCRIPTION

3.8 Reach **"Jungle Junction"** (elev. 3,480 feet) and southern junction with the **Sherburne Pass Trail**, which leads to **Pico Camp** and **Pico Link** and rejoins the A.T. north of Sherburne Pass (see Vermont Section Three). **13.6**

5.3 Reach height of land on Snowden Peak. **12.1**

6.1 Pass junction with **Bucklin Trail** (elev. 3,770 feet). **11.3**

6.2 Pass swampy glade hiding the abandoned **Killington Carriage Road**. **11.2**

Pico Link

S-N

Cooper Lodge →

A closed, stone-and-frame cabin built in 1939 by the Vermont Forest Service and the Civilian Conservation Corps (CCC), this is the highest shelter on the A.T. in Vermont. Maintained by GMC. Accommodates 12 at the shelter and 10 on two tent platforms. Composting privy. Water source is a spring 100 feet south on the A.T. *Fires prohibited.* A GMC caretaker may be present and an overnight fee charged. Next shelter or campsite: south, 4.3 miles (Governor Clement); north, 3.0 miles (Pico Camp by way of Sherburne Pass Trail).

Killington Spur Trail →

Leads 0.2 mile steeply to summit of Killington Peak.

Killington Peak →

Killington Peak (elev. 4,235 feet) is the second-highest mountain in Vermont. From the summit, the Green Mountains from Glastenbury Mountain in the south to Mt. Mansfield in the north are visible, as well as the Taconic and Adirondack ranges in New York and the White Mountains in New Hampshire. To the southeast is Mt. Ascutney, and to the west is Rutland. The summit can also be reached in season by the Killington Ski Area Gondola, which leaves from the base lodge at the end of the Killington access road off Vt. 100.

Shrewsbury Peak Trail →

Leads 2.1 miles east to Shrewsbury Peak (elev. 3, 720 feet) and 4.0 miles to a dirt CCC road (closed in winter) that is 3.0 miles compass-northeast of North Shrewsbury.

Governor Clement Shelter →

Stone shelter on a dirt road in an overgrown field, built in 1929 by the family of William H. Field of Mendon and named for Percival W. Clement, governor of Vermont from 1919 to 1921. Maintained by GMC. Accommodates 10. Privy. Water source is a stream across the road. *Due to its close proximity to a public road, this shelter has a long history of visits by local partiers, creating serious problems with vandalism and harassment of hikers.* The road was gated in

N-S

TRAIL DESCRIPTION

South of Cooper Lodge

6.3	Pass **Cooper Lodge** (elev. 3,900 feet). South on the A.T. 100 feet, the **Killington Spur Trail** to **Killington Peak** comes in from east.	**11.1**
7.6	Reach high point on Little Killington Ridge.	**9.8**
8.0	Pass junction with **Shrewsbury Peak Trail** (elev. 3,500 feet).	**9.4**
8.4	Cross two small brooks.	**9.0**
10.3	■ SOUTHBOUND hikers turn right onto logging road and descend with stream to the east. ■ NORTHBOUND hikers turn left off logging road and enter woods.	**7.1**
10.6	Pass **Governor Clement Shelter** (elev. 1,850 feet). ■ SOUTHBOUND hikers turn right into woods and, in 25 feet, turn left off road. ■ NORTHBOUND hikers ascend on road behind the shelter.	**6.8**

S-N

2008 in an ATC/GMC attempt to solve the problems. Move on if you encounter problems. Next shelter or campsite: south, 5.9 miles (Clarendon); north, 4.3 miles (Cooper Lodge).

Overgrown clearing →
Former site of the Haley Farm, described in the GMC's 1920 *Guide Book of the Long Trail* as providing "good beds and board; telephone."

Upper Cold River Road →
From the Trailhead, it is 2.4 miles east to North Shrewsbury and 7.3 miles west to U.S. 7 in North Clarendon.

Cold River Road (Lower) →
From the Trailhead, it is 2.4 miles east to North Shrewsbury and 7.3 miles west to U.S. 7 in North Clarendon. Limited parking is available on the north side of the road, east of the bridge.

Keiffer Road →
From the Trailhead, it is 0.4 mile west to Cold River Road (Lower) and 1.7 miles east to Lincoln Hill Road in Shrewsbury.

Coolidge Range →
The range is named in honor of John Calvin Coolidge, Jr., thirtieth president of the United States, a Vermont native. The range includes, from north to south, Pico Peak, Little Pico, Killington Peak, Mendon Peak, Little Killington, Shrewsbury Peak, Smith Peak, Bear Mountain, and Salt Ash Mountain.

Lottery Road →
From the Trailhead, it is 1.9 miles east to the village of Shrewsbury and then 2.5 miles on Lincoln Hill Road to Vt. 103.

Clarendon Shelter →
Built by the GMC Killington Section in 1952 and maintained by

N-S	TRAIL DESCRIPTION	
10.7	Cross Robinson Brook on a bridge.	**6.7**
11.0	Cross an **overgrown clearing** with a stone wall.	**6.4**
11.4	Junction with gravel Town Highway 13. ■ SOUTHBOUND hikers turn sharply left, cross bridge over Sargent Brook, turn sharply right, and follow the brook downstream. ■ NORTHBOUND hikers turn sharply left, cross bridge over Sargent Brook, and turn sharply right to reenter woods.	**6.0**
12.0	Cross unpaved **Upper Cold River Road** (elev. 1,630 feet).	**5.4**
12.7	Cross Gould Brook *(elev. 1,480 feet). This crossing can be hazardous in times of high water.*	**4.7**
13.5	Cross **Cold River Road (Lower)**, elev. 1,400 feet. ■ SOUTHBOUND hikers turn right, cross over concrete bridge, and turn left to reenter woods. ■ NORTHBOUND hikers turn right, cross over concrete bridge, and turn left to reenter woods.	**3.9**
13.6	Reach western bank of Cold River.	**3.8**
13.8	Cross unpaved **Keiffer Road**. ■ SOUTHBOUND hikers turn left, reenter woods on right through swampy area, and ascend beside stone wall. ■ NORTHBOUND hikers turn left and reenter field on right, with views of the **Coolidge Range**.	**3.6**
14.8	Reach ridgecrest.	**2.6**
15.1	Pass Hermit Spring (unreliable) on west.	**2.3**
15.5	Cross unpaved **Lottery Road**.	**1.9**

S-N

GMC. Accommodates 12 at the shelter and 20 at tentsites. Privy. Water source is a stream 50 feet east. Next shelter or campsite: south, 3.8 miles (Minerva Hinchey); north, 5.9 miles (Governor Clement).

Crown Point Military Road →

Built in 1759–1760 during the French and Indian Wars, this road was a vital military supply link between Fort No. 4 at Charlestown, New Hampshire, and the Fort at Crown Point on Lake Champlain on the Vermont–New York border. Much of the road has now disappeared, either reclaimed by the forest or plowed under to meet the needs of an expanding population.

Southern end of section →

The A.T. crosses Vt. 103 at the Green Mountain Railroad crossing by Clarendon Gorge, 2.4 miles compass-east of U.S. 7, 7.3 miles compass-south of Rutland, and 6.0 miles compass-west of East Wallingford. A large parking lot is available on the south side of Vt. 103, but long-term parking is not recommended. Theft and vandalism have been reported; do not leave valuables in vehicles. A telephone and groceries are 1.0 mile east. It is 7.3 miles to Rutland Town, with motels, restaurants, a supermarket, outfitters, and a local bus stop, and 9.7 miles to Rutland (see northern end of section).

N-S

| | TRAIL DESCRIPTION | |

15.9 Reach airplane beacon on top of Beacon Hill (elev. **1.5** 1,760 feet).

16.3 Cross brook. **1.1**

16.4 Side trail to **Clarendon Shelter** leads 400 feet east on old **1.0** town road, formerly the **Crown Point Military Road** (elev. 1,350 feet).

17.0 Reach Clarendon Lookout, a rock promontory with views **0.4** below of Vt. 103 and Rutland Airport.

17.1 Pass through boulder-filled ravine. **0.3**

17.3 Pass under power line. **0.1**

17.4 Cross two stiles and reach Vt. 103 at a railroad crossing, **0.0** the **southern end of section** (elev. 869 feet). *Use caution when crossing Vt. 103; traffic moves at high speeds.* ■ SOUTHBOUND hikers cross Vt. 103 and railroad tracks and descend to Clarendon Gorge (see Vermont Section Five). ■ NORTHBOUND hikers cross Vt. 103 and railroad tracks, cross a stile, enter a field, and cross another stile.

S-N

Vt. 103 to Danby–Landgrove Road (USFS 10)

14.6 MILES

The Trail in this section passes through a variety of landscapes, from the crossing of Clarendon Gorge on a suspension bridge, to vistas of the Taconic Range from rock outcrops, to overgrown clearings housing old cellar holes and stone walls, to old woods roads used as cross-country ski trails in winter. It passes just west of the summit of White Rocks Mountain and along idyllic Little Rock Pond, then descends through beaver-challenged stretches along Little Black Branch. South of Vt. 140, the Trail is in the Green Mountain National Forest. The A.T. and the Long Trail coincide throughout this section. The elevation at Vt. 103 is 869 feet; at Danby–Landgrove Road, 1,500 feet. The highest elevation is at the junction with the White Rocks Cliff Trail, at 2,400 feet.

Road Approaches—Both ends are accessible by vehicle. Road access is also available at Vt. 140 (mile 6.3/8.3) and Sugar Hill Road (mile 6.4/8.2).

Maps—For route navigation, refer to Maps Six and Seven with this guide or GMC's *Long Trail Guide* Long Trail Maps 4 and 5, or "Vermont's Long Trail Waterproof Hiking Map (revised third edition)," For area detail, refer to the USGS 15-minute topographic quadrangle for Wallingford, Vermont, or its 7½-minute quadrangle for Rutland, Vermont.

Shelters and Campsites—This section has four shelters—Minerva Hinchey Shelter (mile 2.7/11.9), Greenwall Shelter (mile 7.8/6.8), Little Rock Pond Shelter (mile 12.2/2.4), and Lula Tye Shelter (mile 12.9/1.7)—and one campsite, Little Rock Pond Tenting Area (mile 12.6/2.0). The GMC stations a caretaker in summer at Little Rock Pond to help hikers and supervise shelters and camping in the vicinity of the pond; a fee is charged to help defray costs.

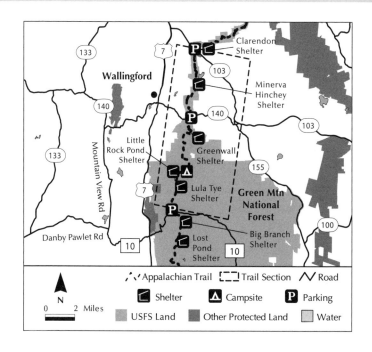

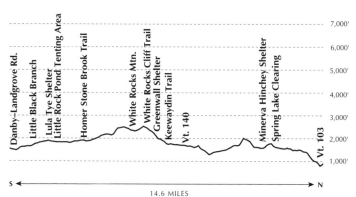

14.6 MILES

Northern end of section →

The A.T. crosses Vt. 103 at the Green Mountain Railroad crossing by Clarendon Gorge, 2.4 miles compass-east of U.S. 7, 7.3 miles compass-south of Rutland, and 6.0 miles compass-west of East Wallingford. A large parking lot is available on the south side of Vt. 103, but long-term parking is not recommended. Theft and vandalism have been reported; do not leave valuables in vehicles. A telephone and groceries are 1.0 mile east. It is 7.3 miles to Rutland Town, with motels, restaurants, a supermarket, outfitters, and a local bus stop, and 9.7 miles to Rutland.

Suspension bridge →

Built in 1974 to replace a similar structure swept away in a 1973 flood. It is dedicated to the memory of Robert Brugmann.

Taconic Range →

A part of the Appalachian mountain system, this range extends southward for 150 miles from a point southwest of Brandon, Vermont, to northern Putnam County, New York. It rises to Mt. Equinox (elev. 3,816 feet) near Manchester, Vermont, and includes Mt. Frissell (elev. 2,380 feet), the highest point in Connecticut. In Massachusetts, the range constitutes the western Berkshire Hills. *Taconic* is an Algonquian word referring to a tree, a wood, or a forest.

Spring Lake Clearing →

Controlled burns were once used as a tool to retain vistas and provide a clearing for wildlife. Now, the forest is reclaiming this highland meadow, and views of nearby Spring Lake are limited.

N-S

| TRAIL DESCRIPTION |

0.0 Where Vt. 103 (Rutland–Bellows Falls Highway) crosses **14.6**
the Green Mountain railroad tracks is the **northern end
of section** (elev. 869 feet). *Use caution when crossing Vt.
103; traffic moves at high speeds.* ■ SOUTHBOUND hikers
descend left to Clarendon Gorge. ■ NORTHBOUND hikers
cross Vt. 103 and railroad tracks (see Vermont Section
Four).

0.1 Cross high **suspension bridge** over the Mill River in Clar- **14.5**
endon Gorge (elev. 800 feet).

0.4 Cross gravel Knipes Road (gated). **14.2**

0.8 Airport Lookout on west offers vistas of the **Taconic Range** **13.8**
in New York (elev. 1,400 feet).

1.0 Pass an overlook. **13.6**

1.1 Pass an overlook. **13.5**

2.0 Pass under the airport-beacon power line. **12.6**

2.1 Reach **Spring Lake Clearing** (elev. 1,620 feet). **12.5**

Clarendon Gorge

S-N

SECTION HIGHLIGHTS

Minerva Hinchey Shelter →
Open-front, frame structure constructed by GMC Killington Section in 1969 and renovated by Killington Section volunteers in 2006; formerly known as Sunnyside Camp and renamed for Minerva Hinchey in tribute to her 22 years of service as GMC's corresponding secretary (1955–1977). Maintained by GMC. Accommodates 8 at the shelter and 10 at tentsites. Privy. Water source is a spring 150 feet south. Next shelter or campsite: south, 5.3 miles (Greenwall); north, 3.8 miles (Clarendon).

Patch's Hollow →
In the early nineteenth century, five families lived here. On May 11, 1831, a band of "rioters," in a display of resentment for the extramarital indiscretions of one Rolan Wheeler, attempted to tar and feather and ride him out of town on a rail. In the darkness, a scuffle ensued, and a knife was drawn. One of the rioters was killed by his own posse, and Mr. Wheeler escaped into the night. Soon thereafter, all the families moved away.

Bear Mountain →
The northernmost of three Bear mountains the Trail crosses between Maine and Georgia. The others are in Connecticut and New York.

Domed Ledge vista →
Views of White Rocks Cliff and Dorset Peak to south and west.

Vt. 140 →
The Trail crosses Vt. 140 2.7 miles compass-east of U.S. 7 in Wallingford and 3.3 miles compass-west of Vt. 103 and Vt. 155 in East Wallingford. The parking lot is off a steep driveway on the northern side of Vt. 140, 0.2 mile east of the Trail crossing. Theft and vandalism have been reported; do not leave valuables in vehicles. Long-term parking is not recommended. It is 3.3 miles east to East Wallingford (ZIP Code 05742), with telephone and groceries, and 2.7 miles west to Wallingford (ZIP Code 05773), with B&Bs, restaurants, groceries, a hardware store, and a dentist.

N-S

TRAIL DESCRIPTION

2.7	Spur trail (elev. 1,530 feet) leads 200 feet east to **Minerva Hinchey Shelter**.	11.9
2.8	■ Southbound hikers turn left off a woods road and enter woods. ■ Northbound hikers turn right onto woods road.	11.8
3.0	Pass under power line.	11.6
3.6	Reach **Patch's Hollow** at northern end of beaver pond (elev. 1,800 feet).	11.0
4.2	Reach height of land on **Bear Mountain** (elev. 2,240 feet).	10.4
5.3	Spur trail leads 300 feet west to **Domed Ledge vista** (elev. 1,575 feet).	9.3
5.7	Cross abandoned Bear Mountain Road. ■ Southbound hikers turn right, join road for 50 feet, and then turn left, leaving road. ■ Northbound hikers turn right, join road for 50 feet, then turn left, leaving road.	8.9
6.2	Pass through Trailhead parking lot. ■ Southbound hikers turn right and reenter woods at western end of parking lot. ■ Northbound hikers walk to eastern end of parking lot and turn left, uphill, on woods road.	8.4
6.3	Cross **Vt. 140** (Wallingford Gulf Road) and bridge over Roaring Brook (elev. 1,160 feet).	8.3
6.4	Cross gravel Sugar Hill Road, which descends 2.7 miles west to Wallingford.	8.2

S-N

SECTION HIGHLIGHTS

Robert T. Stafford White Rocks National Recreation Area →

On June 19, 1984, Congress passed the Vermont Wilderness Act, designating 36,400 acres of the GMNF as the White Rocks National Recreation Area (WRNRA), containing two congressionally designated wilderness areas: Big Branch and Peru Peak, both of which were expanded by Congress in late 2006. In 2007, Congress renamed the WRNRA the "Robert T. Stafford White Rocks National Recreation Area" to honor a man who served as Vermont governor, U.S. representative, and U.S. senator. The land is rich in cultural history. Both native Americans and European settlers relied on its natural resources. Until the 1930s, the entire area was used for farming, intensive logging, iron mining, and settlement. The forest you see may be the third or fourth to dominate the area.

Keewaydin Trail →

Descends 0.4 mile west to White Rocks Picnic Area on USFS 52 (day-use area, gated at dark).

Greenwall Shelter →

Built in 1962 by USFS, maintained by GMC and USFS. Accommodates 8. Privy. A spring 600 feet northeast of shelter may fail in dry seasons. Next shelter or campsite: south, 4.6 miles (Little Rock Pond); north, 5.3 miles (Minerva Hinchey).

White Rocks Cliff Trail →

Descends steeply 0.2 mile west to a viewpoint at the brink of a cliff, with sightings of peregrine falcons possible.

White Rocks Mountain →

The west side of the peak is a jumbled talus slope, the remains of an immense avalanche of quartzite boulders that occurred 10,000 or more years ago. Both Indians and European settlers relied on the local quartzite rock. The effects of Indian quarrying operations can be seen around the talus slopes; native people used the quartzite for arrowheads and other lithic tools. Many stone artifacts are scattered throughout the WRNRA.

| | TRAIL DESCRIPTION | |

7.0 Cross Bully Brook. ■ SOUTHBOUND hikers enter **Robert T. Stafford White Rocks National Recreation Area**. ■ NORTH- BOUND hikers leave Robert T. Stafford White Rocks Na- tional Recreation Area. — **7.6**

7.1 Reach junction with the **Keewaydin Trail** (elev. 1,380 feet). ■ SOUTHBOUND hikers turn left and ascend. ■ NORTH- BOUND hikers turn right and descend to Bully Brook. — **7.5**

7.8 Spur trail leads 0.2 mile east to **Greenwall Shelter** (elev. 2,020 feet). ■ SOUTHBOUND hikers turn right. ■ NORTH- BOUND hikers turn left. — **6.8**

8.3 Pass junction with **White Rocks Cliff Trail** (elev. 2,400 feet). — **6.3**

9.1 Pass west of the summit of **White Rocks Mountain** (elev. 2,680 feet). — **5.5**

White Rocks

SECTION HIGHLIGHTS

Aldrichville clearing →

Aldrichville, a sawmill village established by local businessman/logger Barney Aldrich in the 1880s, operated for more than 20 years before being abandoned in favor of a new location in the valley, nearer to Wallingford's downtown and railroad. At the time of its peak operation, the village consisted of a steam-powered mill, a store, school, blacksmith shop, boardinghouse, and roughly a dozen households—divided into French- and English-speaking neighborhoods.

Little Rock Pond Shelter →

Built in 1962 by USFS and relocated from the pond's island in 1972. Maintained by GMC and USFS; caretaker; fee. Accommodates 8. Moldering privy. Water source is a spring 0.3 mile south on the A.T. Next shelter or campsite: south, 0.4 mile (Little Rock Pond Tenting Area); north, 4.6 miles (Greenwall).

Green Mountain Trail →

Follows the northern and western shores of Little Rock Pond and reaches the summit of Green Mountain (elev. 2,500 feet) in 1.0 mile, then continues 4.1 miles to USFS 10.

Homer Stone Brook Trail →

Descends 2.3 miles west to Homer Stone Road in South Wallingford, near U.S. 7.

Little Rock Pond Tenting Area →

Caretaker; fee. Tent platforms accommodate 28. Moldering privy. Water source is the spring 0.1 mile north on the A.T. Next shelter or campsite: south, 0.3 mile (Lula Tye); north, 0.4 mile (Little Rock Pond).

Little Rock Pond Loop Trail →

The original route of the A.T./Long Trail, this side trail skirts the western side of the pond and rejoins the A.T. by way of the Green Mountain Trail at the northern shore of pond.

N-S   │ TRAIL DESCRIPTION │

11.1	Cross South Wallingford–Wallingford Pond Road (snow-mobile trail).	**3.5**
11.3	Cross Homer Stone Brook on footbridge (elev. 1,900 feet).	**3.3**
11.5	Reach **Aldrichville clearing**.	**3.1**
12.2	Spur trail leads 100 feet east to **Little Rock Pond Shelter** (elev. 1,820 feet).	**2.4**
12.3	Reach northern end of Little Rock Pond and northern junctions with the **Green Mountain Trail** (elev. 1,854 feet) and the Little Rock Pond Loop Trail. The **Homer Stone Brook Trail** leaves the Green Mountain Trail 100 yards west of the A.T.	**2.3**
12.5	Pass spring.	**2.1**
12.6	Spur trail leads 100 feet east to **Little Rock Pond Tenting Area**.	**2.0**
12.7	Reach southern end of Little Rock Pond (elev. 1,854 feet) and southern junction with **Little Rock Pond Loop Trail**, which rejoins the A.T. at mile 12.3/2.3.	**2.9**

Lula Tye Shelter →

Built in 1962 by USFS. It was relocated from the current site of the caretaker platform on the pond in 1972 and named in memory of Miss Lula Tye, the GMC corresponding secretary from 1926 to 1955. Maintained by the GMC and USFS; caretaker; fee. Accommodates 8. Moldering privy. Water source is a spring 0.4 mile north on the A.T. Next shelter or campsite: south, 3.0 miles (Big Branch); north, 0.3 mile (Little Rock Pond Tenting Area).

Southern end of section →

The Trailhead on Danby–Landgrove Road (USFS 10) is 0.5 mile east of the Big Branch Picnic Area, 3.2 miles compass-east of Danby on U.S. 7, and 10.6 miles compass-west of North Landgrove. The road is not maintained in winter. It is paved from Danby but changes to gravel toward North Landgrove. Parking is available at both junctions with the road, 0.2 mile apart. At the northern junction on USFS 10, the primary parking lot is paved. At the southern junction, the parking area lot is smaller and pull-off style. Theft and vandalism have been reported; do not leave valuables in vehicles. Long-term parking is not recommended. Danby (ZIP Code 05739) is 3.2 miles west, with telephone, B&Bs, restaurants, and groceries. It is 5.5 miles, by way of U.S. 7 North in Danby, to Otter Creek Campground, with tentsites, shower, groceries, and long-term parking.

N-S

TRAIL DESCRIPTION

12.9   Spur trail (elev. 1,865 feet) leads 100 feet east to **Lula Tye Shelter**.   **2.7**

13.8   Rock hop across Little Black Branch.   **0.8**

14.0   Cross Little Black Branch over an I-beam bridge.   **0.6**

14.6   Reach northern junction with Danby–Landgrove Road   **0.0**
(USFS 10), just west of the bridge over Black Branch, and
the **southern end of section** (elev. 1,500 feet). ■ SOUTH-
BOUND hikers turn left over bridge and ascend 0.2 mile
on road before reentering woods on the right (see Vermont
Section Six). ■ NORTHBOUND hikers enter woods on old
logging road.

> ***Regulations***—*Camping and fires are restricted to
> shelters and designated campsites. Camping is
> prohibited in the vicinity of Clarendon Gorge.
> Camping within 0.5 mile of Little Rock Pond is
> limited to the following designated sites: Little Rock
> Pond Shelter, Little Rock Pond Tenting Area, and
> Lula Tye Shelter.*
>
> *The southern half of the section, from Vt. 140
> to Danby–Landgrove Road, lies within Green
> Mountain National Forest (GMNF). Throughout
> the GMNF, dispersed camping is allowed at least
> 200 feet from water and 100 feet from any trail;
> fires must be built in the fireplaces provided. No
> campfire permits are required. Cutting or damaging
> living trees, shrubs, and plants is prohibited. Only
> dead material on the ground may be used for fires.
> All trash must be carried out.*

S-N

Danby–Landgrove Road (USFS 10) to Vt. 11/30

17.8 MILES

The Trail in this section closely follows the crest of the Green Mountains through hardwood and spruce forests in the Green Mountain National Forest (GMNF). It traverses four summits: Baker Peak, Peru Peak, Styles Peak, and Bromley Mountain. It skirts the eastern shore of Griffith Lake and passes through the Big Branch Wilderness and the Peru Peak Wilderness. The A.T. and the Long Trail coincide throughout this section. The elevation at Danby–Landgrove Road (USFS 10) is 1,500 feet; at Vt. 11/30, 1,840 feet. The highest elevation is on Styles Peak, at 3,304 feet.

Road Approaches—Both ends are accessible by vehicle. Road access is also found at gravel Mad Tom Notch Road (USFS 21), mile 12.3/5.5.

Maps—For route navigation, refer to Map Seven with this guide or GMC's *Long Trail Guide* Long Trail Maps 3 and 4. For area detail but not current trail routes, refer to these USGS 15-minute topographic quadrangles: Wallingford and Londonderry, Vermont.

Shelters and Campsites—This section has five shelters—Big Branch (mile 1.3/16.5), Old Job (mile 1.5/16.3), Lost Pond (mile 3.0/14.8), Peru Peak (mile 7.7/10.1), and Bromley (mile 15.8/2.0)—and one tenting area, Griffith Lake Tenting Area (mile 7.2/10.6). The GMC stations a caretaker in the summer at Peru Peak Shelter and at the Griffith Lake Tenting Area to help hikers and supervise shelters and camping. At those sites, a fee is charged to help defray costs. Camping within 0.5 mile of Griffith Lake is limited to the Griffith Lake Tenting Area and Peru Peak Shelter.

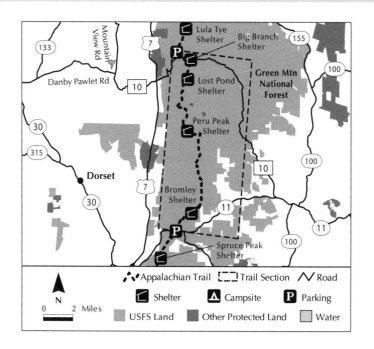

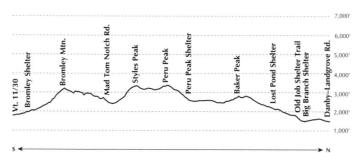

SECTION HIGHLIGHTS

Northern end of section →

The Trailhead on Danby–Landgrove Road (USFS 10) is 0.5 mile east of the Big Branch Picnic Area, 3.2 miles compass-east of Danby on U.S. 7, and 10.6 miles compass-west of North Landgrove. The road is not maintained in winter. It is paved from Danby but changes to gravel toward North Landgrove. Parking is available at both junctions with the road, 0.2 mile apart. At the northern junction on USFS 10, the primary parking lot is paved. At the southern junction, the parking area lot is smaller and pull-off style. Theft and vandalism have been reported; do not leave valuables in vehicles. Long-term parking is not recommended. Danby (ZIP Code 05739) is 3.2 miles west, with telephone, B&Bs, restaurants, and groceries. It is 5.5 miles, by way of U.S. 7 North in Danby, to Otter Creek Campground, with tentsites, shower, groceries, and long-term parking.

Big Branch Wilderness →

Congress designated the Big Branch Wilderness in 1984 and expanded it in 2006. It now has a total of 6,767 acres and is managed by the USFS. Named after Big Branch Stream, this area provides a home for wild turkeys, beavers, and moose. It is part of the Robert T. Stafford White Rocks National Recreation Area.

Big Branch Shelter →

This frame shelter was built in 1963 by USFS and is maintained by the GMC and USFS. Accommodates 8 at the shelter and 12 at tentsites. Moldering privy. Water source is Big Branch. Next shelter or campsite: south, 1.2 miles (Old Job by way of the Lake Trail) or 1.7 miles (Lost Pond); north 3.0 miles (Lula Tye).

Suspension bridge over Big Branch →

May be replaced soon, requiring a temporary reroute of the A.T./Long Trail. Look for updates at <www.greenmountainclub.org>.

N-S

TRAIL DESCRIPTION

0.0 The northern junction with Danby–Landgrove Road (USFS **17.8**
10), just west of the bridge over Black Branch, is the
northern end of section (elev. 1,500 feet). ■ SOUTHBOUND
hikers turn left over bridge and ascend 0.2 mile on road
before reentering woods on the right. ■ NORTHBOUND
hikers turn right and reenter woods on old logging road
(see Vermont Section Five).

0.2 Reach the southern junction with Danby–Landgrove Road **17.6**
(USFS 10) (elev. 1,530 feet). ■ SOUTHBOUND hikers enter
woods on right and descend. ■ NORTHBOUND hikers turn
left onto Danby–Landgrove Road, descend, and cross
bridge over Black Branch.

0.3 ■ SOUTHBOUND hikers enter the **Big Branch Wilderness**. **17.5**
■ NORTHBOUND hikers leave the Big Branch Wilderness.

1.3 Reach **Big Branch Shelter** (elev. 1,470 feet). **16.5**

1.4 Cross **suspension bridge over Big Branch** (elev. 1,500 **16.4**
feet). ■ SOUTHBOUND hikers cross bridge, turn left, and
follow Big Branch upstream. ■ NORTHBOUND hikers cross
bridge, turn left, and follow Big Branch to the west.

S-N

Old Job Trail →

Used as a lowland alternative between the Big Branch bridge and Griffith Lake, a distance of 5.4 miles (see mile 7.0/10.8).

Old Job Shelter →

On the Lake Trail. Built in 1935 by CCC and maintained by GMC and USFS. Accommodates 8 at the shelter shelter and 12 at tentsites. Privy. Water source is Lake Brook. Next shelter or campsite: south, 2.5 miles (Lost Pond); north, 1.2 miles (Big Branch).

Lost Pond Shelter →

The original shelter, a gift of Louis Stare, Jr., was built in 1965 on Cape Cod, dismantled, transported to this site, and reassembled. It was burned by vandals in November 2001 and rebuilt by GMC volunteers in 2002. It was burned again in November 2006. Plans to replace the shelter began in January 2007. Tenting is allowed at the site; tentsites accommodate 10. Privy. Water source is Stare Brook in a ravine below the site. Next shelter or campsite: south, 4.2 miles (Griffith Lake Tenting Area); north, 1.7 miles (Big Branch).

Baker Peak →

Views of the U.S. 7 valley. Danby and the north-flowing Otter Creek are directly below. Across the valley is Dorset Peak and its well-known marble quarry. Emerald Lake and Mt. Equinox are to the south, and the firetower on Stratton Mountain can be seen just behind the ridge of Peru Peak. Pico and Killington peaks are to the north; the Adirondacks, to the northwest. A Baker Peak bad-weather bypass leads east around the summit of Baker Peak; recommended in windy or slippery conditions.

Baker Peak Trail →

Descends 0.9 mile west to the Lake Trail, which leads 2.9 miles to U.S. 7 (see mile 6.9/10.9).

N-S

TRAIL DESCRIPTION

1.5 Reach northern junction (elev. 1,525 feet) with the **Old** **16.3**
Job Trail, which leads 1.0 mile east to **Old Job Shelter**
and rejoins the A.T. at mile 7.0/10.8. ■ SOUTHBOUND hikers bear right and begin steady ascent. ■ NORTHBOUND
hikers bear left along Big Branch to suspension bridge.

3.0 Spur trail leads 100 feet west to site of **Lost Pond Shelter** **14.8**
(elev. 2,150 feet).

3.2 Intersection with wide, grassy fire road. ■ SOUTHBOUND **14.6**
hikers turn right onto road, follow it for 100 yards, and
turn left into woods. ■ NORTHBOUND hikers turn right on
road, follow it for 100 yards, and turn left into woods on
old woods road.

4.5 Reach height of land. **13.3**

5.0 Cross summit of **Baker Peak** (elev. 2,850 feet). **12.8**

5.1 Pass junction with **Baker Peak Trail** to west (elev. 2,760 **12.7**
feet).

Baker Peak

S-N

Lake Trail →

Leads 3.3 miles west to South End Road at a point 0.5 mile east of U.S. 7 and 2.1 miles south of Danby.

Old Job Trail →

From its southern junction with the A.T., leads east along Lake Brook, crosses USFS 30 in 3.4 miles, reaches Old Job Shelter in 4.3 miles, and rejoins the A.T. in 5.4 miles at mile 1.5/16.3. Used as a lowland alternative between the Big Branch suspension bridge and Griffith Lake.

Griffith Lake Tenting Area →

Caretaker; fee. Tent platforms accommodate 20. Composting privy. Water source is at Peru Peak Shelter, mile 7.7/10.1. Next shelter: south, 0.5 mile (Peru Peak Shelter); north, 4.2 miles (Lost Pond).

Griffith Lake →

A 15-acre, spring-fed lake with a depth of about 22 feet. This was the private trout pond of Vermont's first millionaire, Silas Griffith (1837–1903), "Lumber King," who built a hotel on the shores to entertain his business guests.

Peru Peak Shelter →

This log structure originally was built by the CCC in 1935, rebuilt by the Youth Conservation Corps and USFS in 1979, and rebuilt again by the Long Trail Patrol and USFS in 2000. Maintained by the GMC and USFS; caretaker; fee. Accommodates 10; tent platform. Composting privy. Water source is the adjacent brook. Next shelter or campsite: south, 8.2 miles (Bromley Shelter); north, 0.5 mile (Griffith Lake Tenting Area).

Peru Peak Wilderness →

Congress designated the Peru Peak Wilderness in 1984, and it now has a total of 7,672 acres managed by the USFS. Peru Peak Wilderness takes its name from the highest mountain in the area. The A.T./L.T. crosses the southern end of the wilderness, which is part of the Robert T. Stafford White Rocks National Recreation Area.

N-S

TRAIL DESCRIPTION

6.0   Cross an old woods road.   **11.8**

6.1   Cross an old woods road.   **11.7**

6.9   Reach junction with the **Lake Trail** (elev. 2,620 feet).   **10.9**

7.0   Reach northern end of **Griffith Lake** and southern junction   **10.8**
         with the **Old Job Trail** (elev. 2,600 feet). The Griffith Lake
         Trail here leads 2.0 miles west to USFS 58. ■ SOUTHBOUND
         hikers leave **Big Branch Wilderness**. ■ NORTHBOUND hik-
         ers enter Big Branch Wilderness.

7.2   Pass to west of **Griffith Lake Tenting Area** on bog bridg-   **10.6**
         ing (elev. 2,600 feet).

7.4   Reach eastern shore of Griffith Lake (elev. 2,600 feet).   **10.4**

7.7   Pass **Peru Peak Shelter** (elev. 2,550 feet). ■ SOUTHBOUND   **10.1**
         hikers cross wooden bridge over brook and turn to the
         northeast of the shelter. ■ NORTHBOUND hikers cross a
         wooden bridge over the brook.

7.8   ■ SOUTHBOUND hikers enter **Peru Peak Wilderness** and   **10.0**
         ascend to Peru Peak. ■ NORTHBOUND hikers leave Peru
         Peak Wilderness and descend to Peru Peak Shelter.

8.6   Pass spring.   **9.2**

9.0   Reach wooded summit of Peru Peak (elev. 3,429 feet),   **8.8**
         with a short spur trail east to a lookout.

SECTION HIGHLIGHTS

Mad Tom Notch Road (USFS 21) →

This Trailhead is 4.0 miles west of Peru, Vermont. From Peru's J.J. Hapgood Store (0.3 mile north of Vt. 11, 3.5 mile east of the junction of Vt. 11/30 South, or 4.4 miles west of the junction of Vt. 11 and Vt. 100 South), follow the Landgrove Road–Hapgood Pond Road 1.0 mile to North Pond Road. Follow the initially paved North Pond Road 0.5 mile beyond the end of the pavement to the second left, which is gravel Mad Tom Notch Road (USFS 21). Follow this road for 2.1 miles to the height of land in Mad Tom Notch. A gravel parking lot on the south side of the road is just beyond the Trail crossing. The last mile is not plowed in winter. A large parking lot, maintained at the end of the plowed portion of the road, is popular with snowmobilers and open for all winter-recreation activities. The USFS Hapgood Pond Recreation Area, located on Hapgood Pond Road, is 3.0 miles east, 0.7 mile compass-north of North Road, with camping. It is 4.0 miles to Peru (ZIP Code 05152), with groceries.

Mad Tom Notch →

The nearby Mad Tom Brook got its name from the tumbling rush it makes as it flows westward down the mountain into Dorset.

Bromley Mountain →

The summit station of the Big Bromley chair lift, the ski-patrol warming hut, and an observation tower are 100 feet to the east, with views in all directions, including Stratton Mountain and Mt. Equinox. Moldering privy on the west. Bromley Ski Area generously allows hikers to use its ski-patrol warming hut. This use depends on respect for the facility, and its availability is subject to change.

N-S	TRAIL DESCRIPTION	

10.7	Reach rock outcrop on the summit of Styles Peak (elev. 3,394 feet), with views east and south toward **Bromley Mountain**.	**7.1**
12.2	■ SOUTHBOUND hikers leave **Peru Peak Wilderness**. ■ NORTHBOUND hikers enter Peru Peak Wilderness and ascend steeply.	**5.6**
12.3	Cross gravel **Mad Tom Notch Road (USFS 21)** at height of land in **Mad Tom Notch** (elev. 2,446 feet). ■ SOUTH-BOUND hikers pass to the west of a water pump, cross gravel road, and ascend Bromley Mountain. ■ NORTH-BOUND hikers cross road and pass to the west of a water pump.	**5.5**
14.3	Pass over northern summit of **Bromley Mountain** (elev. 3,120 feet).	**3.5**
14.8	Reach summit of **Bromley Mountain** (elev. 3,260 feet). ■ SOUTHBOUND hikers turn right, descending on western-most, wide, novice ski trail. ■ NORTHBOUND hikers continue along western edge of clearing, turn left past an old outhouse, and leave northern side of open summit, descending steeply.	**3.0**
15.0	■ SOUTHBOUND hikers turn right off wide novice ski trail, enter woods, and descend. ■ NORTHBOUND hikers turn left on wide novice ski trail and follow it uphill.	**2.8**

Bromley Shelter →

This post-and-beam structure was built by Erik and Laurel Tobiason and the GMC Manchester Section in 2003 and is maintained by GMC and USFS. Accommodates 12 at the shelter and 10 at four tent platforms 0.1 mile north on the Trail. Handicap-accessible, composting privy. Water source is a spring just below the shelter on an extension of the spur trail. Next shelter or campsite: south, 5.0 miles (Spruce Peak); north, 8.2 miles (Peru Peak).

Southern end of section →

The Trail crossing is 5.8 miles compass-east of Vt. 7A in Manchester Center, 4.5 miles compass-east of the U.S. 7 interchange, and 0.5 mile compass-west of the junction of Vt. 11 and Vt. 30 South. A large, paved parking lot is located on the north side of the road. A hotel and restaurant are 1.8 miles east, groceries are 2.5 miles east, an inn and restaurant are 2.7 miles east, and Peru (ZIP Code 05152) is 4.4 miles east, with groceries. Manchester Center (ZIP Code 05255) is 5.8 miles west, with telephone, motels, inns, B&Bs, restaurants, supermarkets, outfitters, bookstore, cobbler, coin laundry, doctor, dentist, pharmacy, and a local bus stop. Marble Valley Regional Transit community bus, (802) 773-3244, serves the U.S. 7 corridor from Manchester to Rutland and U.S. 4 to Killington. Green Mountain Express, (802) 447-0477, has daily bus service to Bennington.

N-S

| | TRAIL DESCRIPTION | |

15.7	Pass Bromley Shelter tent platforms.	2.1
15.8	Spur trail leads 100 yards east to **Bromley Shelter** (elev. 2,500 feet).	2.0
17.1	Cross bridge over Bromley Brook (elev. 2,080 feet).	0.7
17.5	Pass under power line.	0.3
17.6	Cross bridge over brook on I-beam bridge.	0.2
17.7	Cross gravel road. ■ SOUTHBOUND hikers turn right onto road and follow it to parking lot. ■ NORTHBOUND hikers turn left off road and enter woods.	0.1
17.8	The parking lot on Vt. 11/30 is the **southern end of section** (elev. 1,840 feet). ■ SOUTHBOUND hikers pass through parking lot, cross Vt. 11/30, climb highway bank, and reenter woods (see Vermont Section Seven). *Use caution when crossing Vt. 11/30; traffic moves at a high rate of speed.* ■ NORTHBOUND hikers follow gravel road (abandoned old Vt. 11) from the northern end of the parking lot.	0.0

> *Regulations*—This section lies within the Green Mountain National Forest (GMNF). Camping is restricted to shelters and designated campsites or at least 200 feet from any water and 100 feet from the Trail, if not at those sites. Fires at designated sites must be built in the fireplaces provided; campfire permits are not required. Only downed wood may be used for fires. Cutting or damaging living trees, shrubs, and plants is prohibited. All trash must be carried out.

S-N

Vt. 11/30 to Stratton–Arlington (Kelley Stand) Road

17.5 MILES

The most notable features in this section are Stratton Pond on the western slope of Stratton Mountain and the summit itself. In the mid-nineteenth century, Stratton Mountain was the hub of a prosperous farming community. The area has since reverted to woodland, but cellar holes, apple trees, and lilac bushes are reminders that people once lived in this remote part of the Green Mountains. The Trail passes through the Lye Brook Wilderness and is mostly forested with northern hardwoods. Thickets of small spruce dot the area. Remnants of railroad grades and old logging roads remain. Many marshy areas are close to the Trail, and the over-all ecological balance is quite fragile. Be prepared for muddy trails and an intense black-fly season in the spring and early summer. The A.T. and the Long Trail coincide throughout this section. The elevation at Vt. 11/30 is 1,840 feet; at Stratton–Arlington (Kelley Stand) Road, 2,230 feet. The highest elevation is the summit of Stratton Mountain, at 3,936 feet.

Road Approaches—Both ends are accessible by vehicle.

Maps—For route navigation, refer to Maps Seven and Eight with this guide or GMC's *Long Trail Guide* Map 3. For area detail, refer to the USGS 15-minute topographic quadrangle for Londonderry, Vermont, or the 7½-minute quadrangles for Manchester and Sunderland, Vermont.

Shelters and Campsites—This section has three shelters—Spruce Peak (mile 2.8/14.7), William B. Douglas (mile 5.8/11.7), and Stratton Pond (mile 10.6/6.9)—and one tenting area, North Shore (mile 10.4/7.1). The GMC stations a caretaker at Stratton Pond to supervise camping in the vicinity, so a fee is charged to help defray costs.

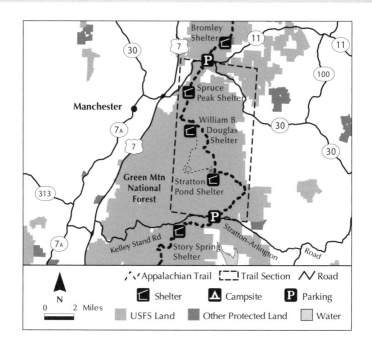

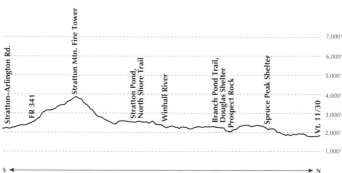

SECTION HIGHLIGHTS

Northern end of section →

The Trail crossing is 5.8 miles compass-east of Vt. 7A in Manchester Center, 4.5 miles compass-east of the U.S. 7 interchange, and 0.5 mile compass-west of the junction of Vt. 11 and Vt. 30 South. A large, paved parking lot is located on the north side of the road. A hotel and restaurant are 1.8 miles east, groceries are 2.5 miles east, an inn and restaurant are 2.7 miles east, and Peru (ZIP Code 05152) is 4.4 miles east, with groceries. Manchester Center (ZIP Code 05255) is 5.8 miles west, with telephone, motels, inns, B&Bs, restaurants, supermarkets, outfitters, bookstore, cobbler, coin laundry, doctor, dentist, pharmacy, and a local bus stop. Marble Valley Regional Transit community bus, (802) 773-3244, serves the U.S. 7 corridor from Manchester to Rutland and U.S. 4 to Killington. Green Mountain Express, (802) 447-0477, has daily bus service to Bennington.

Spruce Peak Shelter →

Log structure with a sliding door, front porch, and woodstove, constructed in 1983 by the Brattleboro Section of GMC, USFS, and a work crew from the Rutland Community Correctional Center. Maintained by GMC and USFS. Accommodates 16 at the shelter and 10 at tentsites. Composting privy. Water source is a reliable piped spring 100 feet beyond the shelter at the end of the spur trail. Next shelter or campsite: south, 3.6 miles (William B. Douglas); north, 5.0 miles (Bromley Shelter).

Prospect Rock →

Blue-blazed spur descends 50 yards west (elev. 2,079 feet) to views of Manchester and Mt. Equinox (elev. 3,848 feet).

Old Rootville Road →

Descends (straight ahead) to a gate near a water tank at 1.8 miles and, 0.2 mile beyond, to East Manchester Road 100 yards east of Vt. 11/30 at a point 2.0 miles east of Manchester Center at U.S. 7A.

N-S

	TRAIL DESCRIPTION	

0.0 The parking lot on Vt. 11/30 is the **northern end of section** (elev. 1,840 feet). ▪ Southbound hikers pass through the parking lot, cross Vt. 11/30, climb the highway bank, reenter the woods, and pass among large boulders. *Use caution when crossing Vt. 11/30; traffic moves at a high rate of speed.* ▪ Northbound hikers follow gravel road (abandoned old Vt. 11) from the northern end of the parking lot (see Vermont Section Six).   **17.5**

0.4 Cross abandoned old Vt. 30 and a bridge over a stream.   **17.1**

0.5 Cross a stream.   **17.0**

1.9 Cross a woods road, under a power line, and a small brook.   **15.6**

2.4 Spur trail leads 100 yards west to Spruce Peak (elev. 2,040 feet), with views of the Taconic Range and valley below.   **15.1**

2.8 Spur trail leads 0.1 mile west to **Spruce Peak Shelter** (elev. 2,220 feet).   **14.7**

3.2 Pass west of a summit.   **14.3**

4.9 Reach junctions with spur trail to **Prospect Rock** and with **Old Rootville Road** (elev. 2,150 feet). ▪ Southbound hikers turn left, ascending on Old Rootville Road, follow it for nearly a mile, and turn right off road at a clearing. ▪ Northbound hikers turn sharply right off the road, ascend on stone steps, and reenter woods.   **12.6**

S-N

SECTION HIGHLIGHTS

Branch Pond Trail →
Leads west 0.5 mile to William B. Douglas Shelter, 4.0 miles to Lye Brook Trail junction at Bourn Pond, and, by way of Lye Brook Trail, back to A.T. at Stratton Pond in 6.5 miles—or 6.8 miles to USFS 70 and 8.3 miles to Stratton–Arlington (Kelley Stand) Road.

William B. Douglas Shelter →
An original closed shelter at this site was Swezey Camp, built in 1935. Another shelter was built in 1956 and renamed to honor a GMC trail-maintainer from Brattleboro who headed the construction team. It was extensively renovated in 2005. Maintained by GMC and USFS. Accommodates 10. Privy. Water source is a spring 50 feet south. Next shelter or campsite: south, 5.6 miles (North Shore); north, 3.6 miles (Spruce Peak).

Lye Brook Wilderness →
Congress established the Lye Brook Wilderness in 1975, and it now has a total of 17,841 acres managed by the USFS. This area is named after Lye Brook, which flows through its western half. Most of the wilderness is above 2,500 feet on a high plateau with several ponds and bogs. The western section is extremely steep, facing west-north-west toward U.S. 7 and Manchester. The A.T./Long Trail crosses the northwest tip of the wilderness area and may be more challenging to follow due to the minimal trail maintenance and minimal blazing prescribed for wilderness areas.

North Shore Trail →
Leads west 0.5 mile to North Shore Tenting Area and 0.7 mile to Lye Brook Trail at the outlet of Stratton Pond.

North Shore Tenting Area →
Caretaker; fee. Three tent platforms accommodate 24. Composting privy. Water source is Stratton View Spring, 0.1 mile west. Next shelter or campsite: south, 0.7 mile (Stratton Pond); north, 5.6 miles (William B. Douglas).

N-S

TRAIL DESCRIPTION

5.8 Cross brook on bridge and, 100 feet south on A.T., at Lye   **11.7**
Brook Wilderness northern boundary (elev. 2,280 feet),
reach junction with **Branch Pond Trail**, which leads west
to **William B. Douglas Shelter** and rejoins the A.T. by way
of the Lye Brook Trail at mile 10.5/7.0. ■ SOUTHBOUND
hikers follow old woods road, in and out of the woods,
and enter **Lye Brook Wilderness**. ■ NORTHBOUND hikers
leave Lye Brook Wilderness, cross brook on bridge, enter
clearing, turn left on Old Rootville Road, and follow it
for nearly a mile.

8.6 Cross footbridge over the Winhall River (elev. 2,175   **8.9**
feet).

10.4 Reach northeastern corner of Stratton Pond (elev. 2,555   **7.1**
feet). The **North Shore Trail** leads west to the **North Shore
Tenting Area**. ■ SOUTHBOUND hikers leave the **Lye Brook
Wilderness**. ■ NORTHBOUND hikers bear right, leave shoreline (coinciding with the Catamount Trail), follow a woods
road, and enter the Lye Brook Wilderness.

S-N

SECTION HIGHLIGHTS

Willis Ross Clearing→

Former site of Willis Ross Camp, built in 1929 and burned in 1972. The foundation stones are visible at the eastern end.

Stratton Pond →

Stratton Pond, the largest pond on the Long Trail, is a popular spot for swimming and fishing and receives the heaviest overnight use of any campsite on the L.T. Overuse has had serious impacts on the pond's fragile shoreline. A GMC caretaker stays near Willis Ross Clearing during prime hiking seasons to assist and educate hikers, help maintain the local trails and campsites, and compost sewage to protect water quality.

Lye Brook Trail→

Leads west 0.1 mile to a spring, 0.6 mile to the North Shore Trail on Bourn Pond, and 9.7 miles to Manchester. It crosses the Branch Pond Trail, which leads to the William B. Douglas Shelter in 6.0 miles and rejoins the A.T. 0.5 mile farther at mile 5.8/11.7.

Stratton Pond Trail→

Leads west 50 yards to trail to Stratton Pond Shelter and 3.7 miles to Stratton–Arlington (Kelley Stand) Road.

Stratton Pond Shelter →

This post-and-beam structure, built by the GMC Worcester Section in 1999, is dedicated to the memory of Robert Humes, longtime GMC Worcester Section volunteer and past GMC president. Maintained by GMC and USFS; caretaker; fee. Accommodates 20. Composting privy. Water source is Bigelow Spring, 0.1 mile west of Willis Ross Clearing on the Lye Brook Trail. Next shelter or campsite: south, 10.6 miles (Story Spring); north, 0.7 mile (North Shore).

N-S

TRAIL DESCRIPTION

10.5	Reach **Willis Ross Clearing** at **Stratton Pond** and intermittent spring (unreliable) 25 feet north on Trail (elev. 2,555 feet). The **Lye Brook Trail** leads west to Bigelow Spring (unreliable) and rejoins the A.T. by way of the Branch Pond Trail at mile 5.8/11.7. ■ Southbound hikers turn left. ■ Northbound hikers turn right.	**7.0**
10.6	Pass junction (elev. 2,620 feet) with **Stratton Pond Trail**, which leads west to a 100-yard spur trail to **Stratton Pond Shelter**.	**6.9**
11.0	Pass a beaver pond.	**6.5**
11.1	Cross a bridge over a brook.	**6.4**
11.7	Cross gravel International Paper (IP) road.	**5.8**
13.0	Pass view to west of Stratton Pond, Lye Brook Wilderness, and Mt. Equinox.	**4.5**
13.5	Pass spring to the east.	**4.0**

Stratton Pond

S-N

SECTION HIGHLIGHTS

Fire tower →

Provides views of the surrounding mountains: to the north, Stratton's north peak and gondola station and, on a clear day, Killington Peak; to the northeast, Mt. Ascutney; to the southeast, Mt. Monadnock in New Hampshire; to the south, Sommerset Reservoir and Mt. Snow; to the southwest, Glastenbury Mountain; to the west, the Taconics, including Mt. Equinox, the highest peak in the range.

Stratton Mountain →

A GMC summit caretaker may be on duty to assist hikers. From the firetower, an old service road leads straight ahead, following the ridge 0.7 mile to the north peak of Stratton Mountain, with its gondola and access to Stratton Ski Area and Stratton Village below. In 1909, James P. Taylor was on the mountain when he conceived the idea of a "footpath in the wilderness" from Massachusetts to Canada, which became the Long Trail in 1910. While on the summit, he once wrote, Benton MacKaye imagined a trail spanning the Appalachian range, an idea fleshed out in his 1921 proposal for "an Appalachian Trail."

Stratton–Arlington (Kelley Stand) Road →

This road was once used for travel between Boston and Saratoga Springs, New York. Kelley Stand was a stage stop for travelers.

Southern end of section →

The Trail crosses the Stratton–Arlington (Kelley Stand) Road 200 feet east of the East Branch of the Deerfield River, 11.5 miles southwest of Stratton, 6.8 miles west of West Wardsboro on Vt. 100, and 13 miles east of Arlington. Parking is on the northern side of the road, just beyond the bridge over the East Branch. Much of the road east to West Wardsboro is paved. To the west to Arlington, it is a narrow gravel road not maintained in winter or "mud season" (mid-May, usually). Regular maintenance begins June 1 and ends on November 1. The GMNF Grout Pond Campground is 0.7 mile east. West Wardsboro (ZIP Code 05360) has a small grocery store. Arlington (ZIP Code 05250) has inns and groceries.

N-S

	TRAIL DESCRIPTION	

13.7 Reach **fire tower** on south peak of **Stratton Mountain** (elev. 3,936 feet). *Camping is prohibited.* **3.8**

14.3 Pass spring on the west. **3.2**

14.8 Reach col between Stratton and Little Stratton mountains. **2.7**

15.5 Pass vista to south. **2.0**

16.1 Cross gravel International Paper road (elev. 2,520 feet). **1.4**

17.5 Reach **Stratton–Arlington (Kelley Stand) Road** at former site of Grout Job, an old logging camp, and the **southern end of section** (elev. 2,230 feet). ■ SOUTHBOUND hikers turn right and follow road over East Branch of the Deerfield River (see Vermont Section Eight). ■ NORTHBOUND hikers enter woods on the northern side of the road and follow a fairly level route, passing a beaver pond. **0.0**

Regulations—Camping within 0.5 mile of Stratton Pond is limited to the following designated sites: North Shore Tenting Area and Stratton Pond Shelter. Fires are prohibited at Stratton Pond Shelter. Camping is not allowed on Stratton Mountain.

The Trail from Prospect Rock to the Winhall River is in the Green Mountain National Forest's Lye Brook Wilderness. Camping and fires are regulated. Camping in the wilderness is restricted to designated campsites and shelters or dispersed to sites 200 feet from water and 100 feet from any trail. Throughout GMNF, fires at designated sites must be built in the fireplaces provided. Campfire permits are not required. Cutting or damaging living trees, shrubs, and plants is prohibited. Only wood on the ground may be used for fires. All trash must be carried out.

S-N

Stratton–Arlington (Kelley Stand) Road to Vt. 9

22.6 MILES

This is the longest section of the Trail in Vermont that does not cross a road and can be best described with one word, "remote." From both ends of this section, the Trail ascends to and follows a rolling ridge through a backcountry of hardwoods and evergreens to the summit of Glastenbury Mountain in the center of the section. The summit, completely covered in tall spruce, was believed by some early native Americans to be an evil spirit that swallowed interlopers. To the south of Goddard Shelter, the Trail enters the Glastenbury Wilderness for eight miles. The A.T. and the Long Trail coincide throughout this section. The elevation at Stratton–Arlington (Kelley Stand) Road is 2,230 feet; at Vt. 9, 1,360 feet. The highest elevation is on the summit of Glastenbury Mountain, at 3,748 feet.

continued on page 268

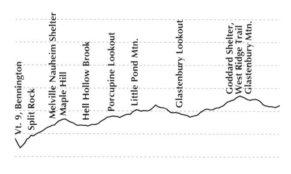

22.6 MILES

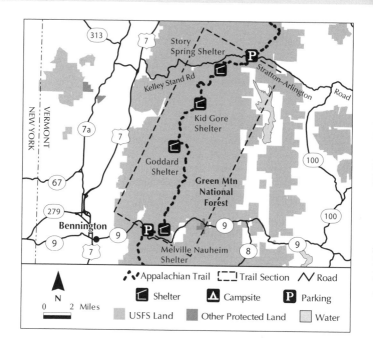

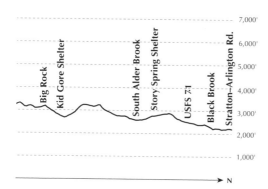

Road Approaches—Both ends are accessible by vehicle.

Maps—For route navigation, refer to Map Eight with this guide, the GMC's *Long Trail Guide* Map 2, or "Vermont's Long Trail: Waterproof Hiking Map (revised third edition)," from the Wilderness Map Company. For area detail but not current trail routes, refer to the USGS 15-minute topographic quadrangle for Londonderry, Vermont, or the 7½-minute quadrangles for Sunderland and Woodford, Vermont.

Shelters and Campsites—This section has four shelters: Story Spring (mile 3.6/19.0), Kid Gore (mile 8.4/14.2), Goddard (mile 12.5/10.1), and Melville Nauheim (mile 21.0/1.6).

Hell Hollow Brook

SECTION HIGHLIGHTS

Northern end of section →

The Trail crosses the Stratton–Arlington (Kelley Stand) Road 200 feet east of the East Branch of the Deerfield River, 11.5 miles southwest of Stratton, 6.8 miles west of West Wardsboro on Vt. 100, and 13 miles east of Arlington. Parking is on the northern side of the road, just beyond the bridge over the East Branch. Much of the road east to West Wardsboro is paved. To the west to Arlington, it is a narrow gravel road not maintained in winter or "mud season" (mid-May, usually). Regular maintenance begins June 1 and ends on November 1. The GMNF Grout Pond Campground is 0.7 mile east. It is 6.8 miles east to West Wardsboro (ZIP Code 05360), with a small grocery store. Arlington (ZIP Code 05250) is 13 miles west, with inns and groceries.

USFS 71 →

Leads west 0.8 mile west to Stratton–Arlington (Kelley Stand) Road and the Stratton Pond Trail trailhead parking lot.

Story Spring Shelter →

Built in 1963 by USFS and named in honor of George F. Story, an active trail worker in the GMC Worcester Section. Maintained by GMC and USFS. Accommodates 8 at the shelter and 16 at tentsites. Privy. Water source is a spring 50 yards north on the A.T. Next shelter or campsite: south, 4.7 miles (Kid Gore); north, 10.6 miles (Stratton Pond).

N-S

TRAIL DESCRIPTION

0.0	The Stratton–Arlington (Kelley Stand) Road at the former site of Grout Job, an old logging camp, is the **northern end of section** (elev. 2,230 feet). ■ SOUTHBOUND hikers follow road from the parking lot right, crossing the East Branch of the Deerfield River. ■ NORTHBOUND hikers enter woods (see Vermont Section Seven).	22.6
0.1	Pass southern junction with Kelley Stand Road (elev. 2,240 feet). ■ SOUTHBOUND hikers turn left off road and enter woods. ■ NORTHBOUND hikers turn right and follow road over East Branch of the Deerfield River to the Trailhead parking lot on northern side of road.	22.5
0.9	Cross Black Brook footbridge (elev. 2,220 feet), rebuilt in 2002 by the volunteer Long Trail Patrol.	21.7
2.0	Cross gravel **USFS 71** (elev. 2,380 feet)	20.6
3.6	Reach **Story Spring Shelter** (elev. 2,810 feet). A spring is 50 yards north on the A.T.	19.0
4.3	Pass old beaver ponds.	18.3
4.5	Cross two adjacent branches of South Alder Brook (elev. 2,600 feet).	18.1
7.5	Pass to the west of an unnamed summit (elev. 3,412 feet) just north of Lydia's Rest (elev. 3,300 feet), which offers views to the west.	15.1
8.0	Cross brook.	14.6

S-N

SECTION HIGHLIGHTS

Kid Gore Shelter and Caughnawaga Tentsites →

Log lean-to built in 1971 by GMC and Camp Najerog alumni. Named in memory of Harold M. ("Kid") Gore, who ran Camp Najerog. Maintained by GMC and USFS. Accommodates 8 at the shelter and 12 at the tentsites. Privy. Water sources are a spring 30 feet north of shelter (unreliable) and a reliable brook north on the Trail in Glen Haven. Next shelter or campsite: south, 4.4 miles (Goddard); north, 4.7 miles (Story Spring).

Glastenbury Mountain →

This remote summit lies in the center of the unincorporated town of Glastenbury in Bennington County. The township is now almost entirely in the GMNF, but, for much of the last century, it was owned by one family. Timber magnate Trenor W. Park passed Glastenbury along to his grandson, Hall Park McCullough, whose grandson, Trenor Scott, sold most of his holdings to the Forest Service. By the late 1880s, Glastenbury was completely clear-cut to supply vast quantities of charcoal to the iron industry in nearby Shaftsbury and Troy, New York. Glastenbury is now a rich mosaic of balsam fir, red spruce, white and yellow birch, beech, and mountain ash and supports mature forest. It is interspersed with patches of ferns, raspberries, blackberries, bluebead lily, and dwarf dogwood.

Fire tower →

The abandoned 1927 firetower has been renovated by USFS as an observation deck. The view from the tower has been described as "more wilderness than is to be seen from any other point on the Long Trail." The panorama from the tower includes, to the south, the Berkshires and Mt. Greylock; to the west, the Taconic Range; to the north, Mt. Equinox and Stratton Mountain; and to the east, Somerset Reservoir, Mt. Snow, and Haystack Mountain.

N-S

TRAIL DESCRIPTION

8.2	Reach the northern junction with the loop trail to **Kid Gore Shelter** and the **Caughnawaga Tentsites** in Glen Haven and, 200 feet to the south on the Trail, the southern junction (elev. 2,800 feet) with the loop, which leads 0.1 mile east to the shelter. ■ SOUTHBOUND hikers turn sharply right, cross a brook, and ascend on a wet ledge. ■ NORTHBOUND hikers turn sharply right, descend on a wet ledge, and cross brook.	**14.4**
8.9	Pass Big Rock (elev. 3,250 feet).	**13.7**
11.2	Cross a snowmobile trail.	**11.4**
12.2	Reach the summit of **Glastenbury Mountain** and a former **fire tower** (elev. 3,748 feet). *To protect the water quality of a spring below, camping on the summit is discouraged.*	**10.4**
12.3	Pass site of former firewarden's cabin to west.	**10.3**

Glastenbury fire tower

S-N

SECTION HIGHLIGHTS

Goddard Shelter →

This timber frame lean-to was built in 2005 by Erik and Laurel Tobiason with GMC volunteers, friends, USFS crews, and the Keenan family. It was named in honor of Ted Goddard, former president and treasurer of the GMC. Maintained by GMC and USFS. Accommodates 12. Moldering privy. The water source is a spring 40 feet south on the Trail. Please tent above the shelter, to the west of the A.T. *To preserve the pristine nature of the spring, no tenting is allowed east of the Trail up the mountain.* The view to the south is of Mt. Greylock in Massachusetts. Next shelter or campsite: south, 8.5 miles (Melville Nauheim); north, 4.4 miles (Kid Gore).

West Ridge Trail →

Blue-blazed trail leads 7.8 miles southwest along the ridge, with no water on the southern half, to the Bald Mountain Trail, which leads east 3.1 miles to Vt. 9 or west 3.5 miles to Bennington.

Hell Hollow Brook →

Hell Hollow Brook contributes to the water supply of Bennington.

Power line →

Views to the west of Bennington and Mt. Anthony and to the east of Mt. Snow, Haystack Mountain, and the northern end of the Hoosac Range.

Glastenbury Wilderness →

Congress designated the Glastenbury Wilderness in 2006. It has a total of 22,425 acres and is managed by the USFS. The forestland and extensive stands of mature beech trees provide critical habitat for black bears. The presence of Bicknell's thrush (designated in Vermont and other Trail states as rare and of special concern) has been documented, as has Swainson's thrush, the yellow-rumped and Cape May warblers, winter wren, dark-eyed junco, and white-throated sparrow.

N-S	TRAIL DESCRIPTION	
12.5	Reach **Goddard Shelter**; a spring is 40 feet south on Trail. Also reach junction with the **West Ridge Trail** (elev. 3,560 feet). ■ SOUTHBOUND hikers turn left and descend toward the spring, entering the **Glastenbury Wilderness.** ■ NORTHBOUND hikers leave the Glastenbury Wilderness, turn right behind the shelter, and climb.	**10.1**
13.8	Pass large rectangular boulder near an unnamed summit (elev. 3,150 feet).	**8.8**
14.5	Cross an old woods road.	**8.1**
15.0	Reach Glastenbury Lookout (elev. 2,920 feet), with view of Glastenbury Mountain and West Ridge.	**7.6**
16.0	Pass west of unnamed peak (elev. 3,331 feet).	**6.6**
16.8	Pass Little Pond Lookout (elev. 3,060 feet), with views to the east.	**5.8**
17.1	Reach wooded summit of Little Pond Mountain (elev. 3,100 feet).	**5.5**
18.2	Reach Porcupine Lookout (elev. 2,815 feet).	**4.4**
19.2	Pass through balsam and spruce swamp on puncheon.	**3.4**
19.4	Cross bridge (elev. 2,350 feet) over **Hell Hollow Brook**, last reliable water northbound until Goddard Shelter. *Camping is prohibited along the brook.*	**3.2**
19.7	Cross a small stream.	**2.9**
20.3	Cross the wooded summit of Maple Hill.	**2.3**
20.5	Cross under **power line** on Maple Hill (elev. 2,620 feet). ■ SOUTHBOUND hikers leave the **Glastenbury Wilderness**. ■ NORTHBOUND hikers enter the Glastenbury Wilderness.	**2.1**

SECTION HIGHLIGHTS

Melville Nauheim Shelter→

This frame structure was built in 1977 by the GMC with funds contributed by Mrs. Melville Nauheim of New York City in memory of her husband. Maintained by the GMC and USFS. Accommodates 8. Privy. Water is available from a stream where the spur trail leaves the A.T. Next campsite or shelter: south, 5.9 miles (Congdon); north, 8.5 miles (Goddard).

William A. MacArthur Memorial Bridge→

Built by the USFS in memory of a dedicated volunteer trail maintainer with the Pioneer Valley and Bennington sections of the GMC.

Southern end of section →

From the Trail crossing on Vt. 9, it is 5.0 miles west to downtown Bennington, 2.8 miles east to Woodford (telephone, groceries), and 8.8 miles east to the junction of Vt. 9 and Vt. 8 South. A USFS parking lot with a privy is on the north side of the road, just west of the Trail. Theft and vandalism have been reported here; do not leave valuables in cars. Local bus service is available to the Trailhead from Bennington; call to make arrangements with Green Mountain Express, (802) 447-0477; $2, Monday–Friday. Daily bus service to Manchester also is available. Woodford State Park campground is 4.8 miles east, and the GMNF Red Mill Campground is 0.2 mile beyond that. A diner is 3.4 miles west, and a motel, restaurant, and groceries are 3.9 miles west. Bennington (ZIP Code 05201) offers telephones, motels, restaurants, supermarkets, an outfitter, coin laundry, cobbler, hospital, doctors, pharmacy, hardware store, local bus service, and a number of special hiker-focused activities.

N-S

	TRAIL DESCRIPTION	

21.0 South of a brook crossing (elev. 2,300 feet), a spur trail leads 100 yards east to **Melville Nauheim Shelter**. **1.6**

21.1 Cross a woods road. **1.5**

21.3 Cross a woods road. **1.3**

21.9 Pass through fissure of Split Rock (elev. 1,900 feet). **0.7**

22.6 Cross City Stream on **William A. MacArthur Memorial Bridge** and reach Vt. 9 at **southern end of section** (elev. 1,360 feet). *Use caution when crossing Vt. 9; traffic moves at high rates of speed.* ■ SOUTHBOUND hikers cross road, walk through parking area on south side of the road, re-enter woods, and climb steeply on rock steps (see Vermont Section Nine). ■ NORTHBOUND hikers cross the road, bear right, reach a footbridge over a stream, turn left, follow briefly downstream, and then bear right uphill, for a steep climb on switchbacks. **0.0**

> **Regulations**—This section passes through the Green Mountain National Forest (GMNF). Camping is prohibited between Maple Hill and Porcupine Lookout and along Hell Hollow Brook, to protect the city of Bennington's public water supply. Elsewhere, camp at least 200 feet from water and 100 feet from trails. Fires at designated sites must be built in the fireplaces provided; elsewhere, use camping stoves. Cutting or damaging living trees and plants is prohibited. Only downed wood may be used for fires. All trash must be carried out.

S-N

Vt. 9 to Mass. 2 (North Adams)

18.4 MILES

The southernmost section in Vermont ascends steeply from Vt. 9 to open vistas on Harmon Hill, then follows a rolling ridge to the Vermont–Massachusetts border at an elevation of 2,330 feet. For the convenience of hikers, the Trail route described in this chapter extends south beyond the state border to include the Appalachian Trail in Massachusetts (Massachusetts Section One) to Mass. 2 in North Adams. South from the state line, the Trail passes over the open, rocky ridge of East Mountain, then drops to the Hoosic River, following logging roads through lowland hardwood forests. The A.T. and the Long Trail coincide from Vt. 9 to the state line. The elevation at Vt. 9 is 1,360 feet; at Mass. 2 (North Adams), 650 feet. The highest elevation is a nameless ridge south of Roaring Branch that reaches 3,025 feet.

Road Approaches—Both ends are accessible by vehicle. Road access is also available at seasonal County Road (mile 11.2/7.2).

continued on page 280

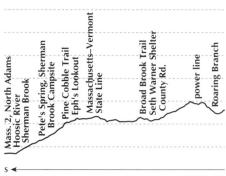

S ◄—

18.4 MILES

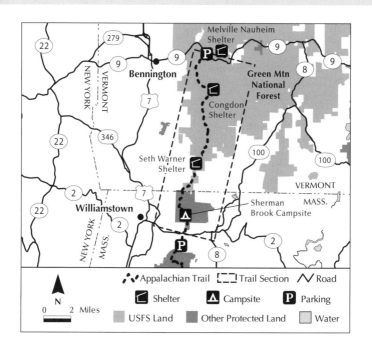

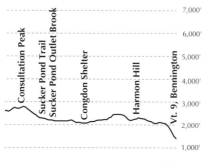

Maps—For route navigation, refer to Map Eight with this guide; the GMC *Long Trail Guide* Map 1; "Vermont's Long Trail Waterproof Hiking Map (revised third edition)," from the Wilderness Map Company; the Williams Outing Club's *North Berkshire Outdoor Guide*; or Map One accompanying the *Appalachian Trail Guide to Massachusetts–Connecticut*. For area detail but not current trail routes, refer to the USGS 15-minute topographic quadrangle for Bennington, Vermont, and the USGS 7½-minute quadrangles for Woodford, Bennington, Stamford, and Pownal, Vermont, and Williamstown, Massachusetts.

Shelters and Campsites—This section has two shelters—Congdon (mile 4.3/14.1) and Seth Warner (mile 11.5/6.9)—and two campsites, Seth Warner Primitive Tenting Area (mile 11.5/6.9) and Sherman Brook Primitive Campsite (mile 16.6/1.8).

Sucker Pond

SECTION HIGHLIGHTS

Northern end of section →

From the Trail crossing on Vt. 9, it is 5.0 miles west to downtown Bennington, 2.8 miles east to Woodford (telephone, groceries), and 8.8 miles east to the junction of Vt. 9 and Vt. 8 South. A USFS parking lot with a privy is on the north side of the road, just west of the Trail. Theft and vandalism have been reported here; do not leave valuables in cars. Local bus service is available to the Trailhead from Bennington; call to make arrangements with Green Mountain Express, (802) 447-0477; $2, Monday–Friday. Daily bus service to Manchester also is available. Woodford State Park campground is 4.8 miles east, and the GMNF Red Mill Campground is 0.2 mile beyond that. A diner is 3.4 miles west, and a motel, restaurant, and groceries are 3.9 miles west. Bennington (ZIP Code 05201) offers telephones, motels, restaurants, supermarkets, an outfitter, coin laundry, cobbler, hospital, doctors, pharmacy, hardware store, local bus service, and a number of special hiker-focused activities.

Harmon Hill →

Views to the north are of Bald and Glastenbury mountains; to the west, of Mt. Anthony, the village of Bennington, and the 306-foot-tall stone obelisk known as the Battle of Bennington Monument, dedicated to the Battle of Bennington during the Revolutionary War in 1777. Controlled burns are used as a management tool by the USFS here to retain the vistas and provide wildlife clearings.

Old Bennington–Heartwellville Road →

This road leads 4.0 miles west to Vt. 9 by way of Burgess Road, 1.0 mile east of U.S. 7 in Bennington. To the east, this road leads to Stamford Stream and the woods road to Dunville Hollow.

N-S	TRAIL DESCRIPTION	

0.0	The **northern end of section** is at Vt. 9 (elev. 1,360 feet). *Use caution when crossing Vt. 9; traffic moves at high rates of speed.* ■ SOUTHBOUNDERS cross road through parking area on south side, enter woods, and climb steeply on rock steps. ■ NORTHBOUND hikers cross road, bearing right, and reach a footbridge over a stream (see Vermont Section Eight).	**18.4**
0.6	■ SOUTHBOUND hikers bear left, and climb more gradually, eventually reaching a clearing. ■ NORTHBOUND hikers bear right and descend more steeply on rock steps.	**17.8**
1.8	Reach open summit of **Harmon Hill** (elev. 2,325 feet).	**16.6**
2.1	Cross a brook.	**16.3**
2.9	Traverse a small clearing. ■ SOUTHBOUND hikers descend steadily and pass two woods roads.	**15.5**
3.6	Cross small stream. ■ NORTHBOUND hikers climb steadily and pass two woods roads.	**14.8**
3.7	Cross **Old Bennington–Heartwellville Road** (elev. 2,220 feet).	**14.7**
4.1	Trail skirts west of a former area of beaver activity.	**14.3**

SECTION HIGHLIGHTS

Congdon Shelter →

This open-front, frame cabin was built by the Long Trail Patrol in 1967 and modified by GMC Pioneer Valley Section volunteers in 1994. It is named for Herbert Wheaton Congdon, a Long Trail pioneer, trail-builder, guidebook editor, and cartographer. Maintained by GMC and USFS. Accommodates 8 at the shelter and 16 at tentsites on the ridge above the privy. The water source is a brook east of the shelter. Next shelter or campsite: south, 7.4 miles (Seth Warner); north, 5.9 miles (Melville Nauheim).

Beaver →

Prior to European settlement, almost every body of water in Vermont had beavers. By the middle of the 19th century, all of the beaver in the state had been trapped out. Beaver were reintroduced in the 1920s and 1930s and have been very successful at recolonizing every area of the state.

Sucker Pond →

Bennington's public water supply. *No swimming or camping.*

Consultation Peak →

Says the GMC *Long Trail Guide*: "Named by volunteer trail workers because of its strategic location for planning maintenance activities."

N-S	TRAIL DESCRIPTION	
4.3	Reach **Congdon Shelter** (elev. 2,080 feet).	**14.1**
4.9	Descend to Stamford Stream.	**13.5**
5.2	Cross woods road.	**13.2**
5.4	Pass the stone foundation of a nineteenth-century tavern.	**13.0**
5.7	Pass over "**beaver**-challenged" puncheon through a wetland in Stamford Meadows.	**12.7**
5.9	Cross Sucker Pond's outlet brook (elev. 2,180 feet).	**12.5**
6.3	Cross a well-traveled woods road that leads 0.2 mile west to a clearing on the eastern shore of **Sucker Pond** and 5.9 miles east to Vt. 9.	**12.1**
7.3	Reach wooded northwest summit of **Consultation Peak** (elev. 2,840 feet).	**11.1**
8.0	Pass over minor knob.	**10.4**
8.3	Pass over minor knob.	**10.1**
8.5	Cross Roaring Branch at the base of a beaver dam (elev. 2,470 feet).	**9.9**

Beaver

SECTION HIGHLIGHTS

County Road →

It is 4.2 miles east by way of Mill Road to Stamford at a point 0.5 mile compass-north of Billmont's Country Store and 6.8 miles compass-south of the junction of Vt. 8 and Vt. 100 in Readsboro. This road is not passable by vehicle 4.0 miles west to the Barber Pond Road junction in Pownal. Parking area for four cars is on the south side of road. The final 0.9 mile is not plowed in winter.

Seth Warner Primitive Camping Area →

Tentsites accommodates 16. Privy. Water source is 600 feet west, beyond Seth Warner Shelter; may fail in dry seasons.

Seth Warner Shelter →

This frame lean-to was built by carpenter trainees organized under the Manpower Development Training Act in 1965. Maintained by the GMC and USFS. Accommodates 8. Privy. A brook that may fail in dry seasons is located 400 feet west of the shelter. Next shelter or campsite: south, 5.4 miles (Sherman Brook); north, 7.4 miles (Congdon).

Broad Brook Trail →

Initially follows the road to the west, then descends 4.0 miles to White Oaks Road 3.0 miles north of Williamstown. Stream crossings along it are difficult in times of high water.

N-S	TRAIL DESCRIPTION	
8.7	Follow along eastern shore of old beaver pond, with good view of Scrub Hill.	**9.7**
9.2	Cross northern summit of nameless ridge (elev. 2,900 feet).	**9.2**
9.4	Pass under power line.	**9.0**
9.8	Reach southern summit of nameless ridge (elev. 3,025 feet), with views to the south and west.	**8.6**
10.0	Pass a lookout, with view south to Mt. Greylock.	**8.4**
10.3	Blue-blazed trail leads east 100 feet to boxed Ed's Spring.	**8.1**
11.2	Cross **County Road** (elev. 2,290 feet).	**7.2**
11.4	Pass under power line.	**7.0**
11.5	Blue-blazed side trail (elev. 2,200 feet) leads 0.1 mile west to **Seth Warner Primitive Camping Area** and 0.2 mile west to **Seth Warner Shelter**.	**6.9**
11.7	Cross narrow dirt road at junction with **Broad Brook Trail** (elev. 2,130 feet). ■ SOUTHBOUND hikers continue along eastern side of ridge, crossing three former logging roads and two small streams.	**6.7**
11.9	Cross a woods road.	**6.5**
12.6	Pass over a bedrock ridge.	**5.8**
13.9	Cross a brook. ■ NORTHBOUND hikers climb to eastern side of low ridge, follow old woods road for some distance, bear left, regain ridge with limited views, and cross three former logging roads and two small streams.	**4.5**

SECTION HIGHLIGHTS

Long Trail →

The state boundary is the southern terminus of the 272-mile Long Trail, maintained by the GMC. The A.T. and Long Trail coincide for more than 105 miles between here and Maine Junction, north of Sherburne Pass and U.S. 4 (see Vermont Section Three).

Southern end of Vermont Section Nine →
Northern end of Massachusetts Section One →

The Vermont–Massachusetts state line is high atop East Mountain. The nearest resupply point is 4.1 miles south in North Adams (see mile 18.4/0.0).

Eph's Lookout →

Named for Ephraim Williams, the founder of Williams College.

'98 Trail →

Leads 1.5 miles west to intersect the Pine Cobble Trail near Bear Spring.

High point →

Located near the southern end of an extensive area on East Mountain that is still recovering from an old forest fire and now covered with blueberry bushes. Provides views to the south of the Berkshire Hills (Hoosac Range on the left and the Taconics on the right) and Mt. Greylock, the highest peak in Massachusetts (elev. 3,491 feet).

Pine Cobble Trail →

Descends 0.2 mile west to Pine Cobble (elev. 1,894 feet) and 1.9 miles farther to Cole Avenue in Williamstown, Massachusetts.

Sherman Brook Primitive Campsite →

Tentsites, with a privy. Water source is Pete's Spring on the A.T. (mile 16.6/2.0). Next shelter or campsite: south, 5.2 miles (Wilbur Clearing); north, 5.4 miles (Seth Warner).

N-S

| TRAIL DESCRIPTION |

14.3 Cross Vermont–Massachusetts state line and reach the southern terminus of the **Long Trail,** the **southern end of Vermont Section Nine,** and **the northern end of Massachusetts Section One** (elev. 2,330 feet). **4.1**

14.9 Pass **Eph's Lookout** (elev. 2,254 feet). **3.5**

15.1 Reach junction with the **'98 Trail**. **3.3**

15.6 Reach **high point** of open, rocky knoll and junction with the **Pine Cobble Trail** (elev. 2,010 feet). ■ SOUTHBOUND hikers turn left and begin descent. ■ NORTHBOUND hikers turn right along ridge. **2.8**

15.7 Skirt marshy pond to the west. **2.7**

15.8 Reach on west the northern junction of a bad-weather route that avoids a steep rock slide and rejoins the A.T. at mile 16.0/2.4. **2.6**

16.0 Pass southern junction on west of bad-weather route that avoids a steep rock slide and rejoins the A.T. at mile 15.8/2.6. **2.4**

16.3 Pass northern end of a loop side trail that leads 100 yards to **Sherman Brook Primitive Campsite** and rejoins the A.T. at mile 16.6/1.8. ■ SOUTHBOUND hikers leave old woods road. ■ NORTHBOUND hikers join and follow old woods road. **2.1**

16.4 Meet Sherman Brook at old bridge abutments. **2.0**

16.6 Reach Pete's Spring (elev. 1,300 feet) on the east at southern end of loop trail that leads 0.1 mile to **Sherman Brook Primitive Campsite** and rejoins the A.T. at mile 16.3/2.1. **1.8**

S-N

Southern end of Massachusetts Section One →

Mass. 2 at the footbridge over the Hoosic River, opposite Phelps Avenue, is 3.0 miles east of the Williamstown business area and 2.4 miles west of the center of North Adams. No parking is available at this Trailhead. Hikers may obtain permission to park at the Greylock Community Club, at the owner's risk, 0.1 mile east of the A.T., or at the Our Lady of Mercy Catholic Church, 100 yards west of the A.T. (permission from the pastor). Berkshire Regional Transit Authority (BRTA), (800) 292-2782, has hourly bus service on Mass. 2, connecting Williamstown to Great Barrington. Buses can be flagged down anywhere on Mass. 2 or 8 and U.S. 7, Monday–Saturday. A telephone, restaurants, supermarket, and coin laundry are 0.6 mile east. The YMCA ($2 showers, pool) is 1.0 mile east. It is 2.5 miles east to North Adams (ZIP Code 01247), with motels, restaurants, supermarket, hospital, doctor, dentist, cobbler, and a local bus stop. To the west, it is 0.4 mile to telephone, lodging, supermarket, and pharmacy; 1.4 miles to motels, restaurants, and groceries; and 2.9 miles to the Williamstown business district (ZIP Code 01267), with inns, restaurants, an outfitter, coin laundry, health clinic, doctor, dentist, pharmacy, Peter Pan Bus Lines (800 343-9999), and local BRTA bus stops.

N-S

TRAIL DESCRIPTION

17.7 ■ SOUTHBOUND hikers reach Sherman Brook and follow it downhill. ■ NORTHBOUND hikers make a short, steep ascent away from the brook and then descend.   **0.7**

18.1 Reach small reservoir on Sherman Brook.   **0.3**

18.2 Northern junction with Massachusetts Avenue. ■ SOUTHBOUND hikers turn right and follow Massachusetts Avenue. ■ NORTHBOUND hikers, just before reaching stone bridge, turn left up driveway and, after 50 feet, turn left onto private road, cross two foot bridges, and enter woods.   **0.2**

18.3 Southern junction with Massachusetts Avenue. ■ SOUTHBOUND hikers turn left and cross footbridge over railroad tracks and Hoosic River. ■ NORTHBOUND hikers turn right onto Massachusetts Avenue.   **0.1**

18.4 Reach North Adams, Massachusetts, on Mass. 2, opposite Phelps Avenue, the **southern end of Massachusetts Section One** (elev. 650 feet). ■ SOUTHBOUND hikers proceed straight ahead on Phelps Avenue (see Massachusetts Section Two). ■ NORTHBOUND hikers cross the footbridge over the Hoosic River and railroad tracks (elev. 650 feet).   **0.0**

> ***Regulations***—*This section passes through the Green Mountain National Forest (GMNF) and the Stamford Meadows Wildlife Management Area and follows a narrow, publicly owned Trail corridor surrounded by private property. In accordance with Vermont law and GMC/landowner agreements, camping and fires are permitted only at designated sites, even on GMNF and Vermont state lands. Small wood fires, although discouraged, are permitted in the shelters' established fire rings.*

S-N

Major side trails and suggested day trips

The A.T. and an extensive side-trail system in New Hampshire and Vermont provide innumerable possibilities for hiking and backpacking trips. The side trails of the White Mountains of New Hampshire and the Green Mountains of Vermont make loop trips possible. The segment of the A.T. between the White and Green Mountains has fewer side trails but offers excellent hiking. Trips in that area often require car shuttling to avoid retracing one's steps.

This chapter lists the major side trails in each section by intersection and briefly describes one possible day-hike per section. For further suggestions and greater detail, we suggest you consult *Best of the Appalachian Trail—Day Hikes,* available from ATC; the Appalachian Mountain Club's *White Mountain Guide;* or the Green Mountain Club's *Long Trail Guide.* For maps, refer to the A.T. maps that accompany this guidebook and maps listed in the introduction to a particular section.

Please see "Questions and Answers about the Appalachian Trail" (page 298) for information on what to pack on a day trip. For more information on a particular side trail, depending on the section, contact either the Appalachian Mountain Club, the Dartmouth Outing Club, or the Green Mountain Club (see "For More Information," page 349).

NEW HAMPSHIRE SECTION ONE

Four side trails can be found in this section: the Success Trail (mile 1.3/15.2), Austin Brook Trail (mile 4.7/11.8), Peabody Brook Trail (mile 6.9/9.6), and Mahoosuc Trail (mile 12.6/3.9).

Mt. Hayes—By way of the Centennial Trail from Hogan Road; 6.6 miles round trip (5 hours); 1,996-foot elevation gain; moderate.

NEW HAMPSHIRE SECTION TWO

This section has a number of side trails that provide interesting side or loop hikes. From N.H. 16 to the west, several side trails provide access to the A.T. To the east, several side trails lead into the Wild River Wilderness of the WMNF. Hikers may ride the Wildcat ski-area chairlift when it is in operation. For more information, consult the AMC's *White Mountain Guide.*

Carter Dome—This domed ledge is the site of a former firetower, with views into Carter Notch. By way of the Nineteen-Mile Brook Trail, Carter Dome Trail, and the A.T., beginning at N.H. 16; return on the A.T. and Nineteen-Mile Brook Trail by way of Carter Notch; 10 miles (8 hours); 3,604-foot elevation gain; loop hike; difficult.

NEW HAMPSHIRE SECTION THREE

This section has a comprehensive system of side trails that offers many possibilities for loop hikes, side trips, and alternate routes; most trails are briefly described in the Trail highlights. For detailed information on the side trails in this section, consult the AMC's *White Mountain Guide.*

Lowe's Bald Spot—A rocky knob with fine views of the Great Gulf Wilderness. Beginning at Pinkham Notch Visitors Center, by way of the Old Jackson Road trail, cross the Mt. Washington Auto Road, reenter woods, and continue on the Madison Gulf Trail; sign will be on the east for spur trail that leads 200 feet east; 4.4 miles round trip (4.5 hours); 950-foot elevation gain; moderate.

NEW HAMPSHIRE SECTION FOUR

This section has several side trails that offer many possibilities for loop hikes, side trips, and alternate A.T. routes and are briefly described in the Trail description. For further information on the side trails in this section, consult the AMC's *White Mountain Guide.*

Franconia Ridge—Superb views from very exposed, above-treeline ridge. Beginning at the Falling Waters trailhead at Lafayette Place East, ascend on the Falling Waters Trail to Little Haystack, turn north on the Franconia Ridge Trail/A.T. to Mt. Lafayette (elev. 5,260 feet); descend on the Greenleaf Trail to Greenleaf Hut; and continue back to Lafayette Place on the Old Bridle Path Trail; 8.7 miles (8 hours); 4,147-foot elevation gain; 4,085-foot elevation loss; loop hike; difficult.

NEW HAMPSHIRE SECTION FIVE

This section has several side trails that offer many possibilities for loop hikes, side trips, and alternate A.T. routes and are briefly described in the Trail description. For further information on the side trails in this section, consult the AMC *White Mountain Guide*.

Lonesome Lake—By way of the Lonesome Lake Trail, Cascade Brook Trail/A.T., Basin–Cascade Trail, and Pemi Trail; 5.6 miles (4 hours); 1,328-foot elevation gain; loop hike; moderate.

NEW HAMPSHIRE SECTION SIX

This section has six side trails: Asquam Ridge Trail (mile 1.9/7.6); Benton Trail (mile 3.4/6.1); Gorge Brook Trail (mile 3.8/5.7); Moosilauke Carriage Road (mile 4.7/4.8); Moosilauke South Peak Spur Trail (mile 4.7/4.8); and Hurricane Ridge Trail (mile 7.3/2.2). For further information on the other trails in this section, consult the AMC *White Mountain Guide,* or contact the Dartmouth Outing Club (DOC) through <www.dartmouth.edu/~doc>.

Mt. Moosilauke—Great views, very exposed, above treeline. From Glencliff by way of the Glencliff Trail/A.T. and Carriage Road/A.T.; spur trail to South Peak (elev. 4,523 feet) adds 0.4 mile; 7.8 miles round trip (5.5 hours); 3,348-foot elevation gain; moderate.

NEW HAMPSHIRE SECTION SEVEN

This section has one side trail, Webster Slide Trail at mile 2.3/7.5.

Wachipauka Pond and Webster Slide Mountain—A spectacular outlook from the eastern ledges and a view of the pond. By way of the Wachipauka Pond Trail/A.T. and Webster Slide Trail, beginning at N.H. 25; 6 miles round trip (4.5 hours); 1,533-foot elevation gain; moderate.

NEW HAMPSHIRE SECTION EIGHT

This section has six side trails: North Cube Side Trail (mile 3.3/12.7), Mt. Cube Section Trail (mile 3.5/12.5), Kodak Trail (mile 3.5/12.5), J Trail (mile 6.3/9.7), Daniel Doan Trail (mile 10.2/5.8), and Smarts Mountain Ranger Trail (mile 10.8/5.2).

Smarts Mountain—Views from an abandoned firetower on the summit. By way of the Lambert Ridge Trail/A.T. and Smarts Mountain Ranger Trail; 7.6 miles (5 hours); 2,130-foot elevation gain; loop hike; moderate.

NEW HAMPSHIRE SECTION NINE

This section has three side trails: Fred Harris Trail (mile 8.8/7.3), Trescott Road Spur Trail (mile 15.0/1.1), and the Velvet Rocks Loop (mile 15.6/0.5).

South Moose Mountain—Views to the east of Mt. Cardigan and Mt. Kearsarge. By way of the A.T. from Three Mile Road, Old Wolfeboro Road, and the Harris Trail; 4.1 miles (3.5 hours); loop hike; easy.

VERMONT SECTION ONE

This section has one side trail, the Tucker Trail at mile 5.1/4.2. For current information on trails in this section, contact the Dartmouth Outing Club.

VERMONT SECTION TWO

This section has no side trails, but many woods and abandoned roads intersect the Trail.

DuPuis Hill—Views of Mt. Ascutney and Pico and Killington peaks from the open, grassy summit. By way of the Pomfret–South Pomfret Road; 2.6 miles round trip (3 hours); 750-foot elevation gain; easy.

VERMONT SECTION THREE

This section has three side trails—Thundering Falls Spur (mile 18.3/5.4), Sherburne Pass Trail (mile 21.8/1.9), and Deer Leap Trail (miles 21.8/1.9 and 22.6/1.1)—and one woods road, Lookout Farm Road (mile 5.4/18.3). For more information on the Long Trail and the A.T. in this section, refer to GMC's *Long Trail Guide*, available from GMC (see "For More Information," page 349).

Deer Leap Overlook—Views of Sherburne Pass and the Coolidge Range. By way of the A.T. on U.S. 4 north to Maine Junction at Willard Gap, take the southern junction of the Deer Leap Trail to the overlook spur, then walk to the northern junction of the Deer Leap Trail, returning southbound on the A.T. to U.S. 4; 4.7 miles (3 hours); 710-foot elevation gain; loop hike; easy.

VERMONT SECTION FOUR

This section has five side trails: Sherburne Pass Trail (mile 3.8/13.6), Pico Link (mile 3.8/13.6), Bucklin Trail (mile 6.1/11.3), Killington Spur Trail (mile 6.3/11.1), and Shrewsbury Peak Trail (mile 8.0/9.4).

Pico Peak—By way of the Sherburne Pass Trail from U.S. 4 to Pico Link to the A.T. at "Jungle Junction," then north on the A.T. to U.S. 4; 8.4 miles (6.5 hours); 1,910-foot elevation gain; loop hike; moderate.

VERMONT SECTION FIVE

This section has four side trails: Keewaydin Trail (mile 7.1/7.5), White Rocks Cliff Trail (mile 8.3/6.3), Homer Stone Brook Trail (mile 12.3/2.3), and Green Mountain Trail (mile 12.3/2.3).

White Rocks Cliff Overlook—Views of Wallingford Valley, west into the Taconics, and north and south along the U.S. 7 corridor. From Vt. 140, return by way of the Keewaydin Trail and Vt. 140; 5.0 miles (3.5 hours); 1,240-foot elevation gain; loop hike; easy.

VERMONT SECTION SIX

This section has three side trails: Old Job Trail (mile 1.5/16.3), Baker Peak Trail (mile 5.1/12.7), and Lake Trail (mile 6.9/10.9).

Baker Peak—By way of the South End Road near U.S. 7 in Danby to Baker Peak, using the Lake Trail, the Baker Peak Trail, and the A.T.; return on the Baker Peak and Lake trails; 5.8 miles (4 hours); 2,130-foot elevation gain; loop hike; moderate.

VERMONT SECTION SEVEN

Five side trails are shown in this section: Old Rootville Road (mile 4.9/12.6), Branch Pond Trail (mile 5.8/11.7), North Shore Trail (mile 10.4/7.1), Lye Brook Trail (mile 10.5/7.0), and Stratton Pond Trail (mile 10.6/6.9).

Stratton Mountain and Stratton Pond—By way of the the A.T. from Stratton–Arlington (Kelley Stand) Road; return by way of the Stratton Pond Trail (former A.T.) and Stratton–Arlington Road; 11.5 miles (6.5 hours); 1,706-foot elevation gain; a long loop hike; moderate.

VERMONT SECTION EIGHT

This section has one side trail, the West Ridge Trail (mile 12.5/10.1).

Split Rock—A steady climb to a huge boulder, split into two upright halves. By way of the A.T. north from Vt. 9; 1.4 miles round-trip (1.5 hours); 540-foot elevation gain; moderate.

VERMONT SECTION NINE

This section has three side trails: Broad Brook Trail (mile 11.7/6.9), '98 Trail (mile 15.1/3.3), and Pine Cobble Trail (mile 15.6/2.8).

Harmon Hill—A seriously steep ascent on a rock staircase of more 500 steps is rewarded with views of the historic village of Bennington from an open field. By way of the A.T. south from Vt. 9; 3.6 miles round-trip (2.5 hours); 965-foot elevation gain; moderate.

Questions and answers about the Appalachian Trail

Preparation

What should I carry?

The A.T. is enjoyable to hike, but inexperienced hikers—even those just out for an hour or two—can quickly find themselves deep in the woods, on steep terrain, and in wet, chilly conditions. Carrying a basic "kit" helps hikers cope with such situations.

Packing for a day-hike is relatively simple:

> Map and compass (learn to use them first!)
> Water (at least 2–3 quarts)
> Warm clothing and rain gear
> Food (including extra high-energy snacks)
> Trowel (to bury human waste) and toilet paper
> First-aid kit, with blister treatments
> Whistle (three blasts is the international signal for help)
> Garbage bag (to carry out trash)

On longer hikes, especially in remote or rugged terrain, add:

> Flashlight (with extra batteries and bulb)
> Heavy-duty garbage bag (emergency shelter or to insulate
> a hypothermia victim)
> Sharp knife
> Fire starter (a candle, for instance) and waterproof matches

If you're backpacking and plan to camp out, we suggest you consult a good "how-to" book for details about what to carry or talk to an experienced hiker. Although we don't have room here to discuss gear in detail, most A.T. backpackers carry the following items, in addition to the day-hike checklist. Some of the items can be shared with a partner to lighten the load:

Shelter (a tent or tarp)
Lightweight pot, cooking utensils
Stove (a small backpacking model, with fuel)
Medium-sized backpack (big "expedition-size" packs
    are usually overkill)
A pack cover or plastic bag (to keep gear dry in rainy weather)
Sleeping pad (to insulate you from the cold ground)
Sleeping bag of appropriate warmth for the season
Food and clothing
Rope or cord (to hang your food at night)
Water filter, iodine tablets, or another method of treating water

Where can I park?
Park in designated areas. Many of them will be indicated in the Trailhead entries for this guidebook and may be marked on Trail maps. If you leave your car overnight unattended, however, you risk theft or vandalism. Many hikers avoid this worry by arranging for a "shuttle" (check <www.appalachiantrail.org> for a list) to drop them off at a Trailhead or arranging to leave their car in the parking lot of a business located near the Trail; ask first, and offer to pay a little something to the business. Some sections of the Trail are served by public transportation. If you decide to park at a Trailhead, hide your property and valuables from sight, or, better yet, leave them at home, so they do not inspire a thief to break in and steal them.

Using the Trail

Where and how do I find water?
Year-round natural water sources are listed in this guidebook; springs and streams are marked on most official A.T. maps. Most (although not all) shelters are near a year-round water source. Some springs and streams dry up during late summer and early fall.

Is the water safe to drink?
Water in the backcountry and in water sources along the A.T. can be contaminated by microorganisms, including *giardia lamblia* and others that cause diarrhea or stomach problems. We recommend that you

treat all water, using a filter or purifier or water-treatment tablets, or by boiling it.

Are there rest rooms?
Many A.T. shelters have privies, but usually you will need to "go in the woods." Proper disposal of human (and pet) waste is not only a courtesy to other hikers, but a vital Leave No Trace practice for maintaining healthy water supplies in the backcountry and an enjoyable hiking experience for others. No one should venture onto the A.T. without a trowel, used for digging a "cathole" 6"–8" deep to bury waste. Bury feces at least two hundred feet or seventy paces away from water, trails, or shelters. Use a stick to mix dirt with your waste, which hastens decomposition and discourages animals from digging it up. Used toilet paper should either be buried in your cathole or carried out in a sealed plastic bag. Hygiene products such as sanitary napkins should always be carried out.

Can I wash up in a mountain stream or spring?
Please don't. Carry water from the water source in a bottle or other container, and then wash your dishes, and yourself, at least 70 paces away from streams, springs, and ponds. Don't leave food scraps to rot in water sources, and don't foul them with products such as detergent, toothpaste, and human or animal waste.

Are bikes allowed on the Trail?
Only where the Appalachian Trail shares the route with the C&O Towpath in Maryland, the Virginia Creeper Trail in the vicinity of Damascus, Virginia, roads in towns, and on certain bridges. They are not permitted on most of the Trail.

Can I bring my dog?
Yes, except where dogs are prohibited (in Great Smoky Mountains National Park, Bear Mountain Zoo, and Baxter State Park). Dogs must be leashed on National Park Service lands and on many state park and forest lands. ATC's Web site, <www.appalachiantrail.org>, offers details about hiking with dogs. Although dogs can be wonderful hiking companions, they can create many problems for other hikers and wildlife if you don't control them. If taken, they should not be allowed to run free; leashing

at all times is strongly recommended and the law on 40 percent or more of the Trail. Keep dogs out of springs and shelters and away from other hikers, their food, and their gear. Not all dogs can stand the wear and tear of a long hike.

How about horses, llamas, or other pack stock?
Horses are not allowed on the A.T., except where the Appalachian Trail coincides for about three miles with the C&O Canal Towpath in Maryland and on about 50 percent of the A.T. in the Smokies (where, by law, the route is open for horses as a historical use). Llamas and other pack animals are not allowed on the A.T., which is designed, built, and maintained for foot travel. Pack animals would seriously damage the treadway, discourage volunteer maintenance efforts, and make the Trail experience less enjoyable for other hikers.

Are any fees required to hike the A.T.?
No. However, there are entrance fees to some of the national parks the Trail passes through, as well as parking fees and campsite fees in popular areas, to help pay for maintenance costs.

Health and safety

Is the Trail a safe place?
In general, yes. But, like many other popular recreational activities, hiking on the A.T. is not without risk. Don't let the following discussion of potential dangers alarm you or discourage you from enjoying the Trail, but remember not to leave your common sense and intuition behind when you strap on your backpack. Prepare mentally and emotionally.

In an emergency, how do I get help?
Much of the A.T. is within range of cellular phone systems, although signal reception is sometimes not good in gaps, hollows, and valleys; shelters are often located in such areas of poor reception. Emergency numbers are included in this guidebook and on maps. If you don't have a phone or can't get through, the standard call for distress consists of three short calls, audible or visible, repeated at regular intervals. A whistle is particularly good for audible signals. Visible signals may include, in

daytime, light flashed with a mirror or smoke puffs; at night, a flashlight or three small bright fires. Anyone recognizing such a signal should acknowledge with two calls—if possible, by the same method—then go to the distressed person to determine the nature of the emergency.

Most of the A.T. is well-enough traveled that, if you are injured, you can expect to be found. However, if an area is remote and the weather is bad, fewer hikers will be on the Trail, especially after dark. As a rule, keep your pack with you, and, even in an emergency, don't leave marked trails and try to "bushwhack" out—you will be harder to find and are more likely to encounter dangerous terrain. If you must leave the Trail, study the guidebook or map carefully for the nearest place where people are likely to be and attempt to move in that direction. If it is necessary to leave a heavy pack behind, be sure to take essentials, in case your rescue is delayed. In bad weather, a night in the open without proper covering could be fatal.

What's the most dangerous aspect of hiking the A.T.?
Perhaps the most serious dangers are hypothermia (see page 304), a fall on slick rocks and logs, or a sprained or broken limb far from the nearest rescue squad or pay phone. Those are also the best arguments for hiking with a partner, who can get help in an emergency.

What sort of first-aid kit should I pack?
A basic kit to take care of bruises, scrapes, skinned knees, and blisters. The following kit weighs about a pound and occupies about a 3" x 6" x 9" space: eight 4" x 4" gauze pads; four 3" x 4" gauze pads; five 2" bandages; ten 1" bandages; six alcohol prep pads; ten large butterfly closures; one triangular bandage (40"); two 3" rolls of gauze; twenty tablets of aspirin-free pain-killer; one 15' roll of 2" adhesive tape; one 3" Ace bandage; one 3" x 4" moleskin or other blister-care products; three safety pins; one small scissors; one tweezers; personal medications as necessary.

Will I encounter snakes?
Poisonous and nonpoisonous snakes are widespread along the Trail in warm weather, but they will usually be passive. Watch where you step and where you put your hands. Please, don't kill snakes! Some are federally protected under the Endangered Species Act.

What other creatures are problems for people?

Allergic reactions to bee stings can be a problem. Ticks, which carry Lyme disease, are also a risk; always check yourself for ticks daily. Poisonous spiders are sometimes found at shelters and campsites. Mosquitoes and blackflies may plague you in some seasons. Porcupines, skunks, raccoons, and squirrels are quite common and occasionally raid shelters and well-established camping areas after dark, looking for food. Mice are permanent residents at most shelters and may carry diseases.

What about bears?

Black bears live along most parts of the Trail and are particularly common in Georgia, the Shenandoah and Great Smoky Mountains national parks, and parts of Pennsylvania and New Jersey. They are always looking for food. Bears that have lost their fear of humans may "bluff charge" to get you to drop food or a backpack. If you encounter a black bear, it will probably run away. If it does not, back away slowly, watching the bear but not making direct eye contact. Do not run away or play dead. If a bear attacks, fight for all you are worth. The best defense against bears is preparing and storing food properly. Cook and eat your meals away from your tent or shelter, so food odors do not linger. Hang your food, cookware, toothpaste, and personal-hygiene items in a sturdy bag from a strong tree branch at least ten feet off the ground, four feet from the tree and branch, and well away from your campsite.

Is poison ivy common along the A.T.?

Yes. It grows plentifully in the wild, particularly south of New England, and can be an annoyance during hiking season. If you have touched poison ivy, wash immediately with strong soap (but not with one containing added oil). If a rash develops in the next day or so, treat it with calamine lotion or Solarcaine. Do not scratch. If blisters become serious or the rash spreads to the eyes, see a doctor.

Will I catch a disease?

The most common illnesses encountered on the A.T. are water-borne, come from ingesting protozoa (such as *giardia lamblia*), and respond well to antibiotics. But, the Lyme-disease bacterium and other tick-borne illnesses are legitimate concerns, too; mosquito-borne illnesses such as the West Nile virus are less common in Trail states. Cases of rabies have been reported in foxes, raccoons, and other small animals; a bite is a serious concern, although instances of hikers being bitten are rare. One case of the dangerous rodent-borne disease hantavirus has been reported on the A.T.: Avoid sleeping on mouse droppings (use a mat or tent) or handling mice. Treat your water, and wash your hands.

Will I encounter hazardous weather?
Walking in the open means you will be susceptible to sudden changes in the weather, and traveling on foot means that it may be hard to find shelter quickly. Pay attention to the changing skies. Sudden spells of "off-season" cold weather, hail, and even snow are common along many parts of the Trail. Winter-like weather often occurs in late spring or early fall in the southern Appalachians, Vermont, New Hampshire, and Maine. In the northern Appalachians, it can snow during any month of the year.

What are the most serious weather-related dangers?
Hypothermia, lightning, and heat exhaustion are all legitimate concerns. Don't let the fear ruin your hike, but take sensible precautions.

Hypothermia—A cold rain can be the most dangerous weather of all, because it can cause hypothermia (or "exposure") even when conditions are well above freezing. Hypothermia occurs when wind and rain chill the body so that its core temperature drops; death occurs if the condition is not caught in time. Avoid hypothermia by dressing in layers of synthetic clothing, eating well, staying hydrated, and knowing when to hole up in a warm sleeping bag in a tent or shelter. Cotton clothing, such as blue jeans, tends to chill you when it gets wet from rain or sweat; if the weather turns bad, cotton clothes increase your risk of hypothermia. Natural wool and artificial fibers such as nylon, polyester, and polypropylene all do a much better job of insulation in cold, wet weather. Remember that, when the wind blows, its "chill" effect can make you much colder than the temperature would lead you to suspect, especially if you're sweaty or wet.

Lightning—The odds of being struck by lightning are low, but an open ridge is no place to be during a thunderstorm. If a storm is coming, immediately leave exposed areas. Boulders, rocky overhangs, and shal-

TEMPERATURE (¼F)

WIND (mph)	40	35	30	25	20	15	10	5	0	-5	-10	-15	-20	-25	-30	-35	-40	-45
5	36	31	25	19	13	7	1	-5	-11	-16	-22	-28	-34	-40	-46	-52	-57	-63
10	34	27	21	15	9	3	-4	-10	-16	-22	-28	-35	-41	-47	-53	-59	-66	-72
15	32	25	19	13	6	0	-7	-13	-19	-26	-32	-39	-45	-51	-58	-64	-71	-77
20	30	24	17	11	4	-2	-9	-15	-22	-29	-35	-42	-48	-55	-61	-68	-74	-81
25	29	23	16	9	3	-4	-11	-17	-24	-31	-37	-44	-51	-58	-64	-71	-78	-84
30	28	22	15	8	1	-5	-12	-19	-26	-33	-39	-46	-53	-60	-67	-73	-80	-87
35	28	21	14	7	0	-7	-14	-21	-27	-34	-41	-48	-55	-62	-69	-76	-82	-89
40	27	20	13	6	-1	-8	-15	-22	-29	-36	-43	-50	-57	-64	-71	-78	-84	-91
45	26	19	12	5	-2	-9	-16	-23	-30	-37	-44	-51	-58	-65	-72	-79	-86	-93
50	26	19	12	4	-3	-10	-17	-24	-31	-38	-45	-52	-60	-67	-74	-81	-88	-95
55	25	18	11	4	-3	-11	-18	-25	-32	-39	-46	-54	-61	-68	-75	-82	-89	-97
60	25	17	10	3	-4	-11	-19	-26	-33	-40	-48	-55	-62	-69	-76	-84	-91	-98

30 min. 10 min. 5 minutes

FROSTBITE TIMES

Wind Chill (¼F) = $35.74 + 0.6215T - 35.75(V^{0.16}) + 0.4275T(V^{0.16})$
Where, T= Air Temperature (¼F)   V= Wind Speed (mph)
National Weather Service and National Oceanic and Atmospheric Administration
Effective 11/01/01

low caves offer no protection from lightning, which may actually flow through them along the ground after a strike. Tents and convertible automobiles are no good, either. Sheltering in hard-roofed automobiles or large buildings is best, although they are rarely available to the hiker. Avoid tall structures, such as ski lifts, flagpoles, power-line towers, and the tallest trees, solitary rocks, or open hilltops. If you cannot enter a building or car, take shelter in a stand of smaller trees or in the forest. Avoid clearings. If caught in the open, crouch down on your pack or pad, or roll into a ball. If you are in water, get out. Disperse groups, so that not everyone is struck by a single bolt. Do not hold a potential lightning rod, such as a fishing pole or metal hiking pole.

Dehydration—Dry, hot summers are common along the Trail, particularly in the Virginias and the mid-Atlantic. Water may be scarce on humid days, sweat does not evaporate well, and many hikers face the danger of heat stroke and heat exhaustion if they haven't taken proper precautions, such as drinking lots of water. Learn how to protect yourself from heat exhaustion. Dehydration also is common in winter, when sweating may not be as obvious. Drink lots of water all year!

Is crime a problem?

The Appalachian Trail is safer than most places, but a few crimes of violence have occurred. Awareness is one of your best lines of defense. Be aware of what you are doing, where you are, and to whom you are talking. Hikers looking out for each other can be an effective "community watch." Be prudent and cautious without allowing common sense to slip into paranoia. Remember to trust your gut—it's usually right. Other tips include the following:

- Don't hike alone. If you are by yourself and encounter a stranger who makes you feel uncomfortable, say you are with a group that is behind you. Be creative. If in doubt, move on. Even a partner is no guarantee of safety, however; pay attention to your instincts about other people.

- Leave your hiking itinerary and timetable with someone at home, but *don't* post it on an on-line Trail journal. Be sure your contacts and your family know your "Trail name," if you use one of those fanciful aliases common on the A.T. Check in regularly, and establish a procedure to follow if you fail to check in. On short hikes, provide your contacts with the numbers of the land-managing agencies for the area of your hike. On extended hikes, provide ATC's number, (304) 535-6331.

- Be wary of strangers. Be friendly, but cautious. Don't tell strangers your plans (and don't post them in real time on the Internet). Avoid people who act suspiciously, seem hostile, or are intoxicated.

- Don't camp near roads.

- Dress conservatively to avoid unwanted attention.

■ Don't carry firearms. Loaded weapons are prohibited on National Park Service lands and in most other areas without a permit, they could be turned against you or result in an accidental shooting, they are extra weight, and most hikers agree they are unnecessary.

■ Eliminate opportunities for theft. Don't bring jewelry. Hide your money. If you must leave your pack, hide it, or leave it with someone trustworthy. Don't leave valuables or equipment (especially in sight) in vehicles parked at Trailheads.

■ Use the Trail registers (the notebooks stored at most shelters). Sign in using your given name, leave a note, and report any suspicious activities. If someone needs to locate you, or if a serious crime has been committed along the Trail, the first place authorities will look is in the registers.

■ Report any crime or harassment to the local authorities and ATC (at <incident@appalachiantrail.org>).

Trail history

Who was Benton MacKaye, and what was his connection to the Appalachian Trail?

He first published the idea. MacKaye (1879–1975) grew up mostly in Shirley Center, Massachusetts, reading the work of American naturalists and poets and taking long walks in the mountains of Massachusetts and Vermont. MacKaye (which is pronounced like "sky") sometimes claimed that the idea for the A.T. was born one day when he was sitting in a tree atop Stratton Mountain in Vermont. After graduating from Harvard, he eventually went to work in the new U.S. Forest Service and began carving out a niche as a profound thinker and an advocate for wilderness. By 1919, his radical ideas had led to him being edged out of the government, and he turned his attention to creating a new discipline that later came to be called "regional planning." His initial 1921 "project in regional planning" was a proposal for a network of work camps and communities in the mountains, all linked by a trail that ran from the highest point in New England to the highest point in the South. He called it "an Appalachian Trail."

Why did he propose it?

MacKaye was convinced that the pace of urban and industrial life along the East Coast was harmful to people. He envisioned the A.T. as a path interspersed with planned wilderness communities where people could go to renew themselves. That idea never gained much traction, but the notion of a two-thousand-mile footpath in the mountains fired the imaginations of hikers and outdoorsmen from Maine to Georgia. Inspired by him, they began building trails and trying to connect them.

What was his connection to the Appalachian Trail Conference?

MacKaye was responsible for convening and organizing the first Appalachian Trail "conference" in Washington, D.C., in 1925. That gathering of hikers, foresters, and public officials embraced the goal of building the Trail. They established the Appalachian Trail Conference, appointed MacKaye as its "field organizer," and named Major William Welch, manager of New York's Harriman Park, as its first chairman.

What happened next?

Some perfunctory scouting of routes took place. A few short sections were marked and connected. New trails were built in New York. Welch designed a logo and Trail markers. Committees met in a few northeastern states and talked about the idea. But, for several years, the idea didn't really go anywhere. MacKaye was much better at inspirational abstract thinking than practical organizing, and it soon became apparent that someone else was going to have to take the lead for the Trail to actually get built.

Who pushed the project forward?

Two men, retired Judge Arthur Perkins of Connecticut and admiralty lawyer Myron H. Avery of Washington, D.C. Perkins took the idea and ran with it, essentially appointing himself as the acting chairman of ATC in the late 1920s and recruiting Avery to lead the effort in the area around Washington. Both began vigorously proselytizing the idea of the Trail in 1928 and 1929, championing MacKaye's ideas to recruit volunteers, establishing hiking clubs up and down the coast, and actually going out to hike, clear brush, and mark paths themselves. As Perkins' health failed in the early 1930s, Avery took over, devoting incredible time, energy, and willpower to establishing a network of volunteers, developing clubs, working with the government, building the organization of the ATC, and setting the Trail's northern terminus at Katahdin in his native Maine. Avery remained chairman of ATC until 1952.

What was the relationship between MacKaye and Myron Avery?

They were cordial at first, but, by the mid-1930s, as Avery took charge of the Trail project, they quarreled over fundamental issues and visions of what the Trail should be. Avery was more interested in hiking and in connecting the sections of the Trail, while MacKaye was more interested in the Trail's role in promoting wilderness protection.

When was the Trail completed?

In 1937. It fell into disrepair during World War II, when Trail maintainers were unable to work on it, and parts of the route were lost. After the war, a concerted effort was made to restore it, and it was once again declared complete in 1951.

What happened after it was completed?

It's useful to look at the Trail's history in three eras: the era of Trail-building, which lasted until the Trail was completed in 1937; the era of Trail protection, which lasted until 1968, when Congress made the A.T. a national scenic trail; and the era of management and promotion, which has lasted until the present day. The first era was dominated by personalities and focused on getting the thing built and blazed from one end to the other. The second era saw the beginning of growth of the clubs taking care of it and the Conference, the construction of shelters, and a continuing battle to keep the route open over the many hundreds of miles of private property that it crossed. The third era saw an explosion of the number of people hiking the A.T. as the government began buying land along the route to guarantee the permanence of the footpath and volunteers shifted their emphasis to the hard work of managing a part of the national park system. In July 2005, the Conference became the A.T. Conservancy, to better express its work of protecting Trail resources.

How was the original Trail different from today's A.T.?
At first, the goal was simply to blaze a connected route. Often, this meant that the Trail led along old forest roads and other trails. Trail maintainers mostly just cleared brush and painted blazes. Today's Trail has mostly been moved off the old roads and onto new paths dug and reinforced especially for hikers. Today's route, although engineered much more elaborately, often requires more climbing, because it leads up the sides of many mountains that the old woods roads bypassed.

How do terms like "Trailway," "greenway," "buffer," and "view-shed" fit into this history?
The idea of a "Trailway" was first embraced by ATC in 1937. It meant that there was more to the Appalachian Trail than just the footpath. The "Trailway" referred to an area dedicated to the interests of those on foot, originally a mile on either side. In some cases, that came to mean a "buffer"—a legally protected area around the path that kept the sights and sounds of civilization, logging, and development away from the solitary hiker. In other cases, it meant a great deal more. It evolved into a notion of a "greenway," a broad swath of protected land through which the Trail ran. Crucial to the idea of a greenway was that of the "viewshed," the countryside visible from the Trail's high points. In the years since the A.T. became a national scenic trail, the Conservancy has worked to influence the development of surrounding areas so that the views from the Trail remain scenic, even when those views are of areas well outside the boundaries of the public Trail lands themselves.

When did Trail protection begin?
The notion of a protected zone was first formalized in an October 15, 1938, agreement between the National Park Service and the U.S. Forest Service for the promotion of an Appalachian Trailway through the relevant national parks and forests, extending one mile on each side of the Trail. Within this zone, no new parallel roads would be built or any other incompatible development allowed. Timber cutting would not be permitted within 200 feet of the Trail. Similar agreements, creating a zone one-quarter-mile in width, were signed with most states through which the Trail passes.

How were Trail lands identified?

Much of the Trail was already in national forests or national parks and state and local parks, but large portions were on private property, with the agreement of the property owners. In 1970, supplemental agreements under the 1968 National Trails System Act—among the National Park Service, the U.S. Forest Service, and the Appalachian Trail Conservancy—established the specific responsibilities of those organizations for initial mapping, selection of rights-of-way, relocations, maintenance, development, acquisition of land, and protection of a permanent Trail. Agreements also were signed between the Park Service and the various states, encouraging them to acquire and protect a right-of-way.

Why has complete protection taken so long?

Getting federal money appropriated was difficult, and not all property owners were willing to sell, which occasionally raised the specter of the government's threatening to condemn land for the Trail—always a politically unpopular action. Slow progress of federal efforts and lack of initiative by some states led Congress to strengthen the National Trails System Act in an amendment known as the Appalachian Trail Bill, which was signed by President Jimmy Carter on March 21, 1978. The new legislation emphasized the need for protecting the Trail, including acquiring a corridor, and authorized $90 million for that purpose. More money was appropriated during the Reagan, Bush, and Clinton administrations. Today, more than 99 percent of the Trail runs across public lands.

What is the relationship between the A.T. and the government, the Conservancy, and the clubs?

In 1984, the Interior Department delegated the responsibility for managing the A.T. corridor lands outside established parks and forests to the ATC. The Conservancy and its affiliated clubs retain primary responsibility for maintaining the footpath, too. A more comprehensive, 10-year agreement was signed in 1994 and renewed in November 2004.

Wildlife along the A.T.

How "wild" is the A.T.?

The well-known plaque at Springer Mountain in Georgia describes the A.T. as "a footpath for those who seek fellowship with the wilderness." What does that mean? The Trail will indeed take you deep into some of the wildest and most remote woodlands of the eastern United States. But, true "wilderness," in the sense of untouched wild country, is rare, even on the A.T. Much of the land that the Trail follows was once farmland—even the steep, stony, remote slopes—and nearly all of it has been logged at some time during the last four centuries. Except for bears, bobcats, and coyotes, most large natural predators have been exterminated.

In the twentieth century, much of the formerly settled land was incorporated into state and national parks and forests. On that land, forests and wildlife have returned. As you walk through what seems like primeval wilderness, you're likely to run across old stone walls or abandoned logging roads or the foundations of nineteenth-century homesteads. The federal government has designated some of those areas as protected wilderness areas, which strictly limits the ways in which they can be used. Today, the mountains teem with creatures of all sorts, from microbes to moose. To the casual hiker who knows only the woods of a suburban park, it can seem very wild indeed.

One good way to look at the "wilderness" of the A.T. is as a series of long, skinny islands of wildness, surrounded by a sea of populated valleys inhabited by working farms and suburban communities. In the vast national forests of the South and the spreading timberlands of northern New England, those "islands" are somewhat broader. But, even in its wildest places, the A.T. hiker is rarely more than a strenuous day's walk from the nearest highway or community.

What large animals might I see?

Moose, the largest animal that hikers encounter along the Trail (often weighing in at more than 1,000 pounds), inhabit deep woodlands and wetlands from Massachusetts north, especially in New Hampshire and Maine. White-tailed deer can be found along the entire length of the Trail. Elk have been reintroduced to Pennsylvania, North Carolina, and Tennessee. Black bears have been spotted in all Trail states and are especially common in Georgia, North Carolina, Tennessee, Virginia, Pennsylvania, and New Jersey. Wild boars live in the Great Smoky Mountains National Park. Bobcats and coyotes are stealthy residents along most of the route of the Trail, although they're rarely seen. Fishers, otters, and beavers are occasionally reported by hikers.

What small animals might I see?
By far the most familiar will be mice, chipmunks, rabbits, and squirrels, but foxes, raccoons, opossums, skunks, groundhogs, porcupines, bats, weasels, shrews, minks, and muskrats are also common. Tree frogs and bullfrogs inhabit wet areas in warm weather, lizards scurry along rocks and fallen logs, snakes (both venomous and not) are common south of New England, and streams and ponds are home to salamanders, bass, trout, bream, sunfish, and crayfish.

Which animals are dangerous?
Few A.T. hikers encounter aggressive animals, but any wild animal will fight if cornered or handled roughly—even timid animals such as deer can be quite dangerous in those circumstances. The large wild animals most likely to be aggressive include moose (during rutting season) and black bears (especially mother bears with cubs). Mountain lions, which have stalked people in western states, have long been rumored to have returned to the Appalachians, but so far scientists have not been able to confirm any sightings in mountains that the A.T. traverses.

When disturbed or stepped on, many other creatures will strike back aggressively, inflicting painful wounds or poisonous stings. Those include timber rattlesnakes and copperheads, hornets, wasps, yellow jackets, Africanized bees, and black widow and brown recluse spiders. Foxes, bats, raccoons, and other small animals susceptible to rabies may bite when suffering from infection. Mice, although not aggressive, may transmit diseases, and biting insects such as mosquitoes and ticks can infect hikers with bacteria. Hikers in more populated sections of the Trail also might encounter aggressive dogs.

What rare or endangered animal species might I see?
Birders might spot rare species such as the Bicknell's thrush, hermit thrush, gray-cheeked thrush, northern raven, olive-sided flycatcher, black-billed cuckoo, spruce grouse, bay-breasted warbler, cerulean warbler, blackburnian warbler, magnolia warbler, blackpoll warbler, alder flycatcher, rusty blackbird, Swainson's warbler, yellow-bellied sapsucker, winter wren, red-breasted nuthatch, sharp-shinned hawk, northern saw-whet owl, golden eagle, peregrine falcon, merlin, bald eagle, and Cooper's hawk.

Harder to find, but also present, are the Carolina northern flying squirrel, Virginia northern flying squirrel, rock vole, Allegheny wood rat, eastern wood rat, water shrew, and fence lizard. The black bear and eastern timber rattlesnake, although not uncommon along the Trail, are on the rare-species list. You may also find a number of rare crustaceans, reptiles, and amphibians, including the zig-zag salamander, northern cricket frog, triangle floater mussel, Jefferson salamander, Appalachian brook crayfish, wood turtle, broadhead skink, pigmy salamander, shovelnose salamander, Shenandoah salamander, Weller's salamander, and squawfoot mussel.

What birds will I see in the Appalachians that I might not see at my backyard feeder?
Birds with summer ranges normally far to the north of where most A.T. hikers live are often found in the mountains, where the altitude makes the climate resemble that of Canada. Insect-eating birds such as whippoorwills, flycatchers, and swallows rarely show up in backyards but are common along the Trail. The songs of deep-woods birds such as the ovenbird, kinglet, veery, pewee, and red-eyed vireo will provide an ongoing chorus for summer hikers. Pileated woodpeckers hammer deliberately on dead trees. Large game birds, such as wild turkey, ruffed grouse, and spruce grouse, forage on the forest floor and surprise hikers as they burst into flight. Many hikers linger to admire the soaring acrobatics of ravens, vultures, hawks, eagles, and falcons on the thermals and updrafts along the rocky crests of the mountains.

Trees and wild plants along the A.T.

How old are the Appalachian forests?

The forests of the Appalachians have been logged heavily for more than three centuries. Photographs from the late nineteenth and early twentieth centuries show many areas almost completely stripped of trees. Many Trail areas were open farmland or pastureland in the 1700s and early 1800s. Lumber is still harvested in national forests and privately owned timberlands along the Trail. Although today's mountains are heavily forested again, it is mostly "second-growth" timber, except in a few isolated coves of "old-growth" forest that date back to precolonial times.

Forest that has grown back from burning or clearing through successive stages to the point at which it reaches a fairly steady state, with dominant full-grown trees, is known as a "climax forest." Several different climax forests appear along the A.T., and they are not mutually exclusive—different types can be found on the same mountain. The kind you encounter will depend on where you are, on what type of soil is underfoot, and the climate. The climate often depends on how high the mountains are—the higher they are, the more "northern" (or boreal) the climate.

What kinds of forests will I encounter along the Trail?

- The *mixed deciduous forest* (also called the *southern hardwood forest*) dominates the foothills of the southern mountains and Trail lands south of New England. Various kinds of broad-leafed trees are dominant, and the understory of small trees and shrubs is profuse. Oak and hickory are the most common large trees, with maple and beech evident in more northerly sections; some sproutings of chestnut (a species that dominated until a blight devastated it early in the twentieth century) can be found as well. Understory trees such as redbud, dogwood, striped maple, and American holly are common, as are shrubs such as witch hazel, pawpaw, and mountain pepperbush.

- The *southern Appalachian forest,* found above the foothills from Georgia to central Virginia, contains more tree species than any other forest in North America and actually takes in a range of different forest types that can vary dramatically according to elevation. Climax hardwood forests of basswood, birch, maple, beech, tuliptree, ash, and magnolia can be found in some coves, while, above about 4,000 feet, the climax forests are typically spruce, fir, and hemlock, particularly on the wetter western slopes. Old-growth forest can be found in isolated parts of the Great Smoky Mountains National Park. Oak forests often predominate on the eastern faces of the mountains, which typically do not receive as much moisture. Pine and oak may mix on some slopes. At higher elevations, the understory is less varied: Shrubs of mountain laurel and rhododendron form nearly impenetrable thickets that are densest where conditions are wettest.

■ The *transition forest* tends to be wetter and more northerly than the mixed deciduous forest. Hikers marveling at the colors of a New England fall are admiring the transition forest. It extends across the hillsides and lowlands of the north and reaches down into the high country of the southern Appalachians. It appears as a mosaic of spruce, fir, hemlock, pine, birch, maple, basswood, and beech forests. The substory of transition forest tends to be more open, with ferns and shrubs of elderberry, hazel, and bush honeysuckle, and often a thick carpet of evergreen needles covers the ground under the trees. Conifers tend to predominate at the higher elevations.

■ The northern or *boreal forest* is the largest North American forest. Most of it is in Canada and Alaska, but A.T. hikers encounter it while traversing the highest ridges of the southern Appalachians and the coniferous uplands of northern New England. Pines and hemlocks characterize its southern reaches, while dwarfed spruces and firs (known as *krummholz*) grow at treeline in New Hampshire and Maine, just as they grow at the borders of the arctic lands farther north. In between is a spruce-fir climax forest. Evergreens such as white pine, red pine, white spruce, balsam fir, black spruce, and jack pine predominate, but hardwoods such as aspen and birch are mixed in as well. The ground of the boreal forest is typically thin and muddy, with little understory, and it includes sphagnum bogs surrounded by a wide variety of aquatic plants, ferns, subalpine plants, blueberry bushes, mountain maple, and ash shrubs.

What wildflowers can I look for, and when will I see them?
Among the small joys of hiking the Trail are the wildflowers that grow along the way. Some poke their heads out of the forest duff in late winter and are gone by the time the spreading canopy of late-spring trees blocks out the sun. Some cluster near the edges of clearings in midsummer, while others hide in the deep shade. And, still others blossom amid the falling leaves and early snows of the Appalachian fall.

Winter/early spring—First to bloom in swampy areas most years is the maroon-colored cowl that shelters the tiny, foul-smelling flowers of skunk cabbage, which may appear while snow is still on the ground. In March and April, along the high, dry ridges, the delicate starbursts of bloodroot appear, along with the corncob-like clusters of squaw root on fallen oak trees; the graceful, lily-like dogtooth violet; the white bunches of early saxifrage; fanlike, purple clusters of dwarf iris in southern sections; the pink-purple flowers and liver-shaped leaves of hepatica; the delicate, white rue anemone; the bee-buzzing carpets of fringed phacelia in the South; and the waxy, pink trailing arbutus farther north.

Spring/early summer—During May and June, as the tree canopy shades the forest floor, the variety of wildflowers blooming along the A.T. becomes too extensive to keep track of. The bubblegum scent and orange blooms of flame azalea shrubs burst out in the southern Appalachians, along with the white and pink blossoms of its close relatives, mountain laurel and rhododendron. The garlicky wild leek, or ramp, flowers in early summer. Hikers may spot the green tubes of jack-in-the-pulpit, dove-like red clusters of wild columbine, vessel-like orchid blossoms of pink lady's-slipper, spade-leaved trillium, bright blue of viper's bugloss, the blue-violet of spiderwort in sunny clearings, black cohosh's delicate cone of tiny blooms, and, in the cold bogs of the northern states, the white blossoms of Labrador tea and the pink pentagons of bog laurel.

Late summer—The heat of July and August in the Appalachians coaxes blossoms from a number of mountain shrubs, shade plants, and meadow plants. The wintergreen shrub blooms white in oak forests, the white starbursts of tall meadow rue appear near open fields, the white petals of the bug-trapping sundew appear in wet areas, mountain cranberry's small bell-like pink blossoms appear in New England, the white-and-yellow sunbursts of oxeye daisy grow along hedgerows, and the greenish-white clusters of wild sarsaparilla appear in the dry, open woods. In the mid-Atlantic states, the understory becomes a waist-deep sea of wood nettle, the delicate white flowers of which belie unpleasant stinging hairs that bristle from the stems and leaves. The succulent stalks of jewel-weed, which has a pale yellow flower, often sprout nearby, and their juice can help ease the sting and itch of the nettles and poison ivy.

Fall and early winter—Certain wildflowers continue blooming late into the fall along the A.T., disappearing from the woods about the same time hikers do. Goldenrod spreads across open fields in September, about the time the leaves start changing color. The intricate white discs of Queen Anne's lace adorn ditches and roadsides until late in the year. Other common fall wildflowers include aster, wood sorrel, monkshood, and butter-and-eggs.

Can I eat wild plants I find?
You could eat certain plants, but, in keeping with the principles of Leave No Trace, you shouldn't. Leave the wild blueberries and raspberries and blackberries of summer for the birds and bears. Resist the temptation to spice up your noodles with ramps in the spring. "Chicken of the woods" mushrooms should stay in the woods. Wild watercress belongs in a stream, not a salad. Rather than brewing your own ginseng or sassafras tea from wild roots, visit the supermarket in town. Many edible plants along the A.T. are rare and endangered, and harvesting them is illegal. Even when the flora are plentiful, remember that the fauna of the Appalachians have no option other than to forage for it; you do.

What rare or endangered plant species might I see?
Most of the federally listed plant species (threatened or endangered) along the Appalachian Trail are found in the high country of the southern Appalachians or the alpine environments of northern New England. There are too many to list here, but typical of those in the southern Appalachians is the spreading avens, a plant with fan-shaped leaves and small, yellow flowers that grows in rock crevices. Although bluets are common along the A.T., a subspecies called Roan Mountain bluet is found in only nine

sites there—the only known sites in the world. Gray's lily is found only on the high balds near Roan Mountain. Although goldenrod is plentiful along the Trail and sometimes considered something of a pest, one rare subspecies, the Blue Ridge goldenrod, is known to exist only on one cliff in North Carolina. Similarly, many of the plants at and above treeline in New England, such as Robbins cinquefoil, are extremely vulnerable to damage from hikers wandering off the A.T. Below treeline, plants such as the small whorled pogonia, an orchid, are threatened by development. Please don't pick the flowers along the A.T.—they might be the only ones of a kind.

The how and why of Trail construction

Who decides which route the Trail takes?

A local Trail-maintaining club, in consultation with the Appalachian Trail Conservancy and the government agency responsible for managing the land in question, determines the route that the footpath follows over a section. According to the National Trails System Act that authorized federal protection of the A.T., the goal is to expose the walker to "the maximum outdoor recreation potential and … enjoyment of the nationally significant scenic, historic, natural, or cultural qualities of the area." In plain language, that means routing the Trail in such a way that walkers have the chance to encounter and appreciate the wildlife, geography, and geology, as well as the historical and natural context of the Appalachians, while merging with, exploring, and harmonizing with the mountain environment.

How is today's A.T. different from the original Trail?

When the A.T. was first built, the main goal was a continuous, marked route, which often meant connecting existing footpaths and woods roads. Long sections of "roadwalks" linked the footpaths. Where no existing routes were available, Trail builders marked out new ones, cleared brush, and painted blazes. But, that was about it, and, for many years, when few people knew about or hiked the Trail, it was enough. Beginning in the 1960s, two things happened: The A.T. became a part of the national park system, and the numbers of people using it began skyrocketing. With increased use, mud and erosion became problems.

As the Trail was moved away from existing footpaths and roads and onto new paths planned and built especially for the A.T. on federal land, Trail builders began "hardening" the path and designing it to stand up to heavier use.

What causes the Trail to deteriorate?

Erosion can damage the footpath quickly. The mineral soil of the footpath is made of very fine particles bound together by clay that, once broken from the ground by boots and hiking poles, is easily washed away by fast-flowing water. (Water moving at two miles per hour has sixty-four times more ability to carry soil particles than water moving at one mile per hour.) Trail builders work to separate water from the treadway. Where that is not possible, they try to slow it down. Since water in rivulets or ruts flows faster than water flowing across the Trail in sheets, trail builders try to channel water off the part that hikers walk on. Where they can't, they slant the path outward so that water will stay "thin" and flow slowly off the sides in a sheet, rather than becoming "thick" and channeling down the middle of the Trail.

Why are parts of the Trail routed over narrow log walkways?

Believe it or not, it's not to keep your feet dry. The goal is to protect the land, not your nice, new boots. Bog bridges, also called "puncheon," allow the Trail to take hikers into an important part of the mountain environment without turning such ecologically sensitive swamp areas into hopeless quagmires, disrupting plant and animal life there. The Trail is supposed to "wear lightly on the land," and this is one way to do so. Walkways may be built on piles driven into the ground, or they may "float" on boggy ground; in both cases, the wetlands are disturbed much less than they would be by mud holes that widen every time a hiker tries to skirt the edges.

Why does the Trail zigzag up steep mountains?

When it was first marked, the Trail often climbed steep slopes by the most direct route, and older parts of today's Trail still tend to have the steepest sections. But, water runs faster down a steeper trail and erodes it more quickly. In recent years, many sections have been rerouted so that the Trail ascends by way of "sidehill" that slants up a mountainside and "switchbacks" that zigzag across its steepest faces. Again, it isn't done to make the Trail easier for hikers, although that's sometimes the effect, but rather to make the footpath itself more durable and less subject to erosion.

How does the Trail cross creeks and rivers?

Bridges take the Trail across all its major river crossings, except for the Kennebec River in Maine (where hikers ferry across in canoes). Most, such as the Bear Mountain Bridge across the Hudson in New York, are highway bridges; a few others, such as the James River Foot Bridge in Virginia, are built especially for foot travelers. A few large creeks require fording, but most are crossed by footbridges or stepping stones. Small streams may require fording when spring floods submerge the rocks and stepping stones that lead across them.

Why are there so many logs and rock barriers in the path?

Unless the logs result from a "blowdown" (a fallen tree) or the rocks from a rockslide, they're probably water-diversion devices, such as waterbars or check dams that have been added to older, eroding sections of the Trail. Avoid stepping on them, if possible: Not only can they be slippery (particularly the logs), but they will last longer if you step over them.

Why is the Trail so rocky?

The Appalachians are the product of erosion, which tends to strip away soil and leave rocks on the surface. Since rocky sections offer a durable surface and often provide spectacular views for hikers, Trail designers don't hesitate to route the footpath along them. This is particularly true from central Virginia through Connecticut and eastern New Hampshire through Maine; many older sections are routed along ridgelines. Typically, the A.T. will climb a ridge on smoother "sidehill" Trail and then follow a rocky ridgeline for some distance, before descending again.

Summary of distances

North–South
CUMULATIVE
MILES

South–North
CUMULATIVE
MILES

Maine Section Thirteen

0.0	Maine 26, Grafton Notch	14.6
3.5	Mahoosuc Trail	11.1
4.6	Speck Pond Campsite	10.0
8.2	Mahoosuc Notch Trail junction	6.4
9.7	Full Goose Shelter	4.9
12.3	Goose Eye Trail	2.3
14.1	Carlo Col Shelter junction	0.5
14.6	N.H.–Maine Line	0.0

Cumulative mileages for the two states can be found in the columns closest to the names of landmarks; cumulative mileages for a particular section can be found in the outside columns.

New Hampshire Section One

0.0	0.0	N.H.–Maine Line	310.7	16.5
1.9	1.9	Mt. Success	308.8	14.6
4.7	4.7	Gentian Pond Campsite and Shelter	306.0	11.8
5.4	5.4	Moss Pond	305.3	11.1
6.9	6.9	Dream Lake	303.8	9.6
9.6	9.6	Trident Col Tentsite side trail	301.1	6.9
10.7	10.7	Cascade Mountain	300.0	5.8
12.9	12.9	Mt. Hayes (eastern summit)	297.8	3.6
16.2	16.2	Androscoggin River	294.5	0.3
16.5	16.5	U.S. 2, Gorham, N.H.	294.2	0.0

New Hampshire Section Two

0.0	16.5	U.S. 2, Gorham, N.H.	294.2	21.1
1.9	18.4	Rattle River Shelter	292.3	19.2
8.0	24.5	Imp Campsite and Shelter side trail	286.2	13.1
9.9	26.4	North Carter Trail	284.3	11.2
12.6	29.1	Zeta Pass	281.6	8.5
14.0	30.5	Carter Dome	280.2	7.1
15.2	31.7	Carter Notch, Carter Notch Hut side trail	279.0	5.9
16.1	32.6	Wildcat Mountain, Peak A	278.1	5.0
18.1	34.6	Wildcat Mountain, Peak D	276.1	3.0
18.4	34.9	Wildcat Mountain, Peak E	275.8	2.7
21.1	37.6	N.H. 16, Pinkham Notch, Pinkham Notch Visitors Center	273.1	0.0

New Hampshire Section Three

0.0	37.6	N.H. 16, Pinkham Notch, Pinkham Notch Visitors Center	273.1	26.0
2.1	39.7	Low's Bald Spot side trail	271.0	23.9
4.0	41.6	West Branch Peabody River	269.1	22.0
4.8	42.4	Osgood Tentsite	268.3	21.2
7.3	44.9	Mt. Madison	265.8	18.7
7.8	45.4	Madison Spring Hut, Valley Way Tentsite on Valley Way	265.3	18.2
8.7	46.3	Thunderstorm Junction, Lowe's Path to Gray Knob Cabin, Spur Trail to Crag Camp Cabin	264.4	17.3
9.3	46.9	Israel Ridge Path to The Perch Shelter	263.8	16.7
10.0	47.6	Edmands Col	263.1	16.0
13.5	51.1	Mt. Washington	259.6	12.5

North–South			**South–North**	
14.9	52.5	Lakes of the Clouds Hut	258.2	11.1
18.8	56.4	Mt. Pierce (Mt. Clinton)	254.3	7.2
19.6	57.2	Mizpah Springs Hut, Nauman Tentsite	253.5	6.4
21.3	58.9	Mt. Jackson	251.8	4.7
22.7	60.3	Mt. Webster	250.4	3.3
26.0	63.6	U.S. 302, Crawford Notch State Park, Dry River Campground	247.1	0.0

New Hampshire Section Four

0.0	63.6	U.S. 302, Crawford Notch State Park, Dry River Campground	247.1	27.7
2.9	66.5	Ethan Pond Campsite and Shelter side trail	244.2	24.8
7.7	71.3	Zealand Falls Hut	239.4	20.0
8.9	72.5	Zeacliff side trail	238.2	18.8
11.9	75.5	Mt. Guyot; Bondcliff Trail to Guyot Campsite and Shelter	235.2	15.8
13.9	77.5	South Twin Mountain	233.2	13.8
14.7	78.3	Galehead Hut	232.4	13.0
16.9	80.5	13 Falls Tentsite side trail	230.2	10.8
17.4	81.0	Garfield Ridge Campsite and Shelter side trail	229.7	10.3
21.3	84.9	Mt. Lafayette, Greenleaf Trail to Greenleaf Hut	225.8	6.4
22.3	85.9	Mt. Lincoln	224.8	5.4
23.0	86.6	Little Haystack Mountain, Falling Waters Trail to Lafayette Place Campground	224.1	4.7
25.1	88.7	Liberty Spring Tentsite	222.0	2.6
27.7	91.3	U.S. 3, Franconia Notch State Park	219.4	0.0

North–South   South–North

New Hampshire Section Five

N-S	N-S	Location	S-N	S-N
0.0	91.3	U.S. 3, Franconia Notch State Park	219.4	16.3
2.9	94.2	Lonesome Lake Hut	216.5	13.4
4.8	96.1	Kinsman Pond Campsite and Shelter side trail	214.6	11.5
5.4	96.7	North Kinsman Mountain	214.0	10.9
6.3	97.6	South Kinsman Mountain	213.1	10.0
8.8	100.1	Eliza Brook Shelter side trail	210.6	7.5
11.7	103.0	Mt. Wolf, East Peak	207.7	4.6
16.3	107.6	N.H. 112, Kinsman Notch	203.1	0.0

New Hampshire Section Six

N-S	N-S	Location	S-N	S-N
0.0	107.6	N.H. 112, Kinsman Notch	203.1	9.5
1.5	109.1	Beaver Brook Shelter side trail	201.6	8.0
3.8	111.4	Mt. Moosilauke	199.3	5.7
8.4	116.0	Jeffers Brook Shelter side trail	194.7	1.1
9.5	117.1	N.H. 25, Glencliff	193.6	0.0

New Hampshire Section Seven

N-S	N-S	Location	S-N	S-N
0.0	117.1	N.H. 25, Glencliff	193.6	9.7
1.9	119.0	Wachipauka Pond	191.7	7.8
2.4	119.5	Mt. Mist	191.2	7.3
4.9	122.0	N.H. 25C	188.7	4.8
7.5	124.6	Ore Hill Shelter side trail	186.1	2.2
8.1	125.2	Cape Moonshine Road	185.5	1.6
9.7	126.8	N.H. 25A	183.9	0.0

North–South			**South–North**	

New Hampshire Section Eight

0.0	126.8	N.H. 25A	183.9	16.0
4.9	131.7	Hexacuba Shelter side trail	179.0	11.1
10.2	137.0	Firewarden's Cabin	173.7	5.8
10.3	137.1	Smarts Mountain Tentsite side trail	173.6	5.7
10.8	137.6	Lambert Ridge Trail	173.1	5.2
16.0	142.8	Lyme–Dorchester Road, Dartmouth Skiway	167.9	0.0

New Hampshire Section Nine

0.0	142.8	Lyme–Dorchester Road, Dartmouth Skiway	167.9	18.1
0.9	143.7	Trapper John Shelter side trail	167.0	17.2
1.4	144.2	Holts Ledge side trail	166.5	16.7
3.4	146.2	Goose Pond Road	164.5	14.7
6.6	149.4	Moose Mountain Shelter side trail	161.3	11.5
11.7	154.5	Etna–Hanover Center Road	156.2	6.4
13.1	155.9	Trescott Road	154.8	5.0
16.1	158.9	Velvet Rocks Shelter side trail (southern jucntion)	151.8	2.0
17.6	160.4	Dartmouth College, Hanover, N.H.	150.3	0.5
18.1	160.9	Connecticut River, N.H.–Vt. State Line	149.8	0.0

Vermont Section One

0.0	160.9	Connecticut River, N.H.–Vt. State Line	149.8	9.3
1.8	162.7	Elm Street (south Trailhead)	148.0	7.5
5.3	166.2	Happy Hill Shelter side trail	144.5	4.0
8.7	169.6	Tigertown Road at Podunk Road, I-89	141.1	0.6
9.3	170.2	Vt. 14, West Hartford, Vt.	140.5	0.0

North–South   South–North

Vermont Section Two

0.0	170.2	Vt. 14, West Hartford, Vt.	140.5	12.6
3.3	173.5	Joe Ranger Road	137.2	9.3
4.8	175.0	Thistle Hill Shelter side trail	135.7	7.8
7.1	177.3	Cloudland Road	133.4	5.5
8.9	179.1	Pomfret–South Pomfret Road	131.6	3.7
11.1	181.3	Woodstock Stage Road	129.4	1.5
12.6	182.8	Vt. 12	127.9	0.0

Vermont Section Three

0.0	182.8	Vt. 12	127.9	23.7
3.8	186.6	Wintturi Shelter side trail	124.1	19.9
7.9	190.7	Lakota Lake Lookout	120.0	15.8
9.0	191.8	Chateauguay Road and Locust Creek	118.9	14.7
13.7	196.5	Stony Brook Shelter side trail	114.2	10.0
14.8	197.6	Quimby Mountain	113.1	8.9
18.0	200.8	River Road	109.9	5.7
20.4	203.2	Vt. 100, Gifford Woods State Park	107.5	3.3
21.8	204.6	Sherburne Pass Trail northern junction	106.1	1.9
22.7	205.5	Maine Junction; Long Trail to Tucker–Johnson Shelter	105.2	1.0
23.7	206.5	U.S. 4	104.2	0.0

Vermont Section Four

0.0	206.5	U.S. 4	104.2	17.4
1.9	208.4	Churchill Scott Shelter side trail	102.3	15.5
3.8	210.3	Jungle Junction; Sherburne Pass Trail (southern junction) to Pico Camp Shelter	100.4	13.6

North–South			**South–North**	
6.3	212.8	Cooper Lodge, Killington Peak Trail junction	97.9	11.1
10.6	217.1	Governor Clement Shelter	93.6	6.8
12.0	218.5	Upper Cold River Road	92.2	5.4
13.5	220.0	Cold River Road (Lower)	90.7	3.9
15.5	222.0	Lottery Road	88.7	1.9
15.9	222.4	Beacon Hill	88.3	1.5
16.4	222.9	Clarendon Shelter side trail	87.8	1.0
17.4	223.9	Vt. 103	86.8	0.0

Vermont Section Five

0.0	223.9	Vt. 103	86.8	14.6
0.1	224.0	Clarendon Gorge, Mill River Bridge	86.7	14.5
2.7	226.6	Minerva Hinchey Shelter side trail	84.1	11.9
6.3	230.2	Vt. 140	80.5	8.3
6.4	230.3	Sugar Hill Road	80.4	8.2
7.1	231.0	Keewaydin Trail	79.7	7.5
7.8	231.7	Greenwall Shelter side trail	79.0	6.8
8.3	232.2	White Rocks Cliff Trail	78.5	6.3
12.2	236.1	Little Rock Pond Shelter side trail	74.6	2.4
12.3	236.2	Homer Stone Brook and Green Mountain Trail	74.5	2.3
12.6	236.5	Little Rock Pond Tenting Area	74.2	2.0
12.9	236.8	Lula Tye Shelter side trail	73.9	1.7
14.6	238.5	Danby–Landgrove Road (USFS 10), northern parking lot at Big Black Branch	72.2	0.0

Vermont Section Six

0.0	238.5	Danby–Landgrove Road (USFS 10), northern parking lot at Big Black Branch	72.2	17.8
1.3	239.8	Big Branch Shelter	70.9	16.5
1.5	240.0	Old Job Trail (northern junction) to Old Job Shelter	70.7	16.3
3.0	241.5	Lost Pond Shelter side trail	69.2	14.8
5.0	243.5	Baker Peak	67.2	12.8
7.0	245.5	Old Job Trail (southern junction) to Old Job Shelter	65.2	10.8
7.2	245.7	Griffith Lake Tenting Area	65.0	10.6
7.7	246.2	Peru Peak Shelter	64.5	10.1
9.0	247.5	Peru Peak	63.2	8.8
10.7	249.2	Styles Peak	61.5	7.1
12.3	250.8	USFS 21, Mad Tom Notch	59.9	5.5
14.8	253.3	Bromley Mountain	57.4	3.0
15.8	254.3	Bromley Shelter side trail	56.4	2.0
17.8	256.3	Vt. 11/30	54.4	0.0

Vermont Section Seven

0.0	256.3	Vt. 11/30	54.4	17.5
2.4	258.7	Spruce Peak side trail	52.0	15.1
2.8	259.1	Spruce Peak Shelter side trail	51.6	14.7
4.9	261.2	Old Rootville Road, Prospect Rock side trail	49.5	12.6
5.8	262.1	Branch Pond Trail to William B. Douglas Shelter	48.6	11.7
8.6	264.9	Winhall River footbridge	45.8	8.9
10.4	266.7	Stratton Pond, North Shore Trail to North Shore Tenting Area	44.0	7.1

North–South			**South–North**	
10.6	266.9	Stratton Pond Trail to Stratton Pond Shelter	43.8	6.9
13.7	270.0	Stratton Mountain firetower	40.7	3.8
17.5	273.8	Stratton–Arlington (Kelley Stand) Road at East Branch of the Deerfield River	36.9	0.0

Vermont Section Eight

0.0	273.8	Stratton–Arlington (Kelley Stand) Road at East Branch of the Deerfield River	36.9	22.6
2.0	275.8	USFS 71	34.9	20.6
3.6	277.4	Story Spring Shelter	33.3	19.0
8.2	282.0	Kid Gore Shelter	28.7	14.4
12.2	286.0	Glastenbury Mountain firetower	24.7	10.4
12.5	286.3	Goddard Shelter	24.4	10.1
16.8	290.6	Little Pond Lookout	20.1	5.8
21.0	294.8	Melville Nauheim Shelter side trail	15.9	1.6
22.6	296.4	Vt. 9, Bennington–Brattleboro Highway, City Stream	14.3	0.0

Vermont Section Nine

0.0	296.4	Vt. 9, Bennington–Brattleboro Highway, City Stream	14.3	14.3
1.8	298.2	Harmon Hill	12.5	12.5
4.3	300.7	Congdon Shelter	10.0	10.0
7.3	303.7	Consultation Peak	7.0	7.0
11.5	307.9	Side trail to Seth Warner Shelter and Primitive Tenting Area	2.8	2.8
14.3	310.7	Vt.–Mass. State Line, southern terminus of Long Trail	0.0	0.0

North–South		**South–North**

Massachusetts Section One

North–South		South–North
0.0	Mass.–Vt. State Line, southern terminus of Long Trail	4.1
1.3	Pine Cobble Trail	2.8
2.3	Pete's Spring, Sherman Brook Primitive Campsite side trail	1.8
4.1	Mass. 2, North Adams	0.0

Index

U

V

For more information

Appalachian Trail Conservancy
ATC's central offices are located in Harpers Ferry, West Virginia. Membership services, administration of conservation and other programs, and requests for information about the Trail are all handled there. The public Information Center is also located there. Regular business hours are 9 a.m.–5 p.m. ET, Monday–Friday, but the center generally is open weekends and holidays except in the winter.

P. O. Box 807
799 Washington Street
Harpers Ferry, WV 25425-0807
Telephone: (304) 535-6331
Fax: (304) 535-2667
<www.appalachiantrail.org>

ATC New England Regional Office
18 on the Common, Unit 7 (P.O. Box 312)
Lyme, NH 03768-0312
(603) 795-4935
<atc-nero@appalachiantrail.org>

The Ultimate Appalachian Trail Store
The ATC sales distribution center is located in:
179 East Burr Boulevard, Unit N
Kearneysville, WV 25430
For customer service, call toll-free to (888) AT-STORE (888-287-8673) during weekday business hours (9 a.m.–4:30 p.m. ET).
Fax: (304) 724-8386
<www.atctrailstore.org>

Frequently requested e-mail addresses
Trail & hiking questions: <info@appalachiantrail.org>
ATC membership: <membership@appalachiantrail.org>
Merchandise: <sales@appalachiantrail.org>
Editor, *A.T. Journeys*: <editor@appalachiantrail.org>
Publisher, ATC books: <general@appalachiantrail.org>
Volunteer Trail crew program: <crews@appalachiantrail.org>
Reporting an incident: <incident@appalachiantrail.org>

Appalachian Mountain Club
Pinkham Notch Visitors Center
Route 16
P.O. Box 298
Gorham, NH 03581-0298
(603) 466-2721
Reservations, Monday–Saturday, 9 a.m.–5 p.m. ET
(603) 466-2727
<www.outdoors.org/lodging>

Headquarters
5 Joy Street
Boston, MA 02108
(617) 523-0636
<www.outdoors.org>
info@outdoor.org

Dartmouth Outdoor Programs
Robinson Hall, Box 9
Hanover, NH 03755
(603) 646-2428
<www.dartmouth.edu/~doc>
thedoc@dartmouth.edu

Moosilauke Ravine Lodge
P.O. Box 65
Warren, NH 03279
(603) 764-5858

Green Mountain Club
4711 Waterbury-Stowe Road
Waterbury Center, VT 05677
(802) 244-7037
<www.greenmountainclub.org>
gmc@greenmountainclub.org

USDA Forest Service
Green Mountain National Forest
231 North Main Street
Rutland, VT 05701
(802) 747-6700
<www.fs.fed.us/r9/gmfl/green_mountain>

White Mountain National Forest
719 North Main Street
Laconia, NH 03246
(603) 528-8721
<www.fs.fed.us/r9/forests/white_mountain>

State Parks
Franconia Notch State Park
9 Franconia Notch State Park
Franconia, NH 03580
(603) 823-5563
<www.franconianotchstatepark.com>
nhparks@dred.state.nh.us

Crawford Notch State Park
Dry River Campground
U.S. 302
Harts Location, NH 03812
(603) 374-2272
<www.nhstateparks.com/crawford.html>
nhparks@dred.state.nh.us

Gifford Woods State Park
34 Gifford Woods
Killington, VT 05751
(802) 775-5354
<www.vtstateparks.com/htm/gifford.cfm>

Acknowledgments

Julie Clemons, Assistant Director, Outdoor Programs Office, Dartmouth College

Dave Hardy, Director of Field Programs, Green Mountain Club

Kevin "Hawk" Metheny, Backcountry Management Specialist, Appalachian Mountain Club

Larry Garland, Cartographer, Appalachian Mountain Club

Matt Stevens, ATC New England Regional Office

Mark Suiters

Earle Towne

Kathryn Wendling, local historian, history of place names in Vermont

Matt Robinson, ATC geographical information systems office, section maps

Photography credits

1 Benjamin R. Thompson; 4 Don Whitney; 6 Bill Cooke, ATC; 7 Isaac Wiegmann (2); 32–33 Timothy Cummings; 35 Benjamin R. Thompson; 36–37, 47 Timothy Cummings; 57 Cynthia Taylor-Miller; 59, 67 Timothy Cummings; 69 David Mills; 81 Dan Stone; 83 Benjamin R. Thompson; 85 Timothy Cummings; 89 Benjamin R. Thompson; 91, 93 Timothy Cummings; 99, 101, 105 Dan Stone; 107 Benjamin R. Thompson; 115, 123, 125 Dan Stone; 129 Dave Crandall; 141 Doug Vandenburg; 151 Timothy Cummings; 161 Fred Shirley; 177 Steve Faccio; 186–187 Timothy Cummings; 208 Matt Stevens; 223 Cynthia Taylor-Miller; 225 Lauralee Bliss; 227, 235 Cynthia Taylor-Miller; 239 Benjamin R. Thompson; 249 Laurie Potteiger; 263 Bill Cooke; 269, 273 Laurie Potteiger; 281 Cynthia Taylor-Miller; 285 Fish and Wildlife Service.